DISC

ACKNOWLEDGEMENTS

The NRA would like to acknowledge the efforts of those whose advice, writing or editing activities contributed to the development of this book:

Charles Mitchell, Manager, Training Department, Education & Training Division.

Larry Quandahl, NRA National Instructor Trainer, Training Department, Education & Training Division and co-author of the *NRA Guide to Personal Protection Outside the Home.*

Stanton L. Wormley, Jr., NRA Certified Instructor and author of the *NRA Guide to Personal Protection Outside the Home.*

This book would not have been possible without the assistance and generosity of numerous corporate supporters, among whom are the following:

Beretta USA	Galco Intl.	SIGARMS
Bianchi Intl.	Glock	Smith & Alexander
Blade Tech	Kahr Arms	Smith & Wesson
Blue Ridge Arsenal	Kel-Tec	Milt Sparks
Brownells	MagLite	Springfield Armory
Browning Arms	MidwayUSA	Sturm, Ruger & Co.
Colt's Mfg. Co.	PACT	SureFire
Crimson Trace	Pro Ears	Taurus Intl.
Cyclops	Mitch Rosen	Virginia Arms

Special thanks go to Harry Jaecks, Art Director, Publications Division, for his expert advice, and to the many NRA staff members, their families and friends, and others who modeled for the photographs in this book.

Additionally, the NRA would like to thank the many NRA Certified Instructors, NRA staff, NRA members, the NRA Foundation, and others too numerous to mention whose assistance helped make this book possible.

Finally, the NRA expresses its deep appreciation to Gila Mae Hayes, widely recognized authority on self-defense and concealed carry issues, who thoughtfully critiqued this book.

TABLE OF CONTENTS

PART VI: SPECIAL DEFENSIVE SHOOTING TECHNIQUES

PART VII: CONCEALED CARRY, SELF-DEFENSE AND THE LAW

APPENDIXES

INTRODUCTION

As of early 2006, 38 of the 50 United States permit law-abiding citizens the right to carry a concealed firearm. Millions of people have taken advantage of this right, creating a need for a comprehensive course that covers the full spectrum of issues and information relating to concealed carry and self-defense. This includes not only techniques for properly carrying, presenting and shooting a concealed firearm, but also strategies for preventing violent encounters, and the legal ramifications of using lethal force in self-defense outside the home. The NRA's Personal Protection Outside the Home Course was designed to meet this need.

For many, the term "personal protection" immediately evokes images of martial-arts techniques or a handgun in a nightstand. In truth, however, the use of force is only one of many methods that you can employ to defend life and limb, and is used only as a last resort, when other methods have failed. *For myriad ethical, legal and practical reasons, it is always preferable to escape, evade, deter or otherwise avoid an attack rather than be forced to counter it with force.* Even when planning and skill give you an overwhelming advantage over an assailant, sidestepping a violent confrontation is always the best course. This is especially true when you are legally carrying a concealed handgun in public. Not only is retreat or flight from a confrontation outside the home the most sensible alternative, it is required by statute in most states (as long as you can retreat safely).

There are times, however, when circumstances allow no other option but the use of force to save your life or the lives of others. When you are confronted with such circumstances outside the home, a concealed handgun is unquestionably the most effective defensive tool available, if it is used properly. The ability to draw a handgun from concealment and shoot accurately is not something you are born with; it must be developed through the mastery of a series of interlocking skills, and then must be reinforced through frequent practice.

Note that, in many defensive situations, merely presenting the firearm will deter the threat, without the need for the gun to be fired. The NRA Personal Protection Outside the Home course will help prepare you to make decisions regarding the level of firearm use that is necessary to protect your life or the lives of others.

The main focus of the *NRA Guide to Personal Protection Outside the Home* is on the effective use of a concealed handgun for self-defense outside the home. Included are chapters on concealment techniques and devices, presenting the handgun from concealment, utilizing cover and concealment outside the home, presentation and movement, point shooting, instinctive shooting, low-light shooting, engaging multiple targets, and one-hand shooting. These skills and others presented in this book form the core shooting skills used to counter a life-threatening attack outside the home.

For those who do not wish to incorporate a handgun into their personal protection plans, or who may not always be able to carry a handgun outside the home, the book also presents techniques and strategies to help you avoid, deter, repel or escape an attack without the use of a firearm. Included are ways to make you seem like less of a target to potential attackers. Additionally, the NRA course, Refuse to Be a Victim®, can help you create a personal security plan that does not include firearms.

The *NRA Guide to Personal Protection Outside the Home* is divided into seven parts: Safety; Strategies for Personal Safety Outside the Home; Carrying a Concealed Handgun and Presenting the Handgun from Concealment; Developing Basic Defensive Shooting Skills; Developing Concealed Carry Defensive Shooting Skills for Use Outside the Home; Special Defensive Shooting Techniques; and Concealed Carry, Self-Defense and the Law. Also included are appendixes on resources for additional information, and facts about the NRA.

Although this book has a wealth of information on virtually every aspect of concealed carry and personal protection outside the home, it is meant to be used within the framework of the NRA Personal Protection Outside the Home Course, a hands-on program encompassing 14 hours of classroom and range instruction. (Mastery of the shooting skills taught in the NRA Basic Pistol Course and the NRA Basic Personal Protection in the Home Course are both prerequisites for this course.) You should understand that merely reading a book—any book—will not, in and of itself, make you proficient at the various skills involved in concealed handgun carry and armed self-defense outside the home. For more information on the NRA Personal Protection Outside the Home Course or any other NRA course, call (703) 267-1423.

A Gun Owner's Responsibilities

Americans enjoy a right that citizens of many other countries do not--the right to own firearms. But with this right come responsibilities. It is the gun owner's responsibility to store, operate and maintain his or her firearms safely. It is the gun owner's responsibility to ensure that unauthorized or untrained individuals cannot gain access to his or her firearms. And it is the gun owner's responsibility to learn and obey all applicable laws that pertain to the purchase, possession and use of a firearm in his or her locale. Guns are neither safe nor unsafe by themselves. When gun owners learn and practice responsible gun ownership, guns are safe.

SAFETY NOTE

The NRA's first Rule for Safe Gun Handling is **ALWAYS** **keep the gun pointed in a safe direction.** Implicit in that is the notion that a firearm must never be pointed at another human being (except, of course, in a self-defense situation). This rule must always be observed; it cannot be relaxed even for legitimate education or training purposes.

Many of the photographs in this book illustrate defensive firearm use, handgun presentation techniques, and specific shooting stances or positions. For instructional purposes it often was necessary to position the camera in front of the muzzle of the gun, or to re-create defensive scenarios in which the defender would point his or her firearm at an attacker. At no time was an actual functioning firearm used in these photographs; special deactivated, non-firing training guns, or solid plastic gun simulators, were employed.

Absolute, unvarying adherence to this first and most important of gun safety rules cannot be overemphasized. Real guns—even when clearly unloaded—must never be used in re-creating or practicing self-defense scenarios, or in any other training activity in which the firearm may be pointed at a training partner or other person. If you engage in such activities, always use a non-firing training gun or gun simulator designed for that purpose.

PART I

SAFETY

CHAPTER 1

BASIC FIREARM SAFETY

Safety is fundamental to all shooting activities. Whether you're practicing at the range, cleaning your gun in your workshop, or defending your family from an attack, the rules of firearm safety always apply.

Safe gun handling involves the development of knowledge, skills and attitudes—knowledge of the gun safety rules, the skill to apply these rules, and a safety-first attitude that arises from a sense of responsibility and a knowledge of potential dangers.

Though there are many specific principles of safe firearm handling and operation, all are derived from just three basic gun safety rules.

FUNDAMENTAL RULES FOR SAFE GUN HANDLING

<u>**ALWAYS**</u> **Keep the Gun Pointed in a Safe Direction.** This is the primary rule of gun safety. A safe direction means that the gun is pointed so that even if it were to go off, it would not cause injury or damage. The key to this rule is to control where the muzzle or front end of the barrel is pointed at all times. Common sense dictates the safest direction, depending upon the circumstances. If only this one safety rule were always followed, there would be no injuries or fatalities from accidental shootings.

<u>**ALWAYS**</u> **Keep Your Finger Off the Trigger Until Ready to Shoot.** Your trigger finger should always be kept straight, alongside the frame and out of the trigger guard, until you have made the decision to shoot.

*Fig. 1. **<u>ALWAYS</u>** Keep Your Finger Off the Trigger Until Ready to Shoot*

When holding a gun, many people tend to place their finger on the trigger, even when they are not ready to shoot. This is extremely dangerous. Unintentional discharges can be caused when the trigger of a loaded gun is inadvertently pressed by a finger left in the trigger guard instead of being positioned straight along the side of the gun's frame.

ALWAYS **Keep the Firearm Unloaded Until Ready to Use.** A firearm that is not being used should always be unloaded. For example, at the range, your firearm should be left unloaded with the action open while you walk downrange and check your target. Similarly, a firearm that is being stored in a gun safe or lock box should generally be unloaded (unless it is a personal protection firearm that may need to be accessed quickly for defensive purposes—see Chapter 2: Concealed Carry Safety).

As a general rule, whenever you pick up a gun, point it in a safe direction with your finger off the trigger, engage the safety (if the gun is equipped with one), remove the magazine (if the gun is equipped with a removable magazine), and then open the action and look into the chamber(s) to determine if the gun is loaded or not. Unless the firearm is being kept in a state of readiness for personal protection, it should be unloaded. If you do not know how to open the action or inspect the firearm, leave the gun alone and get help from someone who does.

Fig. 2. ***ALWAYS*** *Keep the Firearm Unloaded Until Ready to Use*

RULES FOR USING OR STORING A GUN

In addition to these three basic Rules for Safe Gun Handling, you must follow a number of additional rules when you use or store your firearm.

Know Your Target and What Is Beyond. Whether you are at the range, in the woods, or in a self-defense situation, if you're going to shoot you must know what lies beyond your target. In almost all cases, you must be sure that there is something that will serve as a backstop to capture bullets that miss or go through the target. Even in an emergency, you must never fire in a direction in which there are innocent people or any other potential for mishap. Think first, shoot second.

Know How to Use the Gun Safely. Before handling a gun, learn how it operates. Read the owner's manual for your gun. Contact the gun's manufacturer for an owner's manual if you do not have one. Know your gun's basic parts, how to safely open and close the action, and how to remove ammunition from the gun. No matter how much you know about guns, you must always take the time to learn the proper way to operate any new or unfamiliar firearm. Never assume that because one gun resembles another, they both operate similarly. Also, remember that a gun's mechanical safety is never foolproof. Guidance in safe gun operation should be obtained from the owner's manual or a qualified firearm instructor or gunsmith.

Be Sure Your Gun Is Safe to Operate. Just like other tools, guns need regular maintenance to remain operable. Regular cleaning and proper storage are a part of the gun's general upkeep. If there is any question regarding a gun's ability to function, it should be examined by a qualified gunsmith. Proper maintenance procedures are found in your owner's manual.

Use Only the Correct Ammunition for Your Gun. Each firearm is intended for use with a specific cartridge. Only cartridges designed for a particular gun can be fired safely in that gun. Most guns have the ammunition type stamped on the barrel and/or slide. The owner's manual will also list the cartridge or cartridges appropriate for your gun. Ammunition can be identified by information printed on the cartridge box and sometimes stamped on the cartridge head. Do not shoot the gun unless you know you have the proper ammunition.

Wear Eye and Ear Protection as Appropriate. The sound of a gunshot can damage unprotected ears. Gun discharges can also emit debris and hot gas that could cause eye injury. Thus, both ear and eye protection are highly recommended whenever you are firing live ammunition in your gun. Safety glasses and ear plugs or muffs should also be worn by any spectators or shooting partners present during live-fire sessions. Obviously, during an actual violent encounter necessitating the use of your firearm, it likely will not be possible for you to use eye and ear protection.

Fig. 3. Eye and ear protection.

Never Use Alcohol or Drugs Before or While Shooting. Alcohol and many drugs can impair normal mental and physical bodily functions, sharply diminishing your ability to shoot safely. These substances must never be used before or while handling or shooting guns. Note that these effects are produced not just by illegal or prescription drugs. Many over-the-counter medications also have considerable side effects which may be multiplied when certain drugs are taken together or with alcohol. Read the label of any medication you take, no matter how innocuous, or consult your physician or pharmacist for possible side effects. If the label advises against driving or operating equipment while taking the medication, you should also avoid using a firearm while taking it.

Store Guns So They Are Inaccessible to Unauthorized Persons. It is your responsibility as a gun owner to take reasonable steps to prevent unauthorized persons (especially children) from handling or otherwise having access to your firearms. You have a number of options for accomplishing this, which are discussed in greater detail in Chapter 3: Safe Firearm Storage. The particular storage method you choose will be based upon your own particular home situation and security needs.

Be Aware that Certain Types of Guns and Many Shooting Activities Require Additional Safety Precautions. There are many different types of firearms, some of which require additional safety rules or procedures for proper operation. These are commonly found in your firearm's owner's manual. Also, most sport shooting activities have developed a set of rules to ensure safety during competition. These rules are generally sport-specific; the procedures for loading your firearm and commencing fire, for example, are different in NRA bullseye shooting than they are in NRA Action Pistol competition (see Chapter 22: Opportunities for Skills Enhancement).

CHAPTER 2

DEFENSIVE SHOOTING SAFETY OUTSIDE THE HOME

The gun safety rules in the preceding chapter are applicable whenever a gun is handled or fired. However, some of these rules need to be reinforced in light of the particular dynamics and characteristics of defensive shooting situations outside the home.

Probably the greatest obstacle to safe gun handling in defensive situations is stress. In the overwhelming confusion of a violent encounter, it is possible to forget or disregard even the most basic gun safety rules. After all, when you are being attacked, your entire being is focused upon just one thing: survival.

Keeping a firearm pointed in a safe direction is fairly easy when at the range. Generally, pointing the gun downrange is safe. In the street, however, when facing an aggressive attack, a safe direction may be harder to

Fig. 4. A typical urban environment, with vehicles passing in the street, pedestrians on the sidewalks, and buildings with windows and doors facing the street. The concealed carrier must be conscious of the potential safety risks of firing in such an environment.

identify. Bystanders, pets in a yard, moving vehicles in the street, or the windows of surrounding buildings must all be considered before you even draw your firearm. In addition, outside the home there may be oil, propane or gas tanks, or other vessels containing flammable substances. Since many handgun bullets can travel a mile or more, anything within that radius is at risk, including airports, rail lines and, of course, people. A stray bullet can also ricochet off a glass, metal, water, stone or concrete surface and cause property damage, injury or death.

In a store or workplace, a "safe direction" may be especially difficult to find, as a violent criminal may be interspersed with customers, employees or other innocent bystanders. Additionally, in most defensive confrontations, people rarely stand still; both attackers and bystanders are usually moving. The scene is dynamic and fluid, and what is a safe direction one second becomes unsafe in another.

In anticipation of the need to fire quickly during an encounter with an aggressor, some people may unconsciously hold their firearm with their finger on the trigger, even when they are not intending to fire immediately. This violation of a basic Rule of Safe Gun Handling—*ALWAYS* **keep your finger off the trigger until ready to shoot**—can have disastrous consequences, as the stress of a real or potential attack can make you prone to an involuntary, reflexive trigger pull if you are suddenly startled. For the same reason, it is particularly important to avoid prematurely putting the trigger finger on the trigger when drawing the gun from a holster.

As was explained in the previous chapter, it is a basic Rule of Safe Gun Handling that *a firearm should be kept unloaded until ready for use.* In the context of personal protection, "ready to use" means more than merely "ready to shoot." A self-defense firearm you keep in a holster on your person is "ready to use" throughout the entire period you wear it. A gun you keep in a pistol lockbox next to your cash register in your shop is "ready to use" during the hours you spend at your shop. When your business is closed, however, the firearm kept there is no longer ready to be used by you or any of your employees, and must then be kept unloaded and secured to prevent theft or access by an unauthorized person.

One of the most important—and problematic—safety rules in relation to defensive shooting situations outside the home is know your target and what is beyond. Knowing your target is critical to prevent shooting any unintended target.

In the home, a threat to your safety is usually fairly easy to recognize; any stranger there is an intruder whose motives are unknown. In public, situations and interactions are more ambiguous. The approach of a panhandler may be no more than an irritation to some, but can seem to be a deadly threat to others. You must exercise good judgement to differentiate between those who are genuine threats to your safety, and those who merely seem threatening. Safety, ethics and the law dictate that you identify your target and verify it is a lethal and imminent threat before you even draw your firearm.

Moreover, never forget that a concealed carry permit does not entitle you to act as a police officer. The right to carry a gun does not confer the right to intervene in any seemingly confrontational situation.

Fig. 5. The responsible carrier of a concealed firearm must not overreact to ambiguous situations, such as in the photo at left in which the man appears to be reaching for a weapon. In reality, he is simply getting one of the promotional flyers he's handing out.

It's equally as important to know what's beyond your target. In the stress of an aggressive attack, you cannot assume that all of your shots will hit your target. Also, depending upon the gun and ammunition you are using, the distance at which a shooting takes place, the size and dress of your attacker, and the location of your hits on your attacker, some of your bullets may completely penetrate your assailant and continue on, presenting danger to persons or objects beyond. In the home, bullets that miss or overpenetrate their target often lodge in a wall or piece of furniture. In the street, however, such bullets can cause property damage or injury.

Fig. 6. Typical street scene with attacker in foreground, pedestrians, cars and buildings beyond.

Never use drugs or alcohol while or before shooting is an important rule, but one that can be difficult to observe outside the home. Many people enjoy a beer at their local bar after work before going home, or a glass of wine with dinner at a restaurant. A person who uses his or her firearm to stop a violent criminal after such an innocent drink may have a positive blood alcohol test. Even though that person's blood alcohol level may be well under the legal limit for sobriety, the fact that any alcohol at all was present may cast doubt upon a claim of legitimate self-defense. Alcohol and drugs can cloud judgment, slow reflexes and alter perceptions, even at low levels of consumption; you should avoid them during periods when you may be carrying a firearm.

Defensive shooting safety outside the home also extends to proper holster selection and use. Holsters that are poorly designed or manufactured, holsters not designed for concealed carry use, or holsters that are improperly used or worn can all cause unsafe situations, such as spilling a loaded gun out on the ground or forcing the user to employ an unsafe drawing motion. Also, some holsters may be deemed hazardous because they hold the gun in an unsafe position (such as pointing straight rearward).

Gun safety must also be observed while you are honing your firearm skills, whether you're shooting live ammunition at the range or performing dry-fire practice at home. Specific safety precautions for these activities are out-

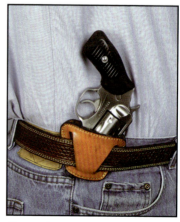

Fig. 7. This holster is unsafe because it doesn't properly fit the gun.

lined in Chapter 22: Opportunities for Skills Enhancement.

It may seem unrealistic to expect a person undergoing an attack to be conscious of the gun safety rules, much less adhere to them. Nonetheless, through constant repetition and mindfulness, safe gun handling skills can become habits that function automatically even during the stress of a violent encounter.

CHAPTER 3

SAFE FIREARM STORAGE

Safe gun storage is an integral part of gun safety. It is one of your prime responsibilities as a gun owner to take all reasonable precautions to prevent unauthorized persons from having access to your firearms. By storing your firearms safely, you not only avoid the possibility of an accidental shooting involving a child or other untrained person; you may also prevent a criminal from using your firearm against an innocent person, including members of your own family.

In addition, some jurisdictions have laws mandating secure firearm storage. Almost all jurisdictions have criminal negligence laws that can be applied to gun owners who do not take reasonable precautions in storing their firearms.

Safe firearm storage is of course critical when you have a gun inside your home, but is even more critical when a gun is taken outside the home. A gun that is stored in a vehicle's glove compartment, a desk drawer, or under the counter at a store may be easier for unauthorized persons to

access than a gun kept in your home in a gun safe or lockbox. Just as you may be held responsible for any damage caused by a gun that is stolen from your home, you may be held equally liable if your gun, taken from your workplace or your automobile, is used to injure or kill an innocent person during a crime.

Fig. 8. Concealed carrier storing handgun in locking gun case in car trunk.

There are two main requirements for the storage of firearms. First and foremost, the storage method chosen must provide an adequate level of protection to prevent unauthorized persons from accessing the firearms. The determination of what is "adequate protection" is a matter of judgment on the part of the gun owner. Temporarily storing your unloaded gun in the locked trunk of your vehicle while you make a quick trip inside a post office may be appropriate in a low-crime suburban or rural area, but may be irresponsible in a high-crime area in which

Fig. 9. When you are visitng places in which you are prohibited from carrying your concealed firearm, as indicated by this notice on the wall of a United States Post Office, you must avail yourself of some means of temporary gun storage.

thieves are known to pop open a trunk in a matter of seconds. Similarly, storing your unloaded gun in a locking desk drawer in your private office—to which only your administrative assistant has access—represents a different level of safety risk than storing it in a locked drawer of a desk on the loading dock, where virtually anyone can easily gain access to it.

The second requirement is that the storage method or device used must allow the gun to be easily retrieved as needed to defend against an intruder or an attack. This is just as important to a shopkeeper behind her counter as it is to a homeowner awakening at night to the sound of an approaching intruder. Again, "easily retrieved" depends upon the particular circumstances of the environment. Be aware that storage methods that provide a high level of security often do not allow quick and easy firearm access; thus, defensive firearm storage inside or outside the home usually involves a compromise between security and access.

Additionally, a firearm storage device should provide some level of concealment. A gun that is not seen is less likely to be stolen. Concealment is achieved by storing the gun in a location or a device where it cannot be seen; ideally, the device itself should not signal to a burglar or thief that a gun is inside. Concealment is especially important when you are storing a gun outside the home, as in a vehicle or workplace. In such locations, many more people can potentially gain access to your gun, and thus there is a greater risk of theft or unauthorized use.

There is no one best method of firearm storage nor one best type of locking or storage device. Each has advantages and limitations. You must choose the firearm storage method that is best for you given your circumstances and preferences.

It is also incumbent upon you as a responsible, law-abiding gun owner to know and observe all applicable state and local laws regarding safe gun storage. For example, if the law in your jurisdiction requires a trigger lock on all stored guns, you must abide by that law no matter what other storage methods you also use, such as a high-security gun safe.

TYPES OF LOCKING MECHANISMS

All storage methods designed to prevent unauthorized access utilize some sort of locking mechanism. Different types of locking mechanisms offer varying degrees of security and accessibility. Keyed locks, such as padlocks and the lockable drawers of desks and nightstands, can offer a reasonable level of security (depending upon the construction of the lock and the storage device). However, under stress or in darkness it may be difficult for some to locate the correct key or to manipulate it in the lock. A lesser concern, but one worth mentioning, is that inserting and turning a key in a gun box lock would likely create some sound—whether it is keys jingling together on a key ring or the movement of the lock's tumblers— that could alert a stealthily approaching attacker.

Combination locks are often found on gun storage boxes, and range from simple triple-rotary-tumbler models to units that rival the mechanisms found on bank vaults. For many people, combination locks are both secure and familiar to operate. Under stress, however, lock combinations can be confused or forgotten by the gun owner, and the tumblers can be challenging to manipulate quickly and accurately. Also, in darkness or even dim light, combination locks can be virtually impossible to operate, making them less than optimal for devices used for emergency firearm storage.

Simplex®-type locks provide a good combination of security and quick access. Such locks feature a number of buttons that are pushed in a specific order to open the device. With only minimal practice, these locks can be easily worked in total darkness. Locks having Simplex®-type mechanisms can be just as strong and tamper-resistant as any other.

Another advantage of a Simplex® lock is that incorrect entry blocks any further attempt to open the lock. A separate clearing code must be entered before the lock will accept the correct combination, making this lock even more resistant to unauthorized attempts to open it.

The basic Simplex®-type lock is a mechanical lock, and thus does not depend upon house current or batteries. Some locking devices combine Simplex® principles with modern electronics. Typically, the storage

Fig. 10. Simplex®-type locking device.

device features a numeric keypad whose numbered buttons are pushed in a specific order to unlock.

A variation on this involves five *fingerpads*, ergonomically placed on the top or front of the device, which can easily be felt in the dark and which are pressed in a sequence (such as thumb, middle finger, little finger, ring finger) to open the device. It is important to note that such locking mechanisms are usually disabled when electric power is lost (as from dead batteries or a failure in house current). There usually is a provision for opening the box with a key under such circumstances, but this could be problematic under stress or in the dark. Some units that use house current have provisions for a backup battery power supply to ensure continuous operation.

Fig. 11. Fingerpad-type locking device. Key provides manual override.

A new type of gun storage device uses biometrics to control access. The most common type of this device features a computer-controlled fingerprint reader to activate unlocking. Though this technology is promising, there are still issues to be resolved (such as the reliability of the reader to distinguish a print on a finger that may be wet with water or blood).

TYPES OF STORAGE DEVICES

There are many different methods for storing firearms safely inside and outside the home, several of which may fit into your defensive plan.

Gun cases are commonly used for the transportation and storage of firearms. Gun cases are typically of synthetic material, though some more costly models are made of aluminum. Some have integral locks; others feature hasps for small keyed or combination padlocks.

Gun cases can be useful in several ways. Where it is legal to transport your gun by air or other common carrier, it must be in a gun case; some specific requirements as to the type and construction of the case may apply. Also, federal law mandates that a gun transported across state lines in your vehicle must be in a "locked container" (such as a gun case) when it cannot be transported in a compartment separate from the driver's compartment. Some states also have additional requirements for transporting guns within state boundaries. Even in jurisdictions or situations in which guns need not be transported in a gun case, it is still a good idea to do so, both to keep them out of sight and to protect them from being jostled together or damaged in your trunk, truck box and so forth. In the home, gun cases

Fig. 12. Plastic gun case secured with padlock.

serve to protect firearms from dust and moisture. Often, guns kept in gun safes for long-term or permanent storage are first put into gun cases.

A *pistol lockbox* allows you to store a gun in your vehicle or workplace so that it is protected from unauthorized access but can still be retrieved quickly. Typically, such boxes are made of steel and feature integral keyed, combination or Simplex®-type locks; a few have electronic numeric keypads or fingerpads. Some lockboxes are designed to store a gun securely out of sight while also providing quick access to that gun if it is needed for defensive purposes. Such boxes are typically located in desk drawers, under countertops, or in the kneewells of desks. Some models are designed for automotive use. These lockboxes are attached using screws or bolts that can be accessed only when the box is open; easy theft of the box is discouraged. Quick-access boxes usually feature locks of the Simplex®, electronic keypad or fingerpad type. Many novel mechanisms exist to provide quick access once the box is opened, from harnesses that swing out and present the gun grip-first to platforms that slide out for easy access.

Fig. 13. Locking pistol box combination lock affords portable handgun security.

Gun safes are designed to offer the greatest level of safety for your guns. Upper-end models provide walls and doors that are virtually impossible to defeat by brute force, high-security mechanical or electronic locks, and complex locking patterns that fasten the door to the frame in multiple locations with thick, hardened steel pins. Most of these models are too heavy and bulky for thieves to carry away easily, even when they are not bolted to the floor; some also offer a degree of fire protection.

Although appropriate for permanent firearm storage, gun safes may not be the best choice for the temporary storage of guns that may need to be quickly retrieved. The weight and size of gun safes often consigns them to the basement of a building, far from your office or work location. Also, gun safes provide little concealment value. No matter where a gun safe is put, almost anyone seeing it will recognize it as a device for the storage of firearms or other valuable items, making it a target for thieves and burglars. Finally, the combination locks and heavy bolting mechanisms typical of such devices make it difficult to access your gun quickly and quietly. Even when equipped with a lighted keypad for quicker access, the sound of the handle

Fig. 14. Gun safe.

being turned and the locking pins retracting will unquestionably alert an intruder in a quiet home or workplace.

There are a few alternative storage methods that should also be mentioned. Many people store guns in a *lockable drawer* of a desk, nightstand, file cabinet or the like. Arguably, under some circumstances in a home or workplace, it may be safe to keep a loaded defensive firearm in an unlocked drawer while the gun owner is actually in the same room and is able to keep the firearm under his or her control. A moment's inattention or carelessness could result in the gun coming under the control of a child, a criminal, a curious co-worker, or some other unauthorized person. The decision to store a gun in this manner must be reached after a careful consideration of the circumstances, needs and risks involved.

Another alternative form of storage is a *lockable gun rack* allowing firearms (particularly long guns) to be displayed or stored openly. This type of device typically features a locking bar (or sometimes a thick, plastic-covered steel cable) that passes through the trigger guard or around the

Fig. 15. Two methods of locking a handgun: top, a padlock around the top strap of a revolver; bottom, a cable lock through the frame and slide of a semi-automatic pistol.

frame, and is secured by a keyed or combination lock. Since a lockable gun rack does not protect a gun from moisture, dust, or fingerprints, and does not conceal a gun from prying eyes, it is best mounted in a locked gun room or gun closet.

Also available are several types of quick-access devices that orient a handgun for a fast grab. Some of these devices are designed for night-time use, and orient a gun in a grip-upward position alongside the mattress. Others place a handgun in a horizontal position directly under a counter, drawer or desktop. These items may be useful in high-threat environments in which there may be no time to work even a Simplex®-type lock—an environment in which life or death may hinge on immediate access to a firearm. These devices do not prevent gun theft or unauthorized access, and are thus not suitable for gun storage.

STORING A GUN SAFELY IN THE HOME

Even a concealed carry gun will be stored in the home part of the time. In some respects, a gun stored in the home is both safer, and more vulnerable, than a gun stored in a vehicle or a typical work environment. Home firearm storage is usually quite safe, as a properly prepared house or apartment can deter most attempts at burglary or theft. In that sense, you can regard your home as a large gun safe or lockbox that represents the first line of defense against any criminal or other unauthorized person.

On the other hand, if a criminal does succeed in breaking into your home, he sometimes has the luxury of taking his time to search for your guns and other valuables. While a person who breaks into your vehicle on the street usually has only a few seconds to complete his crime before a passerby detects him and calls the police, a burglar who entered your home without raising an alarm may have several minutes, a half-hour or even longer to ransack it. This makes a hidden gun more likely to be found, and thus more vulnerable to theft.

There are two types of home gun storage, each with benefits and limitations. Long-term gun storage involves the extended storage of firearms in a device offering extreme protection from theft and sometimes fire and moisture, but delayed access to the firearm. A gun safe is typically used for permanent firearm storage; its size and weight prevent easy theft, and its enclosed environment affords the best possible protection from fire damage, high humidity, etc. This protection is gained, however, at the expense of easy gun access.

Fig. 16. Homeowner retrieving gun from quick-access lockbox in safe room of home.

Quick-access or temporary gun storage does not provide the same degree of protection as long-term storage methods, but gives the ready firearm access that may be needed in the event of a home invasion, nighttime burglary or other defensive emergency. Some quick-access gun storage methods are as simple as putting a gun in an unlocked kitchen or nightstand drawer. However, such measures would not provide appropriate security if you left the room. Greater security can be achieved by using a fingerpad-activated lockbox located by the bed or in the office, basement or TV room.

As general rule, you should avoid storing a gun (loaded or otherwise) in an unlocked drawer, cabinet, etc. when you are not physically present in the home. Even when you are physically present, gun storage in unlocked areas may not be appropriate if you also have children, relatives, friends or others around. You must balance the need for quick access against the need for security.

A few gun safes attempt to provide the best of both worlds by offering, in addition to the heavily-locked main firearm compartment, an auxiliary easy-access compartment containing a single handgun. Access to the auxiliary compartment is by a fingerpad that can be worked quickly, even in the dark. This combination long-term and easy-access storage device can work well if the gun safe is placed in the bedroom or other location in which fast access is most often needed. When situated in a basement, however, the benefit of such a device is greatly diminished.

STORING A GUN SAFELY OUTSIDE THE HOME

Most of the time when you are outside your home, your concealed handgun will be on your person, carried in a holster, handbag, fanny pack or other concealment device. However, there will be occasions when you find it necessary to temporarily remove your gun and store it in a safe manner. For example, in many states allowing concealed carry it is illegal to carry a firearm in an establishment in which alcoholic beverages are served, such as a bar or restaurant. Handgun carry is likewise prohibited in federal buildings (including post offices), as well as in many state and local government offices. Guns are also prohibited in schools and churches, and in many workplaces. Additionally, even in jurisdictions where concealed carry is permitted, businesses may still prohibit legal permit holders from entering with their guns. Thus, a person with a concealed handgun who goes to the post office to buy some stamps, then meets with a teacher at her child's school, and then finally joins her spouse at a restaurant, will need to avail herself of a safe gun storage method several times during the day.

Outside the home, handguns are usually temporarily stored either in a vehicle or in the workplace. Vehicle storage can be necessary when you travel to places where handgun carry is not allowed. Workplace storage may be required when handgun carry is prohibited in your work environment and you must find someplace to put a handgun you carry to and from your place of employment. Additionally, in those work environments in which handgun carry is not explicitly prohibited, there may still be times when carrying a gun on the job is not comfortable, practical or safe.

Vehicle Storage. Many people temporarily store firearms in various areas of a vehicle—the glove box, the trunk or truck box, the map pocket in the vehicle door, or even under the seat. These locations offer some level of concealment and access to the firearm, but little protection against theft or unauthorized access if the vehicle is broken into, or simply left unlocked. In addition, burglars and car thieves make a point of searching these areas for guns. Also, never leave a child alone in a vehicle while you run into a convenience store or gas station if there is an unsecured gun in an accessible area, such as an unlocked glove box or center console.

At the very least, you should store your firearm in a locked gun case inside the vehicle's trunk, cargo box or other lockable area. This method of storage will not prevent the theft of your gun if the vehicle is burglarized, but at least will prevent a criminal from immediately putting your stolen gun to use. Of course, you should unload your gun before locking it inside the gun case, and store the ammunition in a separate locked container.

Greater security and access can be afforded by a special pistol lock box designed for automotive environments. Such devices are usually securely attached to part of the vehicle, such as the floorboard under the seat, the interior of the glove box, the underside of the dashboard or the interior of the storage compartment in the center console. Some of the units may slide or swing out to provide access; all normally require the entry of the proper combination or keypad sequence to access and withdraw the gun. Such a unit, properly installed, will provide no visual clue of the presence of a gun in the vehicle, but will allow ready access in only a few seconds.

The risk of theft inherent in temporary gun storage in your vehicle can be reduced by carefully planning your travels when you are carrying a handgun, and by making sure you have a secure storage method available (such as a locking gun case or pistol box) if you will be visiting places where handgun carry is prohibited. Alternatively, you can choose to not carry a handgun at all on that day, or during that part of the day when you will go to gun-free locations.

Advance planning is also essential when you will be traveling out of your home state and into a state in which your carry permit is not valid, or if you travel in-state on an airplane, train, bus or subway. The carrying of firearms frequently is restricted on public transportation. Always be aware that you are carrying a handgun; you must not become complacent and forget it is there, or inadvertently go someplace where carry is forbidden.

Workplace Storage. Workplace storage can be problematical in several ways. Many companies will frown upon—or simply prohibit—a gun on the premises, even if it is unloaded and secured inside a locking gun case. Even where the presence of a gun is accepted, it may be difficult for you to discreetly transport and store the gun in the workplace. This discretion is important for several reasons. First, the greater the number of people who know that you keep a gun in your desk, tool chest or locker, the greater the likelihood that it will become the target of theft or other unauthorized access. Second, some people are simply uncomfortable around guns, even when they are unloaded and secured in a gun case; keeping your gun out of sight shows consideration for their feelings. Finally, advertising yourself as a gun owner can make you a target of both criminals and of gratuitous and irrational harassment by those who fear both guns and gun owners.

Often a gun is stored in the workplace during the work day primarily because it is safer or more secure there than in an unattended vehicle in a parking lot. In a retail sales environment, however, a handgun may be kept for protection against a violent robber. Such a handgun must be stored so that it can quickly be acquired by authorized employees, but is protected from theft or unauthorized access at all other times.

Thus, as in the home environment, there are two types of workplace gun storage: long-term storage, in which the gun is kept locked up all day with little or no anticipation of defensive use; and quick-access storage, in which the gun is kept readily available to ward off robbers or other violent criminals.

Fig. 17. Both discretion and security are essential in workplace gun storage.

Long-term workplace storage requires, at the very minimum, that you store your gun in a locked drawer or cabinet. This is true even when you store a gun in your private office, to which few have access. Be aware that this minimal level of security may not prevent unauthorized access to your gun, as there may be a number of duplicate keys to your drawer or cabinet, or the key to a similar model elsewhere in the workplace may also unlock yours. Better security (but slower access) is attained when you place your gun in a locked gun case, and then lock it in a drawer or cabinet. This will deter the curious, who generally will not damage a gun case just to satisfy their curiosity, and will also prevent any unauthorized person from being able to use the gun immediately. However, a locked gun case can be stolen and opened later at the thief's leisure.

A locking pistol box securely attached to the inside of a locked desk

Fig. 18. A locked desk drawer can offer both secure storage and quick access in a workplace

drawer or cabinet provides the best practical level of security for long-term gun storage in the workplace. Such a device is highly resistant to theft, and, if equipped with a keypad or fingerpad mechanism, can still be opened relatively quickly if necessary.

This type of device is also highly recommended for the quick-access storage of a handgun kept hidden near a counter or register as protection against criminal attack. Some models feature a locking storage compartment that mounts under a counter and slides outward on rails for easy access. Other models can be mounted inside a drawer, on the side of a counter, under a shelf and so forth.

In some cases, a store owner may keep a small handgun hidden in the cash register drawer itself, on the theory that the drawer will inevitably be opened to give money to a robber. In some cases, however, store robbers have simply grabbed the entire register. Keeping a handgun in the register may ultimately do little more than provide a violent criminal with one more weapon.

Miscellaneous Storage Methods.
There may be occasions when you may consider temporarily storing a gun in locations other than a vehicle or a workplace, such as in a locker at your gym or in a dressing room at a hair salon. While some of these locations are safe, many are not; and you must weigh the convenience of such storage with the very real risk of theft or other unauthorized access.

Fig 19. A gun kept carelessly in an unlocked or open drawer can be easily seen by others.

No single storage method is best. The responsible gun owner will use a mixture of storage methods to prevent any unauthorized access while facilitating easy retrieval when necessary. Research into the various storage options and a carefully thought-out defensive plan will help you decide which firearm storage options are appropriate for your situation.

PART II

STRATEGIES FOR PERSONAL SAFETY OUTSIDE THE HOME

CHAPTER 4

AWARENESS

An awareness of your environment and the real or potential threats that may be in it is one of the most important keys to staying safe. Such an awareness can help you avoid a violent confrontation altogether, or can give you more time to prepare an effective response to an attack that cannot be averted. Remember, it is always best to evade a confrontation by any means possible. Deadly force should be used only as a last resort when no other option is available.

To help in evaluating your alertness at any time, it is useful to identify several different levels of awareness. Readers with military or police experience or prior practical training may have been exposed to this in the form of a four- or five-step "color code" of tactical awareness. The NRA utilizes four levels of awareness: *unaware, aware, alert,* and *alarm.*

UNAWARE

Much of the average person's time in public is spent in an *unaware* condition—a condition in which *one is not alert to the immediate environment.* The ultimate state of unawareness, of course, is sleep, but an unaware state is also common during activities that require attention or concentration, such as watching television, driving a car, carrying on a conversation, or perusing items in a store. People are also often unaware of their surroundings when they are deep in thought or daydreaming, or when they are in the grip of intense emotions. An unaware state (or, at best, a state of markedly reduced awareness) can additionally be caused by fatigue or illness, alcohol, and the use of both illegal and legal drugs (including many over-the-counter medications).

Being in an unaware condition is probably inescapable at least some of the time. Nonetheless, from a practical point of view, unawareness is to be avoided as much as possible, for such a state lessens the likelihood

Fig. 20. A person in an unaware condition on the street, distracted and therefore unconscious of her environment.

that a threat will be perceived or recognized, and also slows your response to danger even after it has been identified. Many criminal attacks are planned for times and circumstances in which the victim feels safe and protected, and is thus likely to be in a state of unawareness.

AWARE

In the *aware* state, a person is *conscious of his or her surroundings, and of those persons around him or her*. However, at this stage, he or she has not identified any potential threats in the environment.

Awareness can involve any of the senses, including sight, hearing, smell and touch; sight and hearing, however, are the most useful in perceiving threats in your environment. Under conditions in which a potential threat is likely to be present, the prudent person avoids anything that may impair the acuity of the eyes or ears. Wearing stereo headphones while walking or jogging may help the time pass more pleasantly, but also prevents you from detecting the sound of an assailant's footsteps, or an automobile, approaching from behind.

While it is relatively easy to operate at a condition of heightened awareness for short periods, particularly under conditions in which a threat is likely, it is much more diffi-cult to maintain awareness for an extended length of time in environments that seem protected or safe, such as your car or office.

Just as a skillful and experienced driver automatically and effortlessly perceives and responds to potential collisions and other road hazards, you can develop an unforced alertness to your surroundings.

Fig. 21. A person in an aware state on the street, her senses open to what is happening in her environment.

ALERT

An individual at the alert level has identified a specific potential threat or threats. This is in contrast to the aware state, in which one has only a gen-eralized consciousness of things in the environment that could be threats.

Potential or hypothetical threats may originate from many sources. Often, certain types of people are perceived as threatening or intimidating. Relying upon stereotypical images to gauge the likelihood of a violent encounter can sometimes make one vulnerable to other, unexpected sources of danger. As you walk on the street, you may keep a wary eye on a group of rowdy teenagers on the corner; but, as a result, you may be totally oblivious to a neatly dressed middle-aged mugger.

Even in the apparent absence of other people, many possible threats in the environment remain. A clump of bushes, a darkened alley or an abandoned car may all conceal a violent assailant. Any unusual or out-of-the-ordinary occurrence, such as a broken stairway light, may also signal a potential threat lurking in the darkness. With practice, you can become more adept at identifying such dangers.

Outside the home, a specific potential threat may take many forms:
- the approach of a stranger;
- an unexpected noise;
- a suspicious-looking person alone with you in an elevator or subway car;
- a stranger asking for assistance with directions, or to borrow a cigarette or some spare change;
- an unfamiliar car with people inside, passing you slowly on the street;
- a flat tire on your car late at night in a poorly-lit parking lot;
- a dark alley or street; or
- a person acting oddly, as though they are drunk or on drugs.

As a general rule, any strangers who approach you may constitute a potential threat, no matter who they seem or claim to be.

Remember that the alert level involves identification of a specific potential threat, not a real or actual threat. Not every panhandler will attack you; not every stranger asking for directions is a mugger.

It is crucial at the alert level of awareness to take two steps immediately after identifying a specific potential threat. Step One is to formulate a hypothetical plan of action to respond to the threat. This plan is absolutely essential; it is always quicker to act than to react. The

Fig. 22. A person in an alert state on the street, having identified a potential threat in her environment. .

planned response can be the evasion of an attack—by means of avoidance, flight, issuing a verbal warning, calling for help, alerting the police and so on—or, as a last resort, the employment of force to defend yourself or others. Implicit in this plan is not only what course of action will be taken (as in, "If he attacks me, I will take cover") but also how ("I will retreat to the mailbox at the corner and assume a kneeling position behind it"). Of course, the plan must be flexible enough to allow you to respond to changing circumstances. Depending upon both your attacker's behavior and the opportunities offered by your environment, you may have to shift between the "evasive" and "defensive" modes of action.

It is always important to have more than one plan of action. In a crisis, plans rarely unfold as anticipated, and having one or more contingency plans may mean the difference between life and death. It is essential to keep thinking and planning, to be continually alert to opportunities that present themselves, and to be flexible enough to adapt your plan of action to changing circumstances.

Note that your plan of action does not have to involve the use of force. Most responses to an attack fall into one of two broad categories: evasion or defense. Evasion, if safely possible, is always preferable. As has been stated above, and as is repeated numerous times in this text, the best course of action is to avoid or evade a violent confrontation altogether. The use of force, deadly or otherwise, should be regarded only as a last resort.

Even when force is used in self-defense, opportunities for evasion may subsequently arise. Your plan should take into account chances that may arise to safely flee a confrontation at any time.

Step Two is to establish a "threshold stimulus" that will initiate your plan of action. Once the potential threat has crossed that threshold, the next level of awareness, *alarm,* is reached and the plan you have formulated immediately goes into effect. A threshold stimulus may be many things: the approach of a threat within a certain distance; the insertion of a potential attacker's hand into his pocket; the presentation of a weapon by the threat; an overt gesture or statement from the threat indicating an intention to do harm, and so forth.

ALARM

At the *alarm* level of awareness, the specific potential threat identified in the alert stage has *crossed one or more of the thresholds previously established, and has become a real threat to your safety.* Your senses are height-

O bserve
O rient
D ecide
A ct

ened, and you will likely feel a high
level of fear and anxiety. The course
of action planned in the *alert* stage is
now implemented.

Often it is appropriate to establish
a cascade of stimuli that sets into
motion an escalating sequence of
actions. For example, you might
establish the following sequence of
stimuli and actions to respond to an
approaching group of teenagers:

Fig. 23. A person in an alarm state on the street, about to react to a threat in her environment that has crossed her threshold stimulus.

• *First Threshhold Stimulus*:
  Approach of a noisy group
  of young men wearing
  gang colors *(alert* level).

• *First Action:* Cross to the opposite side of the street.
• *Second Action:* Establish the next threshhold stimulus and plan
  your response to that stimulus.

• *Second Threshhold Stimulus:* The gang crosses to your side of
  the street *(alarm* level).
• *First Action:* Retreat by reversing your direction, walking away
  from the gang.
• *Second Action:* Look for a means of escaping from or avoiding a
  confrontation, such as a passing empty taxi or police patrol, or a
  store you can go into for refuge.
• *Third Action:* Establish the next threshhold stimulus and plan
  your response to that stimulus.

• *Third Threshhold Stimulus:* The gang follows you into the store.
• *First Action:* Retreat to a position inside the store that provides
  cover and does not allow members of the gang to get behind
  you. Keep in mind that, at this point, you can't assume that
  there is a genuine threat just because the group is in the store.
  Stay alert, but don't overreact.
• *Second Action:* Establish the next threshhold stimulus and plan
  your response to that stimulus.

- *Fourth Threshhold Stimulus:* The gang approaches you, its members making verbal threats and displaying weapons.
- *First Action:* Yell for someone to call the police. This may deter your attackers, and will in any event attract attention to the situation, providing you with witnesses if you must defend yourself.
- *Second Action:* Present your firearm and order them to leave you alone..
- *Third Action:* Establish the next threshhold stimulus and plan your response to that stimulus.

- *Fifth Threshhold Stimulus:* The gang approaches past the threshhold distance.
- *Action:* Utilize your firearm to protect your life.

  Although the foregoing provides a useful succession of steps that can be used to respond to threats in an ever-changing environment, it should not override your own intuition. Never discount or dismiss your instincts about a person or a situation; and do not hesitate to flee if something "doesn't feel right," even in the absence of any overt action that crosses a threshhold you have set.

  As is stressed many times in this handbook, the use of a firearm or other deadly weapon to protect yourself should be an act of last resort when no other option is available. It is always better to evade, escape, avoid or deter an attack than to resolve it through the use of force. By employing your powers of awareness—one of the most important personal protection tools you possess—you will be able to recognize threats in your environment early on, which in turn may enable you to escape or avoid them. If you fail to maintain a state of awareness, you are more likely to become a victim of an attack, or to have to use deadly force to defend yourself.

CHAPTER 5

THE DEFENSIVE MINDSET

As was discussed in Chapter 4, you are often able to avoid or evade violent confrontations through an awareness of the potential threats in your environment. In some situations, however, an attack cannot be averted. Surviving such situations depends not only upon using the appropriate defensive and practical skills, but also upon having a defensive mindset. Your defensive mindset consists of the values, mental techniques, and attitude that maximize the effectiveness of your response to an assault. These attributes also influence the effectiveness of your training regimen, so the development of a defensive mindset is an important initial stage in the NRA Personal Protection Outside the Home Course.

WILLINGNESS TO USE FORCE IN SELF-DEFENSE

The NRA Personal Protection Outside the Home Course teaches the law-abiding citizen how to use a discreetly carried handgun for personal protection when threatened with deadly force outside the home. This entails training to use a firearm as a last resort, if necessary. Any person having personal objections to using deadly force in self-defense should investigate other personal protection strategies, as are presented in the NRA Refuse to Be a Victim® course.

Anyone contemplating the inclusion of a firearm in a personal protection strategy must consider the following questions:

- *Am I prepared to take the life of another human being to save my life or that of another innocent person?*
- *Does my religion permit the taking of a life in self-defense?*
- *Do my personal moral standards permit the taking of a life in self-defense?*
- *Am I prepared to tolerate the judgment of my family, friends, neighbors, co-workers and others if I must defend myself with lethal force?*

Even when it is necessary and justified, shooting a violent criminal is highly stressful. This should be planned for as part of your mental training.

The *willingness* to take a life in self-defense is very different from the *desire* to take a life. No responsible, decent person enjoys taking a life, no matter how depraved or malignant the assailant may be. The willingness to use deadly force in self-defense does not imply a devaluation of human life. In fact, those who include a firearm in their personal protection plans are affirming the value of their own lives and those of other innocent persons. The ethical person does not ever want to use deadly force, but recognizes that there are times when it may be the only option to protect innocent lives.

DETERMINATION TO NEVER GIVE UP

There's an old country saying that runs something like this: "It's not the size of the dog in the fight, but the size of the fight in the dog." The truth of this axiom is apparent to any sports fan who has seen a larger and stronger opponent vanquished by one who is smaller, weaker, and less skilled—but more determined. In war, too, there are innumerable examples of combatants, heavily outnumbered and outgunned, who nonetheless prevailed on the field of battle through sheer will and fighting spirit.

The single most crucial factor in prevailing in a life-threatening encounter is the determination to persevere and win. You must acquire the attitude that if forced to fight, you will never give up.

This attitude of gritty determination is important for several reasons. First, such an attitude, manifested in your speech, eye contact and body language, can throw doubt and fear into a potential assailant, deterring him or her from mounting an attack. If an assault is initiated, sometimes a strong, determined response will cause it to be broken off. Furthermore, even when you are wounded in a confrontation, resolutely continuing your self-defense efforts may stop an attacker before he or she inflicts further injury. There have been many cases of citizens who, though grievously wounded in a criminal attack, refused to give up, and survived their injuries. Finally, your attitude influences your actions. The will to persevere and prevail imbues your efforts with greater power, confidence and effectiveness.

DEVELOPING A PLAN

An important aspect of mental preparedness and an effective defensive mindset is *planning.* If you are concerned with personal protection, you must develop an individual plan to meet your specific needs. Such a plan should take into consideration your personal characteristics, habits, skills and physical capabilities and limitations, as well as the characteristics of the environments outside your home in which you may find yourself.

The most important part of any individualized personal protection plan comprises those steps to avoid having to use deadly force. For example, by staying away from certain streets or areas at night, you may avoid being placed in a situation in which you may have to use force to defend yourself. In a store, a planned escape route may allow a clerk the means to flee a robber's attack without resorting to lethal force. Avoiding a violent confrontation by flight, evasion, deterrence or any other method that can be safely used is always preferable to employing deadly force.

Since the dynamics of any defensive encounter are complex, unpredictable, and changeable, the personal protection plan must offer sufficient flexibility to allow you to make appropriate responses to a wide range of situations. This may involve a series of escalating responses that correspond to different types and levels of threat.

Just as you must regularly practice the shooting and gun handling skills presented in the NRA Basic Personal Protection Outside the Home Course to maintain a high level of preparedness, you should also practice your personal protection plan. Use a training partner to simulate various threats you may find outside the home. Additionally, frequently review your plan in light of changes in individual characteristics or abilities, the defensive environment, or the nature of the threat(s) likely to be encountered.

VISUALIZATION

Visualization is the formation of a mental image of a situation or activity. Visualization is a powerful tool that has been used to improve performance in sports, business and many other aspects of life.

Visualization should be used to imagine different defensive scenarios you may encounter outside the home:

- *What if I suddenly hear a scream down the hall in my workplace?*
- *What if a person in a slowly-passing car suddenly makes a threatening gesture?*
- *What if a stranger on the street suddenly produces a knife or club and demands my wallet?*
- *What if I am stopped at a red light in my vehicle and a stranger attempts to enter by force?*

Visualizing these and similar scenarios gives you a dry run of such situations, and helps reduce the surprise factor should any of the visualized situations actually take place. Through visualization, you will better anticipate potential sources of danger in the environment, and devise practical plans to deal with them.

Visualization should also be used in your range training. Visualize the target not as a piece of paper or cardboard, but as a threat to your life or the lives of others. Using this type of imagery during shooting and gun handling exercises will help you mentally prepare for a real confrontation.

Visualization can additionally be used to build confidence. It has been said that "you can only do what you can see yourself doing." In other words, if you can't picture yourself doing something—whether it is bowling a perfect game, building your own house, or becoming president of a business—you'll probably never be able to do it. Visualization is used this way by many sports psychologists and trainers. They instruct their athletes to visualize themselves not just clearing the hurdles or negotiating the downhill skiing course, but also winning the first place medal. In the same way, when you visualize yourself in a violent encounter, you should complete the mental scenario by visualizing yourself prevailing in that situation. By vividly seeing yourself prevail, and ingraining in yourself the idea that you can and will prevail, you will build confidence in your ability to control a life-threatening situation. That confidence, in turn, will enhance the effectiveness of your defensive actions in a real-life confrontation.

Shooting, gun handling and presentation skills can be critical in helping you prevail in a violent criminal attack, and thus must be diligently practiced. It is equally important, however, to develop and practice the various mental skills, attitudes and techniques—awareness, the willingness to use deadly force, the determination to persevere, planning, and visualization—that together constitute a state of mental preparedness. An individual who possesses only fair marksmanship skills but who has a high level of mental preparedness has a greater likelihood of prevailing in a deadly encounter than a highly skilled shooter who lacks the awareness, will to persevere, planning and other factors that contribute to surviving an attack.

CHAPTER 6

AVOIDING CONFRONTATIONS OUTSIDE THE HOME

It is often repeated in this book that the best way of surviving a life-threatening encounter is to avoid it in the first place. Avoiding a confrontation outside the home doesn't require the foot speed of an Olympic sprinter or the intimidating size of an NFL lineman. Nor does it mean that you've got to be rich enough to afford a bulletproof limousine or an army of bodyguards. Avoiding confrontations is largely a matter of thinking ahead and using some common sense—something anyone can do.

The following are some general guidelines or suggestions for avoiding a confrontation outside the home. This chapter is not intended to present an exhaustive list of violence-avoidance techniques, however. More information on this subject is offered in the NRA Refuse to Be a Victim® Course.,

BE AWARE

Awareness of your environment and the potential threats it contains is the single most important factor that will enable you to avoid a violent encounter outside the home. The more aware you are, the sooner you will recognize a threat, and the more time you will have to retreat, evade or otherwise avoid it. Conversely, you will never take steps to avoid a threat of which you are not aware.

Maintaining a high level of awareness outside the home is difficult to do for long periods of time.

Fig. 24. This person's unaware state makes her an appealing target for a criminal.

When you're taking a walk in the park or waiting for a bus, there is a natural tendency to daydream or become preoccupied with other things rather than scrutinize every approaching stranger. Sometimes you can maintain your level of awareness by making a game of it.

Try engaging in "What If?" games to keep you alert to your surroundings. As you walk down the street, stand in an elevator, or wait in a line at the store, imagine different defensive scenarios and plan your responses to them. What if a mugger jumps out from behind that parked car up ahead? What if that young man at the street corner tries to carjack me when I stop for the light? What if a disgruntled employee in my workplace becomes violent? In addition to keeping you alert, this kind of mental exercise also sharpens your awareness of potential threats in your environment.

Never assume you are safe enough to drift into a state of unawareness outside your home. You have probably seen people reading books or magazines, or even napping, while waiting in a bus or train station. Probably you have also seen people listening to a personal stereo device while walking on a sidewalk or jogging in a park. All of these people have compromised their personal safety to some extent because they believed they were safe enough to let down their guard. As a result, they made themselves vulnerable A full discussion of awareness can be found in Chapter 4: Awareness.

PLAN AHEAD

Plan your daily activities, insofar as is possible, to maximize your safety and minimize the risk of having a violent encounter. If you must go to or

through a high-crime area, plan to do it during a period of relative safety, when many other people are around, for example, or when police patrols are most evident. If you are going to do laundry at an all-night laundromat, don't put it off until 11 p.m., when you may find yourself alone; do it in the middle of the afternoon, when you will be surrounded by many other people.

Fig. 25. Plan ahead to avoid being in a vulnerable situation, such as doing laundry late at night in an empty laundromat.

When you plan ahead, coordinate your activities. For

example, don't plan to drop off some clothes at a church thrift store in a high-crime neighborhood on the way to a formal dinner: your fancy dress will attract attention in that area, and may make you a target.

You should similarly coordinate your concealed carry habits with your activities. If you opt to leave your gun at home one day—perhaps because you will be spending most of your day in a federal building, or because you will be traveling into a jurisdiction in which firearms are not allowed—don't choose that day to also make a business trip into a high-crime area. Wait until the next day, when you will again be wearing your defensive handgun.

AVOID DANGEROUS PEOPLE

Avoiding dangerous people may seem an obvious, even self-evident way to keep out of violent confrontations. Certainly if you avoid criminals, you will avoid crime. However, to maximize your safety in situations outside the home, "avoiding dangerous people" should be interpreted in a much broader way.

Outside the home, there are many types of people who may constitute a threat. Any stranger, for example, may be a mugger. He may seem to be lost, or in need of a light for his cigarette, or he may be in a car and signal you to his open window to ask directions; but these may be ruses to get you to approach within striking distance. While many potential threats are easily identified as such—for example, gang members wearing their colors—more clever criminals hide their true nature behind normal attire and a pleasant demeanor. As a general rule, any

Fig. 26. Associating with dangerous or violence-prone persons will increase your likelihood of being the victim of an attack.

stranger who gets within a certain distance of you and invades your personal space deserves to be regarded with greater vigilance.

Groups of people, particularly teenage boys or young men, are also to be avoided. Studies of social psychology and mob behavior show that the members of a group are capable, collectively, of crimes that no single individual member would commit on his own. During their social development, teenage boys and young men develop a strong group identity that often manifests itself in violence. In areas in which gang activity is prevalent, you should also avoid groups of girls, as they, too, are capable of violent behavior.

Don't assume that just because a person seems to have a good reputation you should trust them with your life. There have been numerous cases of

Fig. 27. Aggressive persons may unpredictably turn on you for little or no reason.

female students at prestigious universities who went to parties at fraternity houses and ended up being assaulted. The members of these fraternities would be regarded by most people as the cream of the social crop: the sons of teachers, lawyers, doctors, bank presidents and so forth. The women who were attacked probably assumed that these fine, upstanding young men—complete strangers in some but not all cases—were not the kind of people to be wary of. They assumed wrong.

Even your friends can be dangerous, at least in some situations. A person who is always noisy or sarcastic, who makes inappropriate or insulting remarks, or who tends to say inflammatory things can get himself and all his companions in serious trouble under certain circumstances. Even in the relatively safe environment of a sports stadium, his disrespectful, caustic remarks about one of the teams can lead to a confrontation with some of that team's fans. If you have a friend such as this, leave him home when you go out in public.

AVOID DANGEROUS SITUATIONS

There is an almost infinite number of situations that are, by their very nature, inherently dangerous. Learn to recognize and avoid these.

Darkness. Many criminals prefer to operate in darkness because low-light conditions hide their activities and facilitate their predations. To

reduce your likelihood of becoming a target, try to avoid being in, or traveling through, areas such as dark parking lots or parking garages, unlit laundry rooms or hallways, dark alleys or streets with broken street-lamps and the like.

Darkness doesn't encourage crime only at night. Even in daytime, the shadows in an alley, under a stair-well, or in a dark corridor can hide a predator.

Whenever possible, plan your activities to take advantage of day-light. If you must travel at night plan your travels to follow well-lit streets;

Fig. 28. Avoid deserted areas at night, especially when you're alone.

park in lighted lots or under streetlamps; and stay away from alleys, dark-ened doorways and other areas in which a criminal may hide. At all times, avoid poorly-lit areas.

Don't Be Alone. Criminals tend to target those who are alone rather than those in a group. Being alone, especially at night or in a deserted area, makes you more vulnerable to attack.

Get in the habit of having company, especially when you're going to be in an area in which there are few other people around. For example, you should have a partner or partners when you go hiking, walking in the woods, or bicycling on a trail. If you are working late at night, have a company security guard walk you to your car. Even when you're walking to the store in broad daylight, you will significantly reduce your chances of being attacked if you are accompa-nied.

Avoiding being out in public alone is especially important for those who the typical male attacker will see, rightly or wrongly, as being easy prey, such as women, the elderly, the

Fig. 29. These women increase their safety by traveling in a group.

handicapped, and those who are of small stature or slight build. If you fall into any of those categories, you should especially avoid traveling alone. Remember, the point is to do everything you can to prevent a confrontation from happening.

Hitchhiking. At all costs, avoid hitchhiking, and avoid picking up hitchhikers; there have been far too many cases of hitchhikers disappearing, and of good samaritans being victimized by hitchhikers.

The only exception to this might be in a situation in which a person was completely stranded, with no shelter, in an extreme environment, such as a desert or a blizzard. Some states, in fact, have laws that make it illegal for a person to refuse to pick up a hitchhiker under certain potentially life-threatening conditions. When there is no threat to life or limb, however, you should always avoid picking up a hitchhiker or engaging in hitchhiking yourself.

Fig. 30. Hitchhiking can put you at risk for attack from a predator in a vehicle.

If you are stranded as the result of a vehicle breakdown, you should stay with your vehicle with the windows rolled up and doors locked and call

the police with your cell phone. Anyone stopping to help should be regarded with suspicion; talk to them only through a small crack between the window and door frame. Refuse all offers of help. If you do not have a cell phone, ask the person to call the police at the first opportunity. Do not leave your vehicle for anyone but a uniformed police officer, or a person known to you whom you were able to call for assistance.

Fig. 31. If you are stranded, stay in your vehicle with the doors locked and windows rolled up, and call for help using a cell phone.

AVOID DANGEROUS PLACES

Most people understand that certain neighborhoods or areas are more dangerous than others. Typically, high-crime inner-city areas are perceived as the areas to avoid, especially at night.

In addition to the "bad neighborhoods" that just about everyone knows about, there are usually many more dangerous places you should avoid if you don't want to become involved in a dangerous encounter. Even in affluent suburban areas, there are certain spots you should stay away from.

Take the time to read the crime reports in your local newspaper; this will often reveal the areas where crime is prevalent. Also, listen to your gut-level reaction. If you sense that something's not right where you are, it probably isn't. Avoid places or areas you know nothing about. If you are new in town, or are unfamiliar with a particular area, ask the locals. People often know where you would or would not be safe.

AVOID MAKING YOURSELF A TARGET

For safety, your goal when you are outside your home should be to blend in with the crowd. Any person who sticks out is more likely to be seen as a target by somebody.

There are many ways in which you can stand out and make yourself a target. Ostentatious behavior—wearing expensive jewelry or clothes, driving an expensive car, or spending large sums of money—often will get you noticed by the wrong people. So, too, will dress or behavior that signifies weakness or vulnerability. An unkempt appearance and a downtrodden, vulnerable look will also attract unwanted attention.

Fig. 32. Wearing a fur coat or excessive jewelry can make you a target.

Be aware that any level of alcohol consumption can dull your senses and cloud your judgement, making you an especially tempting target. In addition, after consuming alcohol your slowed reflexes and skewed perception of reality likely will make you incapable of sensing impending danger, or appropriately responding to an attack.

To blend in with a crowd and avoid being targeted by a predator, wear clothing that is neither extravagant nor shabby, and project a strong and confident image by walking or standing with your head up and your eyes alertly scanning your surroundings. Like most predators, criminals are much less likely to attack if they know you have spotted them and are watching their behavior.

Fig. 33. Avoid performing ATM transactions late at night or at deserted location where a criminal may watch and then assault you.

AVOID HAVING A PATTERN

If you are a person of unvarying habit, you may be making yourself an easier target for a thief, robber, rapist or stalker. Vary your routine; don't fall into a predictable pattern. For example, if you make a night bank deposit after your store closes, vary your route as well as the time of your deposit. Keep in mind that a criminal may observe you for several nights before deciding to rob you. If your routine is predictable, his job is easy; but if he never knows exactly how or when you will arrive at the bank, he'll find it harder to prey on you.

Not everyone has to worry about modifying their life pattern to avoid being targeted. However, those who are the potential victims of stalkers or kidnappers can increase their safety by becoming less predictable.

AVOID ANTAGONIZING OTHERS

Never deliberately antagonize a stranger; you never know who he is, or what he is capable of. However, there are myriad ways in which you can unknowingly antagonize a person and become a target. For example, avoid controversial bumper stickers; they may enrage an unstable motorist, who may try to let you know how he feels about things at the next traffic light. Similarly, T-shirts or sweatshirts with political slogans, moral messages, or even sports team logos can make you the target of an aggressive person with an axe to grind. Wearing unconventional clothing, piercings and other body jewelry, and unusual hair styles can also make you a target of certain people.

Think about how others may respond to your appearance or to any messages on your clothes or your car. You may have to balance your right to free expression with your desire to prevent confrontation.

DON'T RESPOND TO ANTAGONISTIC BEHAVIOR

Even when you don't do anything to antagonize another person, you may still find yourself targeted by an unstable or violent individual. He may not like a person of your social class or ethnicity in his neighborhood; he may be a paranoid person who thinks you're looking at him. You may simply be wearing a shirt or hat whose color symbolizes membership in a rival gang. In all these cases, you may be faced with an aggressive, angry person who confronts you for reasons you don't even understand. Don't feed into his antagonism. Keep your cool; avoid raising your voice or even arguing with him. If possible, don't even respond to his verbal

Fig. 34. When confronted by an aggressive or angry person, avoid arguing or antagonizing him. If necessary, simply walk or run away. This may keep you out of a situation leading to violence.

attacks. Walk away; run if you have to. It may make you look like a coward, but it will keep you out of a situation that may escalate into violence.

LOOK FOR ESCAPE ROUTES

Wherever you are—on the street, in your car, in a store, or at your workplace—you should always look for an escape route to avoid a confrontation. For example, when you're walking to your car in a lonely parking garage, make note of the exits, or even any places where you could jump over a wall and escape. Also, when you pull up behind a line of cars, don't ride the bumper of the car in front of you. Leave enough space—say, a half a car length or more—for you to swing out suddenly in the event of trouble, such as a motorist overcome with road rage. Even when you're in a building—particularly in a strange building—be aware of emergency exits, stairways and elevators. You never know when you might take a wrong turn and suddenly find yourself alone in a darkened hallway, with the sound of stealthy footsteps echoing behind you.

Fig. 35. Whenever confronted by a potential or actual threat, always be aware of potential escape routes (arrow).

CHAPTER 7

RESPONDING TO AN ATTACK OUTSIDE THE HOME

Other chapters in this book contain a variety of strategies and steps to deter, prevent or escape a criminal attack. Even when these strategies are observed, however, you may still be forced to come face to face with an attacker. You may be taken by surprise in a parking lot, in an alley, in a shop, or even right outside your home on the sidewalk.

You must be prepared—through training, prior visualization and mentally playing out scenarios—to be in control of the situation and act decisively. You must be prepared to defend yourself if your assailant presents an imminent deadly threat.

PSYCHOLOGICAL REACTIONS TO A THREATENING ENCOUNTER

The body responds in a number of ways to being threatened with bodily harm. For example, the parts of the brain that control higher thought processes begin to shut down, relinquishing control to more primitive, survival-oriented brain centers.

Every life-threatening encounter is different, and each person responds to an attack in a different way. There is no way to determine ahead of time how a person will react to a particular situation, even if that person has been in a similar situation before.

When confronted with an attack, you may initially delay responding because of denial—you just can't believe that you are being assaulted. Also, many people have an internal resistance to inflicting deadly force in a face-to-face encounter. This inherent reluctance can be overcome through fear, as well as through conditioning and visualization training.

There are five possible responses to any life-threatening encounter: *freeze, submit, posture, flight* or *fight*.

Freeze. The victim of an attack may be so overwhelmed or surprised by being threatened that he or she may freeze and become incapable of any action whatsoever. A momentary freeze resulting from confusion, shock, initial panic or denial of what is occurring is normal and, in fact, should be expected. In some cases, however, the frozen state may persist throughout the encounter.

Fig. 36. Freeze reaction.

Submit. Submission is simply giving in to an attacker. While it is often said that one should accede to an assailant's demands so as not to antagonize him into further violence, some studies indicate that a person using a firearm for self-defense is less likely to be injured by resisting than by submitting.

There may be occasions when submission seems the prudent course of action, such as when you are surprised by an armed assailant who demands only your wallet and not your life. However, it is impossible to predict the outcome of a potentially violent situation, particularly when you are relying upon the good will of a criminal. Crime statistics show that present-day criminals are more willing than their predecessors to maim or kill needlessly, even when the victim is completely compliant. Seemingly pointless murders have been committed to gain status within a gang or to silence or intimidate witnesses. Thus, the

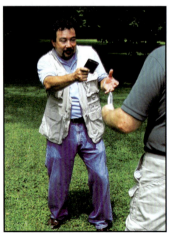

Fig. 37. Submit reaction.

risk of inciting your attacker to greater violence by resisting must be weighed against the danger of putting yourself at the mercy of his or her whims if you submit. Choosing between those alternatives depends upon your moment-to-moment assessment of the situation.

There are some situations you may encounter outside the home in which self-defense experts claim you should never submit. Chief among these is a situation in which you are ordered by an attacker to get into his car. You must resist this at all costs. Police statistics show that persons who comply with this demand quite often end up as fatal victims.

Even under the best of circumstances, submission is never a safe choice. Proper preparation involving training, the defensive mindset, and the development of an effective defensive plan reduces the likelihood of being caught in a situation in which submission seems the best alternative.

Fig. 38. Posture reaction.

Posture. Posturing is combat without contact. Words, sounds, gestures and body language are the weapons used to dominate, intimidate and subdue another. Posturing is frequently seen in the animal world when members of the same species growl, paw the ground, make mock charges and otherwise exhibit aggressive behavior that stops short of actual fighting. Such showdowns usually end with the retreat or submission of one of the animals.

Humans frequently engage in similar behavior. Depending upon the circumstances of the encounter, both attacker and victim may attempt to out-bluster each other until one backs down or flees.

Flight. Flight, also known as retreat, involves removing yourself from the source of the threat. Flight or retreat is a natural instinct when confronted with danger. In some defensive situations, it will not be possible to retreat without the risk of incurring injury.

Fight. In a self-defense context, the fight response involves the use of whatever force is reasonable and necessary to prevent harm from an attacker. In some circumstances, yelling a verbal warning can be a part of the fight response, prior to the utilization of force. Deadly force may be used only when there is an imminent threat of severe harm or death.

Fig. 39. Flight reaction.

Obviously, not every victim of a violent attack will experience all or even most of the above-mentioned psychological reactions. Nor can you predict how you will react in a given situation. It is not uncommon to experience an escalating series of responses—for example, from freeze to flee to posture and finally fight.

Do not forget that your attacker may experience some of the same psychological reactions. If you show determined resistance to your attacker, he may initially posture in an attempt to intimidate you, then eventually take flight. Your attacker very likely has one or more contingency plans for a potential confrontation before he even approaches you on the street. This will give him an advantage over you if you have not developed similar plans.

Fig. 40. Fight reaction.

PHYSIOLOGICAL REACTIONS TO A LIFE-THREATENING ENCOUNTER

No matter what your level of training or how capable you believe yourself to be in handling stressful situations, you will experience, to a greater or lesser degree, a number of involuntary physiological changes during a serious defensive situation.

General Bodily Responses to Imminent Danger. In most cases, there will be a period of time between when you first perceive a threat and an attack actually occurs. This may occur, for example, when you recognize that a mugger or other criminal is stalking you on the street. During this period you probably will experience a number of bodily responses to imminent danger. Your heart rate and respiration will increase (to provide more blood and oxygen to the muscles and brain), your pupils will dilate (to take in more light and see the threat better), and your muscles will be tighter in anticipation of sudden movement.

Adrenaline Rush. One of the ways your body prepares you for flight or fight is through the release of the hormone adrenaline into your bloodstream. This powerful chemical heightens the senses and increases strength, increases heart rate and respiration, and can also cause trembling of the muscles. This trembling can make it more difficult to stand or sit still or, more important, to hold the firearm steady. This trembling can be mistaken for fear by both the assailant and victim. In reality, it is a physical reaction to the excess of adrenaline that has been dumped into the bloodstream in preparation for an attack. This is also what causes the uncontrollable shaking sometimes experienced after a confrontation is over: the body is no longer utilizing all the adrenaline that was released.

Note that although the heightened awareness caused by adrenaline may enable you to more readily perceive a threat, it may also predispose you to overreact to any sudden stimulus.

Loss of Fine Motor Skills. Stress—regardless of its source—results in a loss of fine motor skills. This is often experienced in daily life. For example, it is much harder to unlock your front door with a key when you are rushing to get to a ringing telephone inside. In sports, too, it is common for many athletes to perform better in practice than under the stress of actual competition.

During an attack, your loss of fine motor control will manifest itself in many ways. For example, you will find it more difficult to load a cartridge into a pistol magazine or revolver cylinder, or to open your car door with your key. To compensate for this loss of fine motor control, the NRA Personal Protection Outside the Home Course teaches presentation, shooting and gun handling skills that involve gross motor skills only. This is also why well-designed defensive handguns are simple to operate, and feature controls that are easily and naturally actuated by large muscle movements.

PERCEPTUAL CHANGES DURING A THREATENING ENCOUNTER

Survivors of violent attacks—as well as those who have experienced certain other extremely stressful situations—commonly report that, during the attack or stressful event, their perceptions of visual and auditory stimuli, as well as the passage of time, were altered. These alterations—tunnel vision, auditory exclusion and time dilation—are involuntary, and may have evolved as a survival mechanism to better focus all of one's senses and concentration on an immediate source of danger. While these perceptual changes may have worked extremely well in enabling our ancestors to fight saber-toothed tigers, they do not always provide as much of a benefit when dealing with one or more intelligent, determined human assailants.

Tunnel Vision. Under the stress of an imminent or actual attack, you will be focused almost exclusively on the perceived threat, and will be virtually oblivious to anything going on elsewhere in your visual field. This phenomenon is known as tunnel vision.

It is important to avoid tunnel vision during a defensive shooting situation, because it can cause you to fail to recognize additional threats (or innocent persons) that may lurk just outside your immediate field of view. Tunnel vision can be broken by developing certain training habits (such as lowering the firearm and assessing the area, whether you have fired shots or not).

Auditory Exclusion. During a violent encounter you will also undergo auditory exclusion, a condition during which extraneous sounds may be inaudible. Sounds emanating from outside your visual perception—and even those from within it—may go unheard. People involved in shootings often report that the sound of their own gunshots was no louder to them than a popgun.

You can at least partially counteract the effects of auditory exclusion by screaming your commands to your assailant. Not only does this help break through the veil of auditory exclusion; it also serves to intimidate him.

Keep in mind that you will not be the only one suffering auditory exclusion; your assailant as well as any family members, police officers or innocent bystanders who were involved in the situation will also experience it.

Time Dilation. Time dilation refers to the perception of slowed time that occurs during extreme stress. You may see the movements of both your assailant and yourself as happening in slow motion, and you lose the ability to accurately determine the passage of time. A few seconds of actual time may seem to you to be much longer in duration. The phenomenon of time dilation is the reason why, when you are first alerted to strange sounds or other early warnings of a potential threat, you should wait much longer than you may initially think is necessary before you relax your guard or emerge from hiding.

Temporary Loss of Memory. Highly stressful events can sometimes cause a mental overload that results in a temporary loss of memory. Most often, this is manifested simply in confusion over the details of an incident; occasionally, however, a person may lose all remembrance of the event. The passage of time often restores the accuracy and completeness of the memory.

Because of this phenomenon, comments you make immediately after you have been involved in a life-threatening incident may not be accurate. Thus, if you are involved in a defensive shooting, you should generally tell responding law enforcement officers only that you were unlawfully attacked by a violent adversary and had to use force to defend your life. Avoid making any other statements until you have consulted an attorney.

CONTROLLING AN ENCOUNTER OUTSIDE THE HOME

When you encounter a housebreaker or other intruder in your home, you have the upper hand in certain ways. You are more familiar with the layout of your home; you probably have alarms, deadbolt locks, window bars and reinforced doors to protect you; and, if you have a properly equipped safe room, you have a defensible location to retreat to, in which you may summon help or, if necessary, stop an attack. In a very real sense, if you follow the proper procedure at the first sign of an attack—lock yourself in the safe room, retrieve your firearm and ammunition, and call the police—you can exercise considerable control over a violent encounter.

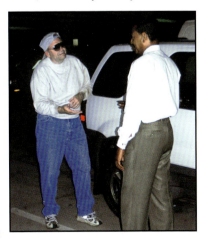

Outside the home, however, the situation is reversed. You are on the criminal's turf: he knows his neighborhood, and he makes sure he has the element of surprise. Moreover, there's often no safe place you can run to. Although the odds appear to be on your attacker's side, there is still much you can do to control the encounter.

Fig. 41. A criminal may close the distance to you by appearing to be a panhandler.

Fig. 42. Safety dictates that you choose an elevator with several people rather than with a single suspicious-looking person.

Keep Your Distance. It is hard to maintain a safe distance from every stranger on a busy sidewalk or crowded elevator, but you should at least maintain an awareness of everyone around you. Try to identify people who may be potential attackers, and make an effort to keep a safe distance from them. This alone may prevent an attack, as a criminal may see you as too difficult a target and turn his attention elsewhere.

Use your common sense when you are in a situation in which physical proximity is likely or unavoidable. Often you are most at risk when you are alone with a stranger who is close to you. For example, avoid riding in an empty elevator with a suspicious-looking person; wait for one carrying a number of people. If you see a loud or unruly group of people approaching you on the sidewalk, unobtrusively cross the street. Don't get on an empty subway car; go to one having several riders.

There may be an interval between the time an attacker has made his intentions clear and he actually begins his attack. For example, he may demand your wallet, claiming he has a weapon, but does not actually brandish it or use it against you. Use this time to increase your distance from him. The best way of maintaining or increasing your distance is, of course, to flee, provided you can do so safely. Even when you are faced with an attacker armed with a firearm, increasing the distance between you and him significantly reduces the likelihood that he will hurt you, particularly if you are moving quickly.

If you are about to be attacked, or are actually being attacked, put obstacles between you and your assailant, such as trees, cars, trash cans, dumpsters and the like. Anything that makes it harder for him to reach you or injure you has the same effect as increasing your distance from him.

Be Wary of Strangers. During the preliminary stages of a threatening or violent encounter, a potential attacker may attempt to engage you in friendly conversation. This can be used to put you off your guard, or to distract you so that you don't notice a hidden accomplice sneaking up on you. Do not be misled by such behavior. Keep any stranger at a distance. A stranger who seems to be unarmed and friendly may suddenly attack you if you let

him get close enough. Also, while he is talking to you, use your peripheral vision to maintain an awareness of additional persons who may be approaching you from the side or the rear.

A potential attacker may attempt to talk his way close to you by asking for a cigarette, the time, or directions to some address. Even when a stranger appears friendly, keep your distance, as well as a high level of awareness. As unfriendly as it may seem, the safest course of action may be to simply walk away from him.

Fig. 43. A person distracted by one seemingly friendly attacker while another sneaks up from behind (arrow).

Yell Your Commands. Once it is clear that a potentially deadly attack is imminent, you are justified in presenting your firearm. Depending upon the circumstances, however, you may not even have to fire it. Your attacker may suddenly stop approaching you, or may begin to back away, for example.

In such a case, it may be appropriate to issue verbal commands to deter further aggression. When giving an attacker instructions, yell your commands as loud as you can. This will both intimidate him and will help overcome his auditory exclusion (explained earlier in this chapter). Keep your commands simple: STOP! GO AWAY! I HAVE A GUN! DROP YOUR WEAPON! LIE DOWN! Yelling at your assailant also will attract the attention of others who may give you assistance, or later serve as witnesses to the attack.

Do not converse or try to reason with your attacker. He will often attempt to gain your sympathy, to appeal to your good nature, or to convince you that you have made a mistake in suspecting him of any criminal intent. He may even try to approach you slowly, talking softly and reasonably. Do not be fooled by this behavior. You must remain in control of the situation. If an attacker continues to approach you and you perceive an imminent threat to your life, you must defend yourself appropriately.

Holding An Attacker At Gunpoint. It is rare that you would hold an uninjured criminal at gunpoint. Numerous studies show that your attacker will usually flee when you present your gun or after a few shots are fired. Let him go. Do not stand between him and an escape route. It is not your job to catch criminals; that is not why you have a concealed carry permit. All you want to do is eliminate the threat to your life.

Holding an attacker at gunpoint is especially problematic outside the home, where you have little control over the environment and the people in it. While you are occupied with a downed or surrendered attacker, it is relatively easy for an accomplice to approach you unawares and mount an attack. Furthermore, outside the home your action of pointing a firearm at another person may be misinterpreted by other civilians and even the

police. It is always better to let an attacker go and let the police capture him later.

In the unlikely event that you do find yourself in the situation of holding an assailant at gunpoint, however, do not approach him or attempt to frisk him. If he has a weapon, have him carefully place it on the ground (muzzle pointing away from you if it is a firearm). If possible, have the assailant kick the weapon some distance away from him. Also, order the attacker to keep his hands high in the air. Don't let him lower his hands

Fig. 44. A person using the proper technique to hold an attacker at gunpoint. The defender uses a cell phone to call police.

to his head or the back of his neck; some hardened and experienced criminals may conceal a weapon in their hat or collar, or between the shoulder blades. Yell all your commands at him in a loud, clear voice. Seek cover; while doing so, make sure his hands stay visible to you at all times. Have him lie face-down on the ground, away from his weapon, chin on the ground and legs spread apart, with his hands held palms-up and stretched straight out from his shoulders.

While you are holding your attacker for the police, you must also remain alert to any other aggressors you have not detected. If possible, seek cover with your back against a wall, dumpster or other solid structure, or otherwise position yourself so that you can cover the intruder while protecting yourself from surprise attack. Use your cell phone to call the police, never taking your eyes off your attacker, or have a bystander call for you.

Note that any assailant you are holding at gunpoint has three choices: run away, comply with your commands, or attack you and get shot. If he chooses flight, let him go.

DEALING WITH AN ATTACK OUTSIDE THE HOME WITHOUT A FIREARM

There may be occasions when you must respond to an attack outside the home without using a firearm. You may not have your defensive firearm with you, for example, or the attack may not threaten your life, and thus does not justify the use of deadly force.

Of course, the best way of dealing with any confrontation is to evade it, escape it, or flee from it. However, if you cannot avoid an attack and you are unable or unwilling to use your defensive firearm to stop it, you may still be able to defend yourself by using martial arts, chemical irritants, or alternative non-gun weapons.

Martial Arts. There are many styles of martial arts instruction currently available, such as karate, judo, aikido, kung-fu, taekwondo, Krav Maga, Sambo, boxing and so forth. While the different types vary as to the actual techniques employed, they all have certain characteristics and limitations in common. All are used essentially at arm's length, potentially increasing the likelihood of injury from an attacker. While the martial arts can be very effective against a single unarmed attacker, they are of uncertain value against an assailant armed with a weapon, or against several attackers.

Most martial arts require some level of strength, speed, coordination and flexibility, and thus may be difficult to master by those who are physically compromised or handicapped. Most importantly, to use the martial arts effectively for defensive purposes normally requires years of rigorous training. This makes the martial arts less than ideal for those who cannot devote the time, money and effort needed to master them, or who have an immediate need for self-protection.

Despite these limitations, martial arts can be a critical component of a complete self-protection strategy. Given that most attacks take place at close range, and that handgun cartridges generally do not produce instant incapacitation, it follows that, even when shot, an assailant armed with a knife, club or other arm's length weapon will have ample opportunity to inflict injury on an armed citizen. Also, close-range attacks may occur so quickly that there is simply no time to present a firearm, even with an instinctive shooting technique. At such times, the ability to effectively ward off or counter the initial stages of an attack with "empty hand" techniques may prevent a serious or potentially fatal injury. These techniques may also give the armed citizen time to present the firearm, or, if shots have already been fired, to wait for hits to take effect.

Martial arts techniques may also be useful to stop or deflect an attack that is not life threatening, and therefore does not justify the use of lethal force. Some shooting schools teach a few basic techniques that can be used in conjunction with firearm presentation. More extensive training can be acquired at martial arts schools that are more defense- than sport-oriented.

Chemical Irritants. Chemical irritants used to deter attackers usually take the form of tear gas or pepper (capsaicin) sprays. When sprayed into the eyes, nose or mouth, these irritants inflame mucous membranes, causing watery eyes, a runny nose, difficulty breathing and an intense burning sensation. Most commonly, these irritants are sold as pocket-size pressurized canisters having a nozzle that can be aimed at an attacker's face.

Chemical irritants can be useful for deterring non-life threatening attacks, or for those persons who do not wish to employ deadly force for self-defense. Unlike martial arts, chemical irritants do not require extensive training for effective use. Chemical irritants can also be effective against non-human attackers, such as aggressive dogs. Nonetheless, they have limitations. In order for a sufficient quantity of irritant to contact the attacker's mucous membranes, he must be fairly close when the spray is activated. This, in turn, can increase the likelihood of receiving an injury from the attacker. Furthermore, in windy conditions, some of the irritant spray can blow back in the user's face. Chemical irritants also vary in effectiveness. According to some estimates, about 10% to 15% of the population is at least somewhat resistant to the effects of tear gas and pepper sprays, and may not be deterred or incapacitated by these products. Finally, carrying chemical irritants is illegal in some jurisdictions. Even in jurisdictions where they are permitted, they may be prohibited in some areas, such as governmental offices.

Non-Gun Options. There are a variety of non-gun options that may be used in lieu of a firearm for self-defense; however, the carry and use of such options is often problematic. Many of these options, such as saps, spring-loaded batons, sword canes and nunchaku are illegal for carry in most jurisdictions, even when firearm carry is permitted. Knives, especially small folding knives, are legal to carry in many jurisdictions, but there are often limitations as to blade length and type.

Some innocuous-looking objects may be used as weapons in an emergency. Canes and umbrellas can be used to ward off an attack, as can a device called a Kubotan, basically an aluminum cylinder about 6" long and $1/2$" thick which is used against pressure points and other vulnerable areas of an attacker. Hung from car or house keys, it attracts little attention. As with other forms of unarmed self-defense, training is required for effective employment of this option.

Similar in size and shape to the Kubotan are some defensive flashlights, which are discussed in greater depth in Chapter 27, Engaging Targets in Low Light Conditions. In addition to being used as contact options, they can also be employed to temporarily blind or disorient a close-range attacker in low-light conditions.

Stun guns, which deliver a disabling but normally non-lethal electrical shock, can be effective in disabling a close-range assailant. There are two major types of these defensive options: one having two exposed electrodes which are simulataneously applied to the body, and the other firing needle-like electrodes which penetrate light clothing and stick in the skin. This latter type allows the defender to stay several feet from an attacker, and is also considered by some authorities to more quickly incapacitate. Both designs rely upon direct contact between the electrodes and the assailant's skin, and thus may not be effective when he is clad in thick, heavy clothing. Note that stun guns are illegal or restricted in many jursidictions.

All non-gun options have some of the same limitations. As with martial arts and chemical irritants, they can only be used when the attacker is at close range, and they vary in effectiveness. Also, training is required to use some of these options effectively. Additionally, some of these items, such as knives and even canes, may be regarded as lethal options by the authorities.

Non-gun weapons have one major advantage, however: they may be carried in a state of readiness that is usually not possible with firearms. A walking stick or umbrella is carried in your hands, and is therefore instantly available; and a Kubotan, canister of pepper spray, or small flashlight can be attached to your key ring, allowing it to be grasped inconspicuously as you walk toward your car or front door. Even a closed folding knife or small stun gun can be held in the hand without drawing attention, unlike a firearm. If you choose to incorporate a non-gun option into your overall defensive strategy, you should train with it as seriously as you do with your defensive firearm.

Because it allows a citizen to stop a threat more quickly, at a greater distance, and with less training than many other tools and techniques, a firearm is the best choice for self-defense outside the home. Adequate proficiency can be acquired by any person regardless of age, size, strength or physical limitation. However, as pointed out previously, there are confrontational situations in which the use of a firearm would not be justified. There are also those who simply do not want to incorporate a firearm into their personal protection strategy. In these cases, non-gun alternatives for personal defense may be appropriate.

CHAPTER 8

IF YOU MUST SHOOT

As is emphasized repeatedly throughout this book, a firearm is a tool of last resort in dealing with a life-threatening encounter. Whenever possible and safe, it is always preferable to prevent, deter, evade or escape an attack. Unfortunately, there may be times when these options are not available, and you must use whatever means are at your disposal—including your defensive firearm—to stop an attack and protect your life or the lives of loved ones.

There is nothing—no shooting sport, no motion picture or instruction manual, and no training regimen—that can fully prepare you for the experience of using your defensive firearm against a violent assailant. Nonetheless, those gun owners who avail themselves of every opportunity to prepare mentally and physically for a defensive situation will almost always fare better than those who don't. A large part of this preparation involves understanding what actually goes on during and after a shooting.

ART DOESN'T ALWAYS IMITATE LIFE

Most people in our society have little or no experience with shooting situations. For many, television and motion pictures are the primary source of information regarding the use of firearms. Regrettably, the portrayals of firearm use in these media bear little resemblance to what actually occurs in real life. Knowing the difference between firearms fact and firearms fiction will enable you to better handle a defensive shooting situation.

Perhaps the greatest misconception fostered by the media lies in the effects of being shot. When a character is shot in motion pictures or television shows, the bullet strike produces a large, easily-seen wound and throws the person violently backward. Often a single shot causes instantaneous collapse.

In reality, this depiction is almost completely inaccurate. Both participants in and witnesses to defensive encounters involving firearms typically report an inability to spot bullet strikes. Also, a bullet hit often produces no discernible effect whatsoever—certainly not the violent backward motion we see in the entertainment media. Furthermore, studies show that one shot rarely stops or instantly incapacitates an assailant. More commonly, multiple shots from a handgun are required to stop an attacker.

Fig. 45. Firing in self-defense at this violent attacker could also endanger bystanders, motorists in passing cars, and others in buildings and roads in the background.

This last point cannot be overemphasized. Even when the first shot is well-placed in the center of mass, incapacitation usually results only after several shots—and several seconds. Hitting a vital area on your assailant may not immediately cause a cessation of the attack, particularly if he or she is under the influence of alcohol or drugs, or is highly motivated to do you harm or take your life. Even when the heart stops, sufficient fresh oxygen remains in the brain and muscles to continue activity for up to 30 seconds—more than enough time for an aggressor to resume or continue an attack. You should assume that your first shot will not immediately stop an attack. This is one of the reasons you need to continue to fire at the assailant until there is no longer any imminent deadly threat.

While there are areas on the body where a bullet hit will produce instant incapacitation, they are very small and unlikely to be hit even by an experienced shooter under the stress and rapid movement of a violent encounter. A solid center of mass hit (or hits) is the surest way to stop an attack quickly.

In television or motion-picture shooting incidents, little concern is given to the consequences of a shot that misses its target. In the media, misses simply splatter against nearby cover or ricochet away harmlessly. In the real world, you must be aware of where every bullet you fire can go—including your misses.

LIKELIHOOD OF INJURY

As discussed above, the great majority of assaults take place at very close range—often a matter of only a few feet. It has also been pointed out that an attacker is unlikely to be stopped immediately with a single shot. These two facts, plus the possibility of encountering multiple assailants in any confrontation outside the home, create a strong likelihood that you will suffer some degree of injury during an attack.

For example, it has been shown that an assailant wielding a knife even as far away as seven yards—21 feet—can usually get to and injure an armed defender before that defender can stop him with a handgun. This is often known as the 21-foot rule. Since most attacks take place at ranges considerably less than seven yards, you can see that an attacker armed with no more than a knife or club (or even his bare hands) often will be able to wound an armed defender.

Fig. 46. Even at a distance of 21 feet, a knife-wielding assailant will likely get to and injure an armed defender before he can be stopped.

The probability of being injured while defending yourself from attack should not, however, deter you from exercising your right of self-defense. Some misguided people believe that resisting an attack makes it more likely that you will be injured. U.S. Justice Department studies show that people who resist an assailant do, indeed, suffer a greater likelihood of injury than those who comply—except for those who resist with a firearm. In these studies, armed citizens who used a gun to protect their lives were considerably less likely to be injured than those who did not fight back. Simply put, if you cannot prevent, deter, evade or escape a violent attack, the effective use of a defensive firearm represents your best choice for minimizing your chances of injury or death.

There are several methods by which you can lessen the likelihood of injury from a violent assailant. The use of cover can protect you from an attacker, or at least slow it down. In any defensive situation, you need to create as much distance as possible between yourself and a violent criminal. This may take you out of the range of

Fig. 47. When attacked, it is important to put oneself behind cover.

edged weapons and contact weapons (hammers, tire irons, clubs, etc.), and decreases the probability of being hit by shots fired by an assailant.

Creating distance does not mean, however, that you delay firing upon an approaching aggressor. As discussed above, a determined assailant starting from seven yards away (a distance a little longer than a typical American-made full-size car) will almost certainly reach you before you can stop him, even with multiple gunshots. You must not wait to fire upon an attacker until the last possible moment in the hope that he will have a change of heart. You should fire whenever there is a clear, unavoidable and immediate threat to life.

Combining the use of both cover and distance can give you more time to react and to put obstacles between you and your assailant. These obstacles—cars, mailboxes, trash cans, trees, streetlight poles and so forth—will slow down your attacker, giving you more time to react. Such obstacles, properly used, can also prevent or delay injury from an attacker armed with an edged or contact weapon.

IF YOU ARE INJURED

Even if you sustain an injury during an attack, it is essential to keep fighting. The indomitable will to prevail is the single most important factor in ensuring your survival in a deadly encounter. Keep in mind that an initial wound from a knife, a club or even a handgun is not likely to be fatal. If you stop fighting when you are first injured, however, you likely will receive additional, possibly lethal, injuries. You must always keep fighting, no matter how badly you think you are hurt. The sooner you stop your attacker, the fewer injuries you or others will receive, and the faster medical attention can be obtained for all injured parties.

To help you deal with the possibility of being wounded during an attack, use mental preparation to help strengthen your resolve to prevail. To some degree, you can control how you react emotionally to situations; practice visualizing yourself during an attack and prevailing despite an injury. Remember that an injury may look worse than it really is, and that many survivors who were wounded in violent attacks report that they did not feel pain or otherwise realize that they were stabbed or shot until later, after the attack was over. In many of the cases in which victims were oblivious to the injuries they sustained, it was because they were completely focused mentally on the struggle to survive and win.

ONCE YOUR ATTACKER IS DOWN

As has been emphasized previously, once you have stopped an assailant's attack, you should do nothing to prevent him from fleeing. It is not your job or responsibility to arrest or detain a criminal. However, if you are forced to shoot an attacker and he goes down, seemingly incapacitated, you may not be able to immediately leave the scene, for reasons of both safety and legality. Under such conditions, you should follow specific procedures to ensure your safety and the safety of loved ones or other innocent bystanders.

Do Not Approach Your Assailant. Once your attacker is down, you must not approach him under any circumstances–not to disarm him, to check on his condition, to render first aid or for any other reason. He may be shamming or only partially incapacitated, and if he has a hidden weapon, he may take advantage of your proximity to try to injure or kill you.

Scan for Threats. Immediately after you fire shots at an assailant that stop his or her attack, lower your firearm slightly to break tunnel vision and to allow you to see the effect of your shots. At that time you should

Fig. 48. After firing shots that stop an attack, lower your firearm slightly and shift your view from side to side to scan for additional threats. If your assailant is down, keep him in your peripheral vision as you scan.

also scan for additional threats.

The technique of scanning for threats outside the home is different from that for scanning in your home. In your home, the advantage should be yours. On the street, you're on your attacker's turf. He knows the alleys, the abandoned buildings and the hidden doorways; he knows how often the police patrol the area, and how likely it is any bystander or resident will hear your cries for help—or even respond.

He will often work with an accomplice who will sneak up behind you while you're distracted. You may think you've stopped an attack when you present your gun and an aggressor backs away, but you have simply allowed yourself to be distracted so that his partner can attack you from the rear.

If your assailant is on the ground, whether he is wounded or has simply surrendered, you should scan by lowering the gun and then shifting your eyes slightly from side to side, keeping your assailant in your peripheral vision. Scan by taking quick glances to each side and to the rear, returning your eyes forward before a hidden adversary can take advantage of your momentary look away. This scanning technique is similar to the "quick peek" technique used to scout for danger around a corner or through a doorway. While you are scanning, keep your gun pointed at your assailant.

In the event that your attacker flees, you still need to scan for threats, but with a different technique. Scan to the left, right, and to the rear as before, but move your gun in the same direction as you scan, so that you are always looking over the sights. Be sure to observe the first rule of safe gun handling (**<u>ALWAYS</u> keep the gun pointed in a safe direction**) and avoid crossing innocent bystanders with your gun's muzzle.

Fig. 49. On this street, cover can be obtained behind cars, the masonry wall, trees, telephone poles, building columns, etc.

Move to Cover. Next, move to cover if you have not already done so. Reload your handgun if necessary. Although it may seem that the danger has passed once your assailant is down and seemingly incapacitated, it is just as important to seek cover after shooting stops as before it starts. Remember, just because an attacker is down does not mean that he is no longer a threat. Even when wounded and on the ground, an assailant may still have the capability and the will to physically threaten you.

Just as importantly, outside the home you are more likely to be confronted by multiple assailants. Thus, even if you have downed an attacker, you may still have his accomplices to deal with. Getting behind cover will allow you to defend yourself against additional attackers.

Contact the Police. After any defensive shooting you must try to contact the police. It is your duty as a citizen to report any violent incident in which you have been involved, as well as to request medical attention for any wounded person.

Even if you believe that a bystander has already called the police, it is still advisable for you to do so as well. You will be

Fig. 50. After a defensive shooting, take cover and use your cell phone to call police.

able to tell the responding officers your side of the incident right from the start, and give them additional information to minimize confusion and the potential for a tragic error resulting from mistaken identity. Also, by summoning the police you indicate that you are a responsible citizen—not a criminal or a person who recklessly abuses his right to bear arms.

You should notify the police only after you have moved to cover. This can be done in several ways. If you possess a cell phone, dial the police with one hand while you keep your handgun pointed at the threat with the other. Don't look at your phone continuously while you're dialing; give it no more than a quick glance or two.

You may not always have a cell phone handy, however. If your defensive shooting incident takes place on a street, it is likely that there will be a pedestrian, shopkeeper, homeowner or the like in the vicinity; ask him or her to lend you a cell phone or to summon the police. Actually, if the shooting takes place in a populated area, it is likely that someone will call the police in any event; but it is important for you to inform the police that you are not the aggressor in this situation.

If the incident occurs in a deserted area, you may have to flag down a passing motorist. Don't lose sight of your attacker, or expose yourself to any more danger than is necessary. Ask to borrow a cell phone from the motorist or, barring that, ask him or her to stop and call the police as soon as possible. In the latter event, make sure the motorist gives the police a good description of you, and emphasizes that you acted in self-defense.

That same point—that you had to shoot in self-defense—should also be emphasized if you are able to talk to the police dispatcher directly. Answer the dispatcher's questions calmly and succinctly. Avoid being excited; not only will your excitement increase the likelihood of garbled communication, but the police officers responding to the call understandably will be leery of dealing with a hysterical person. Do not volunteer any information about the incident other than what is required to answer the dispatcher's questions regarding your immediate safety. Be sure to describe yourself, your attacker and any other people in the the immediate area, so that the police will know who is who when they arrive. Also, notify the dispatcher if your attacker still seems capable of posing a threat. Don't forget to mention that you are armed and are holding your attacker at gunpoint. This will give the responding officers advance warning of what they will find at the scene—a much better alternative than having them unexpectedly be confronted by an armed individual.

Stay on the phone if you can. If you are talking to the dispatcher when the police arrive, you will receive precise directions to allow the officers to safely take charge of the situation. Follow any such directions exactly and immediately; even though you know you're not the aggressor, the police only see you as a person with a gun and, therefore, potentially dangerous. However, if the instructions you receive will clearly increase your risk of being killed or injured, inform the dispatcher why you cannot follow them. They will give you an alternative set of directions.

Most difficult are situations in which you are holding a still-dangerous attacker at gunpoint. In these situations, it is essential to apprise the responding officers of the circumstances so that there is continuity of control of the aggressor.

Wait for the Police. Until the police arrive, wait in your covered position, continue to observe your attacker, and hold your gun in a ready position. Also, continue to scan for additional threats. Do not talk to your assailant except to yell short, decisive commands as necessary to maintain control over him; don't engage in conversation, as this may distract you. Leave cover only if you must do so to maintain your safety, hail a motorist or use a telephone. Do not abandon cover to flee the scene (as to a store) unless you are absolutely certain you can do so in safety. Remember, your attacker may have an accomplice lurking in the vicinity.

If others are with you behind cover, keep them there. Avoid sending them to summon help or to the presumed greater safety of another location, unless this can be done without exposing them to danger from an unseen accomplice.

It may be extremely difficult for you to remain behind cover and watch the assailant you shot. You must mentally prepare yourself for the situation in which a predatory criminal, who just a few moments earlier was intent upon killing you, is now crying out for assistance. For many, this will be the hardest part of a shooting situation.

Regardless, you must keep your distance from that assailant and remain behind cover until police arrive. Your attacker may be shamming, waiting for you to approach so that he or she may use a hidden weapon against you. Alternatively, your shots may have only temporarily incapacitated your assailant, and he may suddenly revive when you come close.

Be On Guard Against a Resumption of the Attack. Sometimes an assailant you are forced to shoot will go down, seemingly incapacitated, then shortly revive. If the revived attacker again constitutes a threat—produces a weapon, for example, or continues to approach—you may have no choice but to again use your defensive firearm.

On the other hand, if the aggressor recovers and flees the scene, do not fire your gun or attempt to stop or follow him. Let him go. It is not your job to capture criminals; in fact, there may be legal ramifications to pursuing your attacker (see Part VI: Concealed Carry, Self-Defense and the Law). Apprehending criminals is the job of the police. Armed with your description of your assailant, and with the knowledge that he will have to seek medical care, the police will have little difficulty in catching him.

Maintain the Integrity of the Shooting Scene. A critical consideration that is often given little thought is the need to maintain the integrity of the shooting scene. When the police arrive, they will commence an investigation that will involve, among other things, all the physical evidence at the scene. It is absolutely essential that all physical evidence be undisturbed. Neither you nor any others at the scene should move or touch anything.

Fig. 51. When a shooting occurs in public and onlookers assemble, it can be difficult to maintain the integrity of the scene.

Bystanders who witness the incident may come to look or to help. Some well-intentioned people may want to give aid to the injured assailant; warn them as strongly as possible of the inadvisability of that act.

Also, it may be a temptation for a bystander to steal the attacker's weapon or, even worse, use it against you. When your attacker goes down, always be aware of the location of his weapon, and of anyone approaching it. Warn bystanders against going near your attacker or his weapon, but do not threaten them; that may be misinterpreted later. Encourage bystanders to keep their distance from both you and your downed attacker. Note that friends of your attacker can make your situation highly unpleasant, such as by inadvertently or intentionally disturbing evidence at the scene.

Greeting the Police. Whether you have contacted the police dispatcher or not, you should follow certain rules when greeting the police to ensure both their safety and yours.

First and foremost, never greet or turn toward a police officer with a gun in your hand. The officers won't know you are the victim; they'll just see the gun swinging toward them.

Also, follow all instructions precisely and immediately. Don't argue, hesitate, stall or give advice. Police officers are trained to take control of situations; if you seem to resist them, they have no choice but to assume you are uncooperative and possibly a threat. All your movements should be slow and precise, and your hands should be visible at all times. The more cooperative and rational you appear to the police officers, the more likely they will be to see you as the innocent victim that you are.

Don't argue with other witnesses at the scene. Some may have an incorrect view of what transpired, or may deliberately give false testimony because they are friends of the victim or hostile to you. Don't protest while the police take their statements; you will have a chance to tell your side of things, and your story will be more readily believed if you stay calm.

In some situations, you may not have an opportunity to call a dispatcher before police arrive. Perhaps a patrol was right around the corner, heard

Fig. 52. Law enforcement officers arriving at the scene of a self-defense shooting will not know who is the attacker and the victim. Under these circumstances, the armed citizen must obey their commands without hesitation.

the shots and responded. Or perhaps you just didn't have a phone or other means of communication at your disposal. When the police arrive on the scene, remember that they don't know that you successfully defended yourself against a threat; all they know is that shots were fired at a particular location and when they showed up, you were standing over a downed man with a gun in your hand. Under those conditions, they have to assume, for their own safety, that you may be a threat. To a police officer, any person with a firearm is a potential threat. Thus, if you behave aggressively, you may survive the criminal attack but still be mistaken for the assailant by the responding officers—with tragic consequences.

The responding officers likely will draw their own guns and order you to put your gun down. Don't argue with them, or try to explain that you were defending yourself. Just comply. You'll have a chance to explain it all later. They may have you lie face down on the ground so that they can handcuff you; don't resist or struggle. The officers' adrenaline levels will be as high as yours. Don't boost them any higher by being uncooperative. No matter what you do, do not point your gun at the officers.

Leaving the Scene. You should stay with a downed assailant until the police arrive, just as you are legally bound to remain at an accident scene. There may be occasions, however, when leaving the scene of a shooting may be appropriate.

As a general rule, you are justified in leaving a shooting scene only when your safety would be compromised if you remained there. For example, if you are attacked by several armed men and you disable one of them, you are not required to remain at the scene if the other men continue to constitute a threat and you are able to flee safely. If they temporarily flee, you should retreat. Similarly, if you fire in self-defense in a neighborhood which contains many friends of your attacker, you may find yourself quickly surrounded by a group of hostile people that threatens to become a mob. Under such conditions, it might be prudent to leave the scene of the incident.

Be aware that the authorities will usually not look favorably on persons who leave the scene of a shooting. If you do leave, immediately contact the police. Go to a police station, flag down a patrol car or use a telephone. If you make contact by telephone, tell the dispatcher who you are, what transpired and where it happened, and follow his or her instructions. You will probably be asked to report to the nearest police station, or to stay at your location until a patrol car meets you. Follow the dispatcher's instructions to the letter.

If you must leave the scene of a shooting incident, do not go home, change clothes, or wash up. Doing any of those things may destroy evidence that may support your claim of legitimate self-defense, or may be perceived as an attempt on your part to tamper or hide evidence.

The same procedure should be followed if you are involved in a shooting that does not result in any injury. For example, you may be confronted by an armed attacker at an ATM machine and exchange shots with nobody apparently being hit. Your assailant runs off, but that does not relieve you of your duty as a responsible gun owner. In the first place, just because your attacker did not seem to be hit does not mean he wasn't; bullet strikes can be extremely hard to spot. Furthermore, there is a good chance that a passerby or resident will report your encounter, possibly even with the tag number of your vehicle.

CHAPTER 9

THE AFTERMATH OF A DEFENSIVE ENCOUNTER OUTSIDE THE HOME

Complete preparation for defensive firearm use outside the home involves more than practicing the shooting fundamentals and positions, handgun presentation and visualization exercises. True, when you are confronted by an assailant, your first concern is prevailing in the encounter, and the skills you have learned are of paramount importance. When the incident is over, however, you may experience emotional turmoil, social ostracism and even legal sanctions. These are all common aspects of the aftermath of a defensive encounter, and require prior mental preparation just as effective shooting and gun handling require physical preparation. Even when you arc justified and forced to do so, shooting an assailant is a distressing experience. Realize this and plan for it in your mental training.

EMOTIONAL AFTERMATH OF A DEFENSIVE SHOOTING OUTSIDE THE HOME

After prevailing in a violent encounter, you may experience a number of emotions. These emotions often occur in the order listed below, but are not universal; some people may not exhibit any of them, while others will experience some or all of the following emotional reactions, but in varying sequences.

Elation. Often there is an immediate feeling of elation at having survived and prevailed in a life-threatening encounter. In today's social and political atmosphere, attack survivors may feel that they should downplay or ignore this emotion. The survivor who feels this elation is experiencing euphoria resulting from both a sense of relief at having survived, and an involuntary biochemical reaction resulting from the release of endorphins and other sensory- and mood-enhancing chemicals into the bloodstream. It is important to realize that there is nothing wrong with a momentary or lasting feeling of elation at having prevailed. Often this emotion is quickly followed by guilt at having felt elation in the first place.

Revulsion. After the initial elation at having survived the violent confrontation, there often arises a feeling of revulsion at what has happened. The victorious victim may become nauseous, vomit, or even faint from the emotional shock of seeing the result of the confrontation. The absence of revulsion does not mean you are a bad or cold person. Your own experiences (such as military combat duty or work as an emergency medical technician) may have given you a greater tolerance for the unpleasant consequences of a shooting. However, in preparing for the aftermath of defensive firearm use, you must recognize that the scene of a shooting contains many disturbing sights and sounds. While you cannot completely steel yourself to what you will see and hear, visualizing potential outcomes may decrease the distress you experience after a shooting.

Although you may not be able to avoid experiencing the emotion of revulsion, you must avoid being overwhelmed by it. Outside the home there are many opportunities for additional aggressors—or even secondary aggressors having no connection to your original assailant—to mount an attack against you after you have stopped an initial assault. If you allow yourself to be overcome by a feeling of revulsion to the point of losing an awareness of your surroundings, you will be extremely vulnerable.

Remorse. Many survivors experience remorse at having hurt or killed an attacker. This has nothing to do with the moral justifiability of their actions. It is simply a normal feeling of sadness or sorrow at having been forced to defend yourself.

Self-Doubt. Those who prevail in a defensive shooting scenario may begin to replay the sequence of events in their minds, and ask themselves questions such as: Did I really have to shoot? Could I have avoided the attack? Was there something else I could have done? Like remorse, this feeling is a natural result of the normal person's aversion to taking a life, even when morally and legally justifiable. Remember, however, that simply by reading this book you are clearly trying to prepare to make such decisions responsibly

Acceptance. This is usually the last of the emotional stages encountered after a defensive shooting. Rationalization is the first step to acceptance, and is often a consequence of the self-doubt described above. As you analyze the circumstances of the shooting, you will conclude that your actions were both justified and necessary.

There is no certainty that you will go through all or any of these emotional stages; nor can you be sure that you will arrive at the acceptance stage. Human emotions are much too complex to encase them in neat psychological boxes, or to arrange them in a simple sequence. Many shooting survivors, in fact, experience residual feelings of remorse and self-doubt, as well as other emotions, such as anger and fear.

As with other traumatic life experiences, you must put a defensive shooting in its proper place and move on. With time, the negative emotions associated with the event usually fade, allowing you to get on with your normal life. Don't dwell on the event, but also do not suppress your feelings about what has occurred. Most mental health experts agree that acknowledging, accepting and expressing your emotions is the first step in dealing with them.

Post-Traumatic Stress Disorder (PTSD). This term has been loosely (and often inappropriately) used in the popular media to describe a wide variety of reactions to stressful life events. Some (but not all) of the symptoms of PTSD include flashbacks, recurrent nightmares, and an inability to function normally (as to hold a job or maintain a stable marriage). Not everyone who has such experiences necessarily has PTSD; that diagnosis can be made only by a trained mental health worker. Nor is it true that everyone who goes through a traumatic event is inevitably afflicted with PTSD. Most people, in fact, who suffer extreme stress—airplane crash survivors, combat veterans, victims of tornadoes and other natural disasters, and the like—do not develop clinical PTSD.

REDUCING THE EMOTIONAL AFTERMATH OF A SHOOTING OUTSIDE THE HOME

Although you cannot avoid experiencing certain emotions as the result of your justifiable use of deadly force, you can prevent those emotions from taking control of your life. Two methods that many have found helpful are counseling and self-reinforcement.

Counseling. Counseling is one of the most effective and widely used ways that human beings have of working out their problems. Although the term may immediately bring to mind formal sessions with a psychotherapist, social worker or clergyman, in actuality counseling goes on everyday in our normal lives. Every time you unburden yourself to another—

whether husband or wife, close friend, neighbor, or co-worker—a kind of informal counseling is going on.

Counseling achieves results in several ways. For one who has used deadly force to survive a deadly attack, talking to another sympathetic person about the experience gives the survivor support and affirmation, as well as the viewpoint of a detached third party. This objective viewpoint can be important in helping a survivor deal with overwhelming self-doubt and remorse, and in finally arriving at an acceptance of his or her actions.

Seeking counseling—whether with a professional or a friend or relative—should never be viewed as a sign of weakness. The survivor who obtains counseling is simply acknowledging two basic human truths: that two heads are often better than one, and that one may sometimes be unable to see the forest for the trees. A gun owner who is involved in a self-defense shooting may be emotionally too close to the event to be able to step back and look at what transpired in a calm, rational, evenhanded manner—as could a friend, pastor or psychotherapist. It is no more a sign of weakness for the survivor of an attack to seek counseling than it is for a physician to get a colleague's advice on a particular surgical procedure. In both cases, counseling provides a fresh and objective point of view that may lead to greater understanding.

Counseling may be obtained from a variety of sources, including:
- psychiatrists, psychologists and other mental health professionals;
- clergy;
- your spouse;
- trusted friends; and
- others who have had similar experiences.

Many police forces have counselors for officers involved in shootings. Such law enforcement agencies may be able to refer you to appropriate counseling resources.

Following any defensive shooting encounter, however, the first type of counseling you should seek is legal counseling. Consult with your attorney before speaking to others about the incident.

Self-Reinforcement. Self-reinforcement is a technique by which you replace negative, self-destructive thoughts with positive, self-affirming ones. In a sense, you are acting as your own counselor, giving yourself support and validating the actions you took in self-defense.

Self-reinforcement can and should be practiced by anyone who has had to defend himself or herself with deadly force. Self-reinforcing statements should take the following form:

- *I am a good person.*
- *I did not choose to attack another law-abiding citizen.*
- *I did not attack anyone. I was attacked by a criminal.*
- *My attacker was the one who chose a lifestyle and sequence of events that led to his injury or death.*
- *I was morally justified in protecting my life with deadly force.*
- *I have quite possibly saved the lives of others by stopping this predator from harming future innocent victims.*
- *I had no choice but to use deadly force to stop my attacker.*
- *I am a moral person.*

Ultimately, you are the only person who can make it possible for you to put a defensive shooting into proper perspective and get on with your life.

LEGAL AFTERMATH OF A DEFENSIVE SHOOTING OUTSIDE THE HOME

The legal ramifications of being involved in a self-defense shooting out-side the home will vary depending upon the laws applicable in your juris-diction. In many areas, both the police and the prosecutor's office have some discretion in the way in which a defensive shooting is handled. If you are involved in an absolutely clearcut case of self-defense, you may only have to answer questions at the police station and make a formal statement. However, if the circumstances around the shooting incident are initially unclear, you could be arrested. In a worst-case scenario, it is possi-ble that you could be charged with a felony, arrested, handcuffed and put into a police car; taken to a police station and fingerprinted, photographed, booked and put into a cell; and held in jail until the charges against you are dropped or bail is arranged. Furthermore, your carry permit likely will be suspended or revoked, and your defensive handgun (and possibly any other firearms in your home) could be confiscated by the police. Additionally, you will undoubtedly incur hefty legal bills in your own defense.

Be aware that your local law enforcement agencies, prosecutors and judges may view a defensive shooting outside the home in a different light than one that occurs inside your home. If the police arrive at your home to find that you have shot an armed stranger who broke into your home, they will be inclined to believe your claim of self-defense: it's the only story that, at first glance, makes sense. If the physical evidence and witness testimony supports that claim, there is a good chance you can avoid arrest. On the other hand, when the same officers respond to a shooting in the street, the situation is much more ambiguous. It may come down to your word against that of your assailant or other witnesses. Some of those witnesses may be friends of your attacker, or may be biased against you simply because you carry a gun. Don't forget, to some people, only criminals carry guns.

Be careful what you say and do immediately after you use your handgun in self-defense. Even though you may feel elation, revulsion, remorse and self-doubt—all natural and understandable reactions—you must not outwardly indulge those emotions after a defensive shooting outside the home. Do not hoot or cheer, or display an elated expression, even if that is how you momentarily feel; do not make audible comments about the incident, to yourself or anyone else. In the street or other public place, there will often be witnesses. Act as though your every word and gesture will later be put on display in a court of law or in the newspaper.

Furthermore, you should understand that many police officers and public officials—particularly in big cities—do not like concealed carry laws. Politically motivated officials may try to portray you as a trigger-happy madman in an attempt to discredit concealed-carry laws and to demonize concealed-carry permit holders.

A more complete discussion of the legal issues revolving around the self-defense use of a firearm is found in Part VI: Concealed Carry, Self-Defense and the Law. The defense-oriented gun owner is strongly encouraged to consult a qualified attorney familiar with the gun laws and self-defense laws of the gun owner's jurisdiction.

SOCIAL AFTERMATH OF A DEFENSIVE SHOOTING

In addition to the emotional and legal aftermath that follows the use of a firearm in self-defense, there are social consequences as well. People will see you being questioned by the police, and quite possibly being handcuffed and taken away in a police car. They may also see your assailant lying on the sidewalk, or being carried off on a stretcher. Some of these people may be your friends, neighbors or co-workers. And those among your friends, family and acquaintances who do not actually witness these events will nonetheless read about them in the paper or see them on the 11 o' clock news.

Even if you are eventually fully exonerated, some may still see you as "that trigger-happy nut" or some other unflattering designation. You may be the target of those who hate guns and distrust gun owners, as well as those who can't stand the thought of anyone acting in self-defense. Some of your co-workers and neighbors will begin to act differently toward you, avoiding you, shunning you or treating you with outright hostility.

At work, your act of self-defense may impact negatively on your job advancement if your superiors don't like, or are afraid of, guns. Additionally, your superiors and co-workers will now be aware that you carry a concealed handgun; that, too, may cause you problems. You may be prohibited from carrying your firearm at work, or bringing your firearm onto company property. Even if company management is firearm-friendly, they may have to eventually give in to the complaints of gun-hating employees.

You may even get anonymous threatening notes at work, or crank calls at home from people who cannot accept what you've done. People may stare at you in stores, and shopkeepers you had amicably dealt with for years may now be unexpectedly cold and standoffish. More importantly, you may find yourself targeted by those who identify with, or were friends with, your assailant.

Worst of all may be the effects on your family. Your spouse may find himself or herself socially ostracized, and your children may have to endure cruel taunts from their classmates at school—or even critical comments from their teachers. You may even have members of your own family who cannot understand what you had to do.

There can be substantial unforeseen consequences when you are forced to use your firearm for self-defense outside the home. Your ordeal will not end merely when the attack is stopped; the emotional, legal and social aftermath probably will continue for weeks, months or even years after the event. This aftermath is one more reason why the seriousness of the responsibility of owning a firearm for self defense cannot be overly emphasized.

Jaime

Use of Lethal Force in Self Defense

I ntent

O portunity

A bility

PART III

CARRYING A CONCEALED HANDGUN AND PRESENTING THE HANDGUN FROM CONCEALMENT

CHAPTER 10

HANDGUN CARRY: HOLSTERS, HOLSTER PURSES AND FANNY PACKS

For people who are properly trained and licensed, there are many ways in which a concealed handgun can be carried. Many of these carry methods involve the use of concealment holsters—devices that are designed to hold a handgun on the body, under the clothing. Handguns can also be discreetly carried in external devices such as handbags, fanny packs, attache cases and the like; many models of these items are available that are specially designed for handgun carry. With such items, the handgun is not concealed under the clothing but inside the device, which outwardly appears to be nothing more than a normal handbag, fanny pack or attache case.

Each specific type of concealment holster or external carry device has strengths and limitations, depending upon the needs and characteristics of the user. What works well for one person in one situation may not be as effective for another person in another situation. Thus, no one device or carry mode is the best for all people. Your selection of the holster, holster purse or other handgun concealment device that is best for you depends upon a careful consideration of a number of factors.

Fig. 53. This ballistic nylon briefcase has a separate compartment for a concealed handgun.

Handgun concealment devices can be judged on the basis of four critical attributes: *concealment, access, retention* and *comfort. Concealment* refers to the degree to which the device hides the gun from observation. *Access* describes the ability of the user of the device to quickly and easily obtain the gun from the device. *Retention* refers to those aspects of design and construction that prevent the loss of the handgun in an attack or during vigorous activity. *Comfort* is probably the least critical of these, but is still important: a handgun concealment device that is uncomfortable to wear will probably be left at home.

HOLSTERS

Holsters are typically constructed of leather or synthetic materials, or a combination of the two. Synthetic holsters can be made of flexible nylon fabric (often called ballistic nylon) or of stiff polymer materials (such as

Fig. 54. A selection of various types of holsters. Top row: pancake holster with safety strap, inside-the-waistband holster with safety strap, open-top pancake holster, vertical shoulder holster. Second row: polymer strong-side belt holster; pocket holster for small handgun; paddle holster with safety strap.

Kydex) that retain their molded shape. Molded polymer holsters are simple, strong and impervious to moisture and solvents, and offer extremely fast presentation. They can be noisy, however, when the gun is drawn

Leather holsters are also available in both soft (flexible) and hard (rigid) versions. Some leather holsters have thin metal strips sandwiched between layers to stiffen the holster in critical areas. With either material, the more rigid holsters are usually shaped or molded to fit a specific make and model handgun, while the flexible ones will accept a variety of handguns of roughly the same size.

In general, no matter what the material, stiff molded holsters are prefer-

NRA Guide to Personal Protection Outside the Home

able, as they do not collapse when the gun is withdrawn, and thus allow one-handed reholstering.

Gun retention is achieved in two primary ways. First, the holster can grip the gun snugly. Most often this method of retention is accomplished through molding the holster to closely fit a particular model of gun. Spring steel inserts or elastic straps are also used on some models to increase the holster's grip on a gun. Additionally, many molded holsters are designed to allow the adjustment of holster friction, through tension screws and other devices.

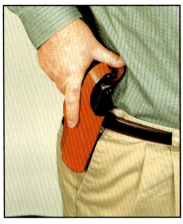

Fig. 55. The most common type of holster safety strap is the thumb-snap, which is disengaged by the thumb during the draw.

Other holsters—usually those of soft synthetic fabric or leather construction—make use of a second type of retention feature, a safety strap (also sometimes called a retention strap) that encircles the hammer, trigger guard or other part of the gun. Safety straps are not, however, a mark of an inferior holster; some top quality molded holsters feature them for added retention. With some designs, such as many shoulder holsters, a friction fit is not sufficient to retain the gun; safety straps are an absolute requirement.

Safety straps slow presentation speed, and can be difficult for the weak hand to manipulate in weak-hand presentation techniques; for these reasons, they are often omitted from "professional" holsters. However, a safety strap can help prevent an assailant from acquiring your firearm in an arm's-length struggle.

Some types of safety straps have closures designed for fast and easy unfastening. A thumbsnap, for example, incorporates a tab of leather or other stiff material that is attached to the snap closure. This tab is positioned on the holster to allow easy unfastening by the thumb during a natural drawing motion.

Shoulder Holsters

In the mind of the general public, shoulder holsters exemplify the typical concealment holster. There are three basic types of shoulder holsters, all named for the position in which they carry the gun: *upside-down shoulder*

Fig. 56. Vertical shoulder holster, seen from the side (above), with harness (right).

holsters, horizontal shoulder holsters, and *vertical shoulder holsters. Upside-down shoulder holsters* hold a handgun—most commonly a small semi-automatic pistol or short-barreled revolver—under the weak-side armpit with the muzzle pointing straight up. Retention is by means of spring steel inserts in the holster, elastic bands or a safety strap. *Horizontal shoulder holsters* hold a handgun in a roughly horizontal position under the weak-side arm.

Depending upon the particular model, the actual gun angle may vary from horizontal to pointing around 45 degrees upward. Thumbsnap-type safety straps are commonly used for gun retention. *Vertical shoulder holsters* hold the gun with the butt upward and facing forward. Many of these holsters feature a clamshell design. One or more pieces of spring steel tensions the two halves of the holster together, retaining the gun. Presentation is accomplished by pulling the gun forward between the spring-tensioned holster halves.

All shoulder holsters feature a harness of leather, fabric or elastic straps to suspend the gun. These harnesses are almost infinitely adjustable, even on economy models, allowing a custom fit for comfort and good access.

Shoulder holsters have the primary advantage of providing good handgun concealment when you're wearing a short, waist length jacket that would reveal most belt-mounted holsters.

Fig. 57. Horizontal shoulder holster, seen from the side (left), with harness (right).

Additionally, they can provide good all-day comfort when you're wearing a large, heavy handgun. Moreover, they allow an easy draw from the sitting position—an important consideration if you are attacked in your vehicle.

These holsters have some significant limitations, however. For most people the draw from a shoulder holster is not as

Fig. 58. A shoulder holster is excellent for carrying a concealed handgun under a short jacket.

fast as from a strong-side hip holster or crossdraw holster; some people with short arms can find it awkward to reach all the way across the body to access the gun. Concealment can also be a problem. The straps that comprise the harness of the holster can easily show or "print" through light clothing. Also, because shoulder holsters need to be placed far enough around on the body to be grasped by the hand on the opposite side, con-

Fig. 59. Shoulder holsters allow an un-impeded draw from the sitting position..

Fig. 60. Shoulder holsters can allow an assailant to block the draw.

cealment can be compromised by anything that causes the covering clothing to open, such as a sudden turn or an errant gust of wind.

This across-the-body presentation movement has two other drawbacks as
well. First, if you are attacked by a criminal at arm's length, he can easily
thwart your draw simply by blocking your arm as it retrieves the gun. With
horizontal and vertical models, additionally, the gun butt is positioned in a
way that makes it possible for an adversary to take your gun. Moreover,
when a gun is withdrawn from a shoulder holster it most often points off to
the side; the gun must be swung in a wide arc to come on target. This
movement could endanger any innocent person who is swept by the muzzle. Proper training can ingrain a safer gun movement to the target.

Finally, pretty much all upside-down and horizontal shoulder holsters
carry the gun in a position that is technically unsafe. A gun in an upside-
down holster points at your own armpit, while a gun carried in a horizontal
shoulder rig points rearward, potentially sweeping any person behind you
with the muzzle. With the vast majority of shoulder holsters, there is little
chance of a gun firing while it is in the holster. However, an overly excited
person drawing from such a holster might prematurely engage the trigger
and fire the gun just as it is being withdrawn.

Hip Holsters

Hip holsters are probably the most varied group of holsters available,
and for good reason: by positioning the gun on the strong-side hip, these
holsters offer the best balance of concealment, access, retention and comfort for most people.

Hip holsters come in many forms and styles. Much of the variance centers around the way in
which the holster attaches
to the belt. In general, hip
holsters go on the belt via
slots in the holster body, or
loops attached to the holster. Pancake holsters—so
called because many mod-
els are roughly the size
and shape of a pancake—
are among the most popu-
lar hip holster. They nor-

*Fig. 61. From left: polymer belt-loop vertical drop
holster; loop/slot belt holster with moderate forward
rake; pancake holster with extreme forward rake.*

mally attach by way of slots, which tend to pull the holster closer to the body. Slots are also used on belt-slide holsters, minimalist designs that only encircle the handgun in a small area just forward of the trigger guard, leaving most of the barrel or slide uncovered. Many hip holsters make use of both slots and loops to offer a variety of gun positions.

Hip holsters are available in a variety of gun angles. Those that put the bore axis straight up and down are called "straight drop" holsters. Others tilt or cant the gun butt forward at an angle. These so-called forward cant or FBI rake holsters are generally more popular with knowledgeable gun carriers, as they allow a more rearward (and thus more concealable) gun position without compromising gun access or draw speed. Some holster models allow adjustment of gun angle. Also popular are high rise or high ride holsters, which carry the gun high on the belt, promoting concealment.

Fig. 62. Paddle holsters have a curved paddle (arrow) that is inserted inside the pants.

Paddle holsters are a type of hip holster that requires neither slots nor loops, nor even a belt. These holsters have a large curved, stiff, paddle-shaped piece on the back of the holster. This paddle is inserted inside the waistband of the pants, and the holster is held in place by simple friction or by tabs. The primary appeal of these holsters is their ability to be put on and taken off quickly and easily, without the need to undo the belt. Some paddle models allow for adjustment of the holster position and cant. The only drawback with paddle holsters is that they require a tight-fitting belt or pair of pants to prevent the holster from being withdrawn with the gun during presentation.

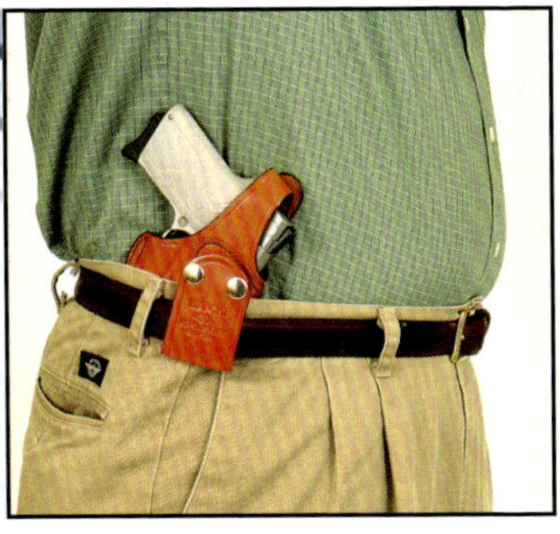

Inside-the-waistband (IWB) holsters are a high-concealment variant of the standard hip holster. The body of the IWB holster fits inside the pants; outside loops fasten it to the belt. IWB holsters give better concealment under short jackets, coats or shirts, especially when the clothing rises up when the arms are lifted. Some people, however, find that IWB holsters carry the gun so tightly to the body that they cannot achieve as fast a draw as with a conventional hip holster. Comfort

Fig. 63. Inside-the-waistband holster.

is also an issue with some; and those with tight-fitting pants will find it hard to accommodate the extra bulk of an IWB holster. Nonetheless, among those who carry guns as part of their professional duties, such as bodyguards and undercover police officers, IWB holsters are often preferred over other designs.

Hip holsters generally provide the fastest and safest gun presentation of all the holster types. The drawing motion is straight and direct: as the gun is rotated toward the target, the muzzle tends to follow a line that points mostly at the ground, reducing the likelihood that a premature discharge would cause injury to any bystanders. Access is excellent with these holsters; the gun is in a position that can be reached with a minimum of body movement. Retention is also excellent. In a close-range attack, a person can turn the strong side away from an attacker, preventing him from either grabbing the gun or blocking the draw. In an attack from the rear,

Fig. 64. Hip holsters provide good retention against an assailant's grab. Here the armed citizen merely clamps his elbow against his side to retain the gun.

with most hip holsters , gun takeaway can be prevented simply by clamping the gun butt to the side with the elbow.

Nonetheless, hip holsters do have a few drawbacks. Comfort is an issue for some, especially with a heavy handgun; some people just never get used to a two-pound weight hung on their belt. With hip holsters that are worn outside the pants, a waist-length bomber jacket will not provide adequate concealment;

Fig. 65. This sequence of photos shows how the muzzle is always pointed in a safe direction when proper techniques are used during presentation from a hip holster.

Fig. 66. Drawing in the seated position can be awkward with a hip holster.

the tip of the holster will protrude below the waist of the jacket, particularly if the jacket rides up, as when you are reaching above your head. Such hip holsters require a long jacket or coat. Persons with large hips also may find it harder to conceal the bulge of a hip holster. Finally, the gun position with a typical hip holster makes it hard to draw from a seated position, such as in a vehicle, and also tends to cause the gun butt to audibly hit the hard back of a chair or bench when the wearer sits.

Standard hip holsters may not accommodate womens' waist/hip angle, with the result that the gun butt digs into the shooter's side. Some companies offer holsters that better meet womens' needs by providing an outward-angled gun butt, a greater degree of cant, and a lower position on the belt.

Crossdraw Holsters

Crossdraw holsters are a type of belt holster that is positioned on the weak-side hip. Just as with a shoulder holster, drawing from a crossdraw holster requires you to reach all the way across your body. Thus, these holsters have the same disadvantages as most shoulder holsters: they can be

Fig. 67. Crossdraw holsters often position the gun with the butt angled forward. This facilitates the draw, but also makes it easier for an assailant to grab it.

awkward to draw from and difficult to conceal well, and position the hand-gun in a way such that an arm's-length assailant can easily block your draw or acquire a grip on the gun butt.

Crossdraw holsters offer somewhat faster presentation than shoulder holsters, but they suffer from the same concealment limitation as conventional hip holsters: they must be worn with long covering clothing (except for IWB-style crossdraw models). Despite their drawbacks, crossdraw holsters are still preferred by some shooters.

Ankle Holsters

Ankle holsters are handgun concealment devices that fit snugly around the ankle or calf area of the leg, usually by means of Velcro® straps or elastic bands. Ankle holsters are available in almost any material; they are limited, however, to small semiautomatic pistols and snub-nosed small-frame revolvers.

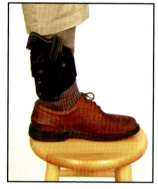

Fig. 68. Ankle holster.

Typically, ankle holsters locate the gun on the inside of the lower weak-side leg. To present from such a holster while standing, the leg must be raised and the pants pulled back to allow access to the gun. A somewhat easier draw can be performed in the sitting position.

Fig. 69. Armed citizen drawing from ankle holster, showing its inherent clumsiness.

Ankle holsters can provide excellent concealment—but only with pants having sufficiently loose legs. Gun retention can be a concern, especially with designs lacking safety straps: the gun could potentially fall out of the holster when you are running or jumping. Basically, their awkward draw—and the limited types of guns they can accommodate—makes ankle holsters suitable only for small backup handguns of the type used primarily by undercover police officers.

Small-of-the-Back Holsters

Small-of-the-back (SOB) holsters position the gun on the belt in the middle of the back, making your gun invisible to anyone scrutinizing you from the front. To present the handgun, the firing hand must go underneath the covering clothing all the way around to the back to grip the gun. SOB holsters come in models affording both a palm-out and a palm-in draw; IWB-type models are also available.

SOB holsters can provide excellent concealment, particularly when smaller, thinner handguns are used and the covering clothing hangs straight down, as with a sport coat or suit jacket. With practice, you can learn to draw quickly with such holsters.

Fig. 70. Small-of-the-back holster.

However, SOB holsters may be easily spotted whenever you bend down and the covering clothing is pulled tightly across your back. Retention can also be a problem: the position of the holster makes it harder to counter—or even be aware of—an attempt by a criminal behind you to take away your gun. Furthermore, during presentation from an SOB holster, most people will cross their own body with the muzzle as they rotate the gun toward the target. An SOB holster also can be uncomfortable if you sit against a hard-backed chair or bench; and it can loudly thump against such a seat when you sit, potentially alerting criminals within earshot. Finally, if you fall rearward onto the holster, serious back injury could result.

Wallet Holsters

Some manufacturers have made holsters designed to look like wallets with a space inside them for a small handgun, such as a two-shot derringer. A hole in the side of the wallet holster gives access to the gun's trigger, allowing it to be fired from within the holster.

These devices were intended to provide a measure of protection if a robber demanded your wallet. Although used by some police officers as a way to carry an undercover firearm, the Bureau of Alcohol, Tobacco, Firearms and Explosives (BATFE) has ruled that wallet holsters cannot be legally carried by civilians, so they should be avoided.

Pocket Holsters

Small handguns are often carried in a pants or jacket pocket. Pocket carry, though common, can be problematical; the gun may rotate to an awkward position, and its outline often prints through the fabric. These problems can be remedied with pocket holsters, flattened holsters that fill the pocket, camouflaging the gun's profile while keeping it in a butt-upward position that facilitates presentation. In use, a well-made pocket holster simply seems to be a thick wallet in your pocket.

Pocket holsters are inexpensive, highly concealable, and comfortable, and provide good retention and reasonably good access. Their chief benefit is that they allow a person to completely conceal a small handgun with virtually any type of clothing or in just about any situation. Pocket holsters may be difficult to draw from when in a seated position, however.

Fig. 71. Pocket holster and gun outside pocket (above) and hidden inside pocket.

Holster Vests/Holster Jackets

Some specialized articles of clothing—typically vests or jackets—feature pockets or compartments containing integral holsters capable of concealing handguns of almost any size. In many cases the gun is retained by a

Velcro® safety strap, and the holster itself may be removed or exchanged for one of a different size.

Holster vests and jackets afford a reasonable level of concealment, access and comfort. However, you must be careful not to carelessly put the jacket aside or hang it up; for your safety and that of all those around you, it must remain

Fig. 72. Holster jacket, closed (left) and open to show handgun in pocket.

under your direct control at all times. Additionally, in many of the models, the gun is carried in a shoulder-holster position on the weak side of the body. This confers upon these garments all the safety and retention problems that accompany shoulder holsters.

Underwear Holsters

Recent years have seen several companies market holsters that essentially fit around your waist over your underwear, with a small pouch in front for a handgun. Concealment can be astonishing with these devices.

While concealment and retention are excellent, these holsters can be dif-

Fig. 73. Underwear holster outside pants with gun (left) and inside the pants, demonstrating concealment.

ficult to draw from quickly. Like ankle holsters, underwear holsters should be reserved for deep-cover situations or for emergency back-up handguns.

Belly Bands

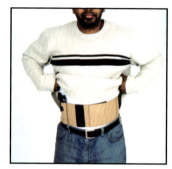

A simple way of carrying a concealed handgun is known generically as a belly band, a wide piece of elasticized fabric that encircles the waist. Fastening is usually by way of a Velcro® closure. The gun—usually a small, flat semiautomatic pistol—is simply tucked into the band, which is then covered with a shirt. Some belly bands have a small integral holster to more reliably position the gun.

Belly bands can give very good concealment and retention, but access to the gun can be slow, as the shirt and other covering clothing must first be unfastened and swept aside. Additionally, some people find it uncomfortable to have an elastic band constantly pushing a handgun against their body. Belly bands, like ankle holsters and underwear holsters, are much better than nothing at all, but should generally be relegated to a back-up gun or situations requiring extreme concealment.

Fig. 74. Belly band with handgun (top), and concealed under sweater.

Holster Accessories

For a holster to do its job properly—to retain the gun, remain in a consistent position on the trousers and freely release the handgun when it is

Fig. 75. A complete concealment rig: holster, magazine pouch and gun belt.

drawn—a gun belt is usually recommended. Thin, narrow leather dress belts just aren't up to the task of stabilizing a pound or two of metal on the hip. A thick leather gun belt resists twisting or sagging, and makes wearing a holster more comfortable.

For proper function, the belt width must exactly match the width of the slots or loops on the holster. If the belt is too large, the holster won't go on; too small, and the holster will move around on the waist, and will tend to follow the gun when it is withdrawn. A proper width gun belt provides consistent gun positioning and a crisp gun release.

Another worthwhile accessory is a magazine or speedloader pouch. Not only will this device provide you with additional ammunition; putting it on the side opposite a hip or shoulder holster may help to balance the pull of a heavy gun. Again, be sure to select a pouch having slots or loops of the exact same width as your gun belt.

HOLSTER PURSES, BRIEFCASES, AND FANNY PACKS

Holsters are simply not appropriate for everybody or for every situation. In business environments, women are often expected to wear a dress; a hip or shoulder holster cannot be used with such a garment. Even when women wear slacks, the waistband often is not stiff enough to support even a small paddle holster.

Moreover, at times men and women both may dress in ways that make holster carry difficult or impossible. For example, it is hard to hide a holster when you are dressed in shorts and a T-shirt, and you're going for your morning run. For such situations, alternative types of handgun concealment devices must be used.

Fig. 76. A few of the many types and styles of holster purses. Item at top left is leather backpack.

Holster Purses and Briefcases

Holster purses are handgun concealment devices that outwardly appear to be conventional handbags, but which have a pocket or compartment dedicated to handgun carry. Frequently the handgun is carried in an internal holster inside the gun compartment: this ensures a proper grip position whenever you go to grip the gun. No other objects should be carried in the gun compartment.

Fig. 77. A ballistic nylon brief-case, which can carry papers as well as a concealed handgun.

Access to the gun compartment may take many forms. One of the more popular types features a hidden, Velcro®-closed slit in the end of the bag, whose sides can be separated by inserting the firing hand fingertips between them. This type of bag is typically hung from a strap on the weak side shoulder; the opening giving access to the gun compartment is thus within easy reach of the firing hand.

Other holster purse designs resemble handbags having top flap closures. With these purses, access to the gun is gained through the top of the bag, after the flap has been opened.

Although this discussion of holster purses naturally focuses on women, many manufacturers also accommodate men whose dress or business environment makes holster carry impossible. Most popular are soft-sided attache cases that hang from the weak side shoulder. Just as with the holster purses of the same design, a Velcro®, snap or zipper closure on the end of the bag gives access to the dedicated gun compartment. Generally, these devices not only provide good handgun concealment; they also are well-designed for use in the office as well. Since the mode of carry and presentation is the same for both types of devices, it will henceforth be understood that the term "holster purse" also applies to gun concealment briefcases and attache cases.

Businessmen can also take advantage of other gun concealment devices, such as day planners and briefcases having separate gun compartments. The access afforded by such devices depends upon the design.

Concealment and comfort are usually quite good with holster purses—as long as they are worn with the appropriate clothing. Carrying an expensive-looking leather bag when you are going horseback riding may draw

Fig. 78. All the women here are carrying holster purses of different types with handguns concealed inside. A properly selected purse is indistinguishable from a regular purse. The purses are carried on the weak-side shoulder with a hand on the strap.

unwanted attention to your holster purse. Access with these devices varies, depending upon the design; shoulder-strap models probably offer the fastest presentation. Also, for proper access, you must always carry the bag in the proper manner.

The main concern with these handgun concealment devices is retention. In the street, you can have both your valuables and your gun taken by a purse-snatcher. And in a cafe, an office or other relaxed setting, you may let down your guard and hang the purse over the back of your chair, where it can be easily grabbed. Not only does this carelessness invite theft, but your gun does you little good if it's in a purse 30 feet away. Nonetheless, a properly-designed and well-crafted holster purse is unquestionably the best alternative for anyone unable to wear a holster in any formal environment.

Fanny Packs

A fanny pack provides the same type of holsterless handgun concealment as does a holster purse—but in a different environment or set of circumstances.

Fanny packs were originally designed to be worn by day hikers over the small of the back—hence the name. They were intended to carry a few small items—perhaps a compass, some first-aid cream, and maybe even a sandwich—for a short outing. Today, they are commonly worn by runners, bicyclists and others whose clothes offer no pockets to carry a wallet and car keys, and they are just as commonly worn to the front or the side as in the back. Fanny packs are also often seen on casually-dressed non-athletes and tourists.

Fig. 79. Fanny pack.

Like holster purses, fanny packs made for concealed carry feature a separate gun compartment sealed by a snap, zipper or Velcro® closure. The fanny pack is worn approximately in front of the belt buckle. To access the gun, the flap to the compartment is pulled open and the firing hand inserted. Some designs simply offer an empty compartment, while others have Velcro® straps to secure the gun in a consistent position for a faster, easier grip.

The better handgun concealment fanny packs look and function just like the models worn by runners, hikers and so forth. Avoid fanny packs with gun company logos; you may want to show your support for your favorite gunmaker, but knowledgeable criminals may pick up on the logo and decide that you've got a gun, and they want it.

As long as your gun fanny pack does not clash with your clothing, it should provide good concealment. Comfort with these devices is also usually quite good, as is access. In fact, fanny packs have an edge over many holsters in that they are relatively convenient to draw from when you're seated in your car. The level of retention a fanny pack provides depends upon the way it is worn and the care the user exercises with it. As with a holster purse, an unbuckled fanny pack hung over a chair or left lying on the ground is an open invitation to a thief. In most instances, however, you should be able to keep your fanny pack around your waist for the entire time you are out.

Fig. 80. A fanny pack can be used to conceal a handgun when an armed citizen is engaged in outdoor activities.

CHAPTER 11

PRINCIPLES OF CONCEALED CARRY

Selecting a suitable carry holster should be only a part of your overall handgun concealment strategy. Your carry holster must be integrated with the proper clothing, and you must constantly be aware of the body positions, actions and activities that promote or hinder handgun concealment. Consequently, there are a number of basic principles, techniques and tips to help you better conceal your handgun.

SELECTING OR MODIFYING A CONCEALED CARRY GUN

There are two objectives when selecting or modifying a gun for concealed carry. First, the gun must be easily concealed. Second, and just as important, the gun design should facilitate a smooth draw from under the clothing.

For maximum concealment, select the smallest gun possible in the caliber you've chosen for your carry firearm. However, some gun dimensions are more critical than others. Handgun width is the most important parameter: the narrower the gun, the less it will protrude from your hip, the small of your back, or wherever you carry your handgun. Thus, semi-automatic handguns are generally more concealable than revolvers. If you do choose a revolver, you may want to opt for a five-shot model over a six-shot gun; a five-

Fig. 81. All of these handguns can be concealed with the proper concealment device, though some models are more easily concealed than others.

Fig. 82. A narrow gun butt can stay closer to the body and is thus more concealable.

shot cylinder is smaller in diameter, and thus is more concealable.

Gun butt dimensions are next in importance to gun width. The gun butt is often positioned by the holster to stick out from the body, so it is the part of the gun that most likely will produce a pronounced bulge in the clothing. The longer, wider and bulkier the butt, the bigger the bulge it will produce. Thus, for concealment purposes, guns with smaller butts (such as round-butt revolvers) are best. Oversize target stocks should be replaced with standard stocks; even better are special minimum-size stocks made specifically for concealment. The best of such models have minimum lateral bulk but are proportioned to fill the hand for a solid grip on the gun.

Concealment pistol stocks should be made of relatively hard, smooth materials, such as wood or hard plastic. Soft rubber grips, although able to absorb some of the recoil of powerful defensive handguns, tend to stick to the covering clothing. This can both complicate the draw, as well as cause the clothing to fold or bunch unnaturally, revealing the gun. Many wood or plastic grips are sharply checkered; to prevent this checkering from catching on the clothing or abrading the lining, the checkered diamonds should be dulled slightly by flattening their tips.

Although gun length is not as critical for concealment as gun width or gun butt size, it is still important. Clearly, a pistol with a 6"- or 8"-barrel is going to be harder to conceal than the same gun with a barrel measuring only 2" or so. The importance of barrel length depends

Fig. 83. A short jacket can ride up and expose a hip holster.

upon the manner in which the gun is carried. When the gun is positioned so that its barrel runs along the long axis of the body (as with a hip holster), a longer barrel is less of a hindrance to concealment than when it is carried in other ways. When carried in a horizontal shoulder holster, for example, even an increase in barrel length from 2" to 3" can seriously affect concealability. Even in a hip holster, a long barrel can be a liability, as it may hit the bottom of a chair, car seat, etc. when you sit. Furthermore,

the longer the gun, the longer it will protrude below the belt line. This, in turn, makes it difficult to use short coats or jackets, and limits the range of movement that is possible without revealing the gun below the hem of the covering clothing. Additionally, the longer the barrel of the gun, the higher the gun must be raised to fully clear the holster. This can create a problem for short-waisted people, or those with limited shoulder flexibility.

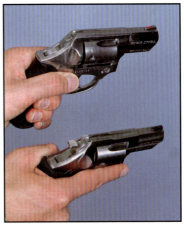

With some guns, dehorning is desirable to enhance concealability. Dehorning is the process of removing all sharp edges and corners from the gun so that it will not tear or abrade the clothing lining as it is carried, or catch on the lining as it is drawn. Dehorning, which is usually performed by a gunsmith, also can make fast gun handling

Fig. 84. A revolver with a dehorned hammer spur (top) compared with a standard hammer.

easier on the hands. Certain guns can be dehorned even further, by removing the spur from an external hammer or by replacing a spurred hammer with a spurless hammer. Some short-barreled revolvers incorporate a hammer shroud, which not only facilitates a snag-free draw, but also allows the gun to be fired repeatedly in the pocket, if necessary, without danger of the fabric being caught between the gun's hammer and frame.

SELECTING CONCEALMENT CLOTHING

The proper clothing is an integral part of the total handgun concealment system. Clothing for concealed carry should both conceal the handgun and facilitate the draw. There are certain basic principles to follow when selecting concealment clothing:

Fig. 85. A heavy, loose garment such as this photographer's vest provides good concealment for a handgun, as well as excellent access.

Wear loose clothing. Loose clothing prevents telltale gun bulges that can signify a gun to an observer. Loose clothing may also make it easier for you to access and draw your gun. However, clothing that is excessively loose can draw attention, and can additionally gather in folds that can actually impede the draw.

Also, if you carry your gun under a jacket, make sure the jacket can be comfortably buttoned or zipped up to keep it from opening on a windy day.

Wear heavy clothing. Where possible and appropriate, a coat or jacket of heavy fabric is preferred over one of light fabric. Light fabric will too easily conform to a protruding holster or gun butt, often revealing the gun's outline. A lightweight fabric will also often reveal the straps of a shoulder holster. Heavy, stiff fabric, such as corduroy or tweed, will tend to hang

Fig. 86. The outline of this handgun concealed in the pocket easily prints through the light fabric of the trousers.

in a way that conceals any irregular shape beneath it, such as a gun. Heavy fabric also tends to be easier to sweep aside to access the firearm.

Avoid very light-colored clothing. Bulges in clothing caused by a concealed handgun create hollows and shadows. These can be more evident when the clothing is light-colored.

Don't wear clothing with regular patterns. Stripes, geometric patterns, plaids and so forth create a visual reference that easily reveals any irregularities in the way the clothing drapes the body. Solid-colored fabric, or fabric with a random pattern, better hides gun or holster bulges.

Fig. 87. When everyone else is wearing short sleeves on a hot day, a jacket worn to cover a handgun can make you conspicuous.

Wear clothing that is appropriate. The clothing you wear when carrying a concealed handgun must also blend in with the style and type of clothing appropriate to the weather and the circumstances. For example, a lightweight sport coat worn over a hip holster may fit in an office or on a city street, but would be totally inappropriate on a beach or a jogging trail. For that matter, any type jacket at all might be out of place on a sweltering summer day. If you're wearing a windbreaker while everyone else is wearing just a T-shirt, you'll certainly attract the attention of any reasonably observant criminal.

Additionally, with certain items of clothing it may be desirable to reinforce the lining in the area that covers the holstered gun. Such a stiffener can prevent the gun from abrading the lining, and also can make it easier for the strong hand to sweep the clothing away to access the gun.

Wearing a Concealment Holster

While having a top quality holster is certainly essential for proper handgun carry, you must also know how to wear that holster to allow maximum concealment, access and retention.

Fig. 88. Proper placement of a hip holster, with handgun butt fairly high and holster roughly aligned with the trouser seam.

Hip holsters. Avoid placing a hip holster too far to the front or the rear. For best concealment under a jacket or loose open shirt, the holster should generally be no further forward than the point of the hip. The further rearward it is, the less likely the gun can be spotted should the jacket open due to a gust of wind or normal activity. On the other hand, a holster that is located too far back is more difficult to draw from, makes retention more difficult, and usually creates a highly visible bulge.

Many people using hip holsters with a forward or FBI rake find that a good balance among concealment, access and retention is achieved when the holster is placed so that the gun butt is under the elbow joint. With the holster in this position, the gun can be clamped tightly between the elbow and the side of the body to thwart any attempt at removal by an assailant.

When you've got to pick up an object while you're wearing a hip holster, bend at the knees rather than at the waist. Bending at the waist will make the butt of the gun visibly protrude to the rear under the clothing;

Fig. 89. Bending improperly to pick up an object (above) can cause a gun in a hip holster to protrude. A hip holster can also place the gun butt in a position to knock loudly against a wood or metal chair back when sitting.

the bulge is a dead giveaway to any reasonably observant person.

Be careful when sitting down on a chair, especially one with a hard back; the gun or holster might audibly knock against it.

Shoulder holsters. There are many shoulder holster designs, and thus many variations in the way these holsters can be worn.

Fig. 90. This shoulder holster puts the handgun too far forward for proper concealment.

Virtually all shoulder holster designs utilize some sort of suspension harness. Proper harness adjustment is extremely important to ensure good concealment, easy presentation and comfort. Make sure the harness fits properly not only when you're just standing with your arms at your sides, but also when you're reaching, turning, bending and so forth. Lean to the front and note how far forward the holster hangs; it may be visible if the jacket billows away from the body. Also, be sure the straps of the harness don't twist or turn; twisted straps will clearly show through most clothing.

Fig. 91. A twisted shoulder holster harness (above) can easily print through the fabric of a jacket.

Be careful not to put the handgun too far forward on the weak

side; although this may make it easier to draw from the holster, it also makes the gun easier to spot, particularly if the coat opens up. Conversely, putting the gun too far rearward will cause a bulge in the back of the jacket.

Fig. 92. Crossdraw holsters may place the gun too far forward for proper concealment or gun retention.

Crossdraw holsters. Some of the comments made in relation to wearing shoulder holsters apply to crossdraw holsters as well. Avoid wearing a crossdraw holster too far forward; not only will the gun be less well concealed, it can also be more easily grabbed by an assailant. Worn too far to the rear, however, the holster will create a visible bulge to the side, and will also be hard to draw from.

Holster Belts. As mentioned in Chapter 9, an important piece of clothing for those wearing a hip, crossdraw or small-of-the-back holster is a gun belt. The belt's width should match exactly the slots or loops in the holster. Additionally, the type of gun belt you wear should match the style and type of clothing you are wearing. Belts for both formal and casual dress are available.

Check Yourself In the Mirror. Your best tool for evaluating the efficacy of your concealed carry system is a full-length mirror. With your holster and gun in place, covered by the shirt, jacket or coat you're planning to wear over it, first examine yourself in the mirror with your arms at your sides. Use light coming from an angle rather than hitting you straight on; oblique light shows irregularities better. Turn 90 degrees to the left and right; look for telltale bulges, lines, creases and so forth. When your holster side faces the mirror, be especially aware of any bulge resulting from a protruding gun butt. Also make sure that the

Fig. 93. Checking yourself in a mirror in different positions can help you determine how concealable your carry rig is.

Fig. 94. A too-heavy handgun, or inadequate holster belt, can allow the pants to droop on one side.

gun or holster does not peek out from under the covering clothing.

Next, try moving around as you watch yourself in the mirror. Bend, stoop, reach forward, reach upward, lean backwards and so forth. In some positions, you likely will observe bulges from the gun or holster; make a mental note to avoid these positions when out in public. In some cases the jacket or coat may ride up and reveal part of the gun or holster underneath; this is especially common when the jacket barely covers the gun or holster to begin with, and you reach above your head (as when you're in a supermarket and reaching for a product on a high shelf).

Observe how far your jacket can be open before your gun and holster are visible. This will tell you how careful you must be in situations in which your jacket may fly open unexpectedly, such as when you're in a strong breeze or when you're running.

When you're wearing a heavy handgun on a hip holster, look to see that it doesn't pull your pants down on one side. A heavy pistol in a shoulder holster can likewise droop, making the harness hang improperly. Counterbalancing the gun with a weight on the opposite side, such as a magazine or speedloader, can help counteract these tendencies.

Holster Purses and Fanny Packs. When you carry a gun in a holster purse or fanny pack, special concealment techniques are usually not necessary; adequate concealment is normally provided by the purse or pack itself. However, you should still observe some common-sense suggestions to maximize access and retention.

Always wear the holster purse or fanny pack in the same manner. In the event of a sudden threat to your life, your draw must be an immediate and instinctive reflex. That reflex is possible only if the purse or pack is carried in the exact same way all the time, both during practice and on the street. If you wear a holster purse that hangs from your

Fig. 95. A fanny pack looks out of place when worn with a business suit.

weak side shoulder, make it a habit to always carry the purse that way. Don't occasionally switch it to the strong-side shoulder, or carry it by its handles. Similarly, don't move your fanny pack around on your waist so that it's in front one time, then to the side or rear the next.

Make sure your holster purse or fanny pack matches or complements

Fig. 96. Carrying a holster purse carelessly makes it difficult to access the gun, and easy for a mugger to grab it.

your clothing. Different occasions demand different styles of dress, and your holster purse or fanny pack should match that style just as your shoes, hat or any other accessory. Carrying an expensive-looking leather handbag when you're in jogging clothes will draw unwanted attention, and thus will defeat the purpose of concealment.

Use the utmost care and control when carrying a holster purse or fanny pack. Avoid dropping the purse or pack on the ground, swinging it so that it bangs against something hard, or carrying it loosely or carelessly.

There are at least three reasons why you must exercise extreme care and control over your holster purse or fanny pack while you are wearing it. First, it contains more than just a wallet, a checkbook, or some cosmetics; it holds a loaded gun that you may need to save your life. Dropping it on hard concrete could disable the gun within or, in extremely rare cases, cause it to discharge.

Second, the more careful you are when carrying your purse or pack, the harder it will be for a mugger or other assailant to take it from you—and with it, your gun. Purse-snatchers have been known to cut the strap of a handbag with a razor to facilitate its theft, or to simply yank the bag off the shoulder. A holster purse that is tightly clenched between the arm and the body is harder for a criminal to take, and actually may deter an assault.

Third, it is extremely difficult to draw quickly and smoothly from a free-swinging holster purse, or a fanny pack that is loosely carried around the waist. Not only will such a purse or pack be inconsistently located, making a quick, reflexive draw impossible, but a loosely-held purse or a loosely-mounted fanny pack will also prevent clean release of the gun when it is drawn.

CHAPTER 12

PRESENTING THE HANDGUN FROM CONCEALMENT

Presenting the handgun safely, smoothly and quickly from concealment is the single most important new shooting skill introduced in the NRA Basic Personal Protection Outside the Home Course. All the other shooting skills you have learned in other NRA courses, such as the Basic Pistol and Basic Personal Protection in the Home Courses, are integrated with that new skill.

Proper presentation technique is critical to responsible gun carry, as poor technique reduces the effectiveness of your handgun in defending your life. Your first concern when carrying a concealed handgun is safety. Safe technique must be ingrained from the very first practice session.

HANDGUN PRESENTATION STEPS

To foster safety and to facilitate learning, the proper technique of handgun presentation is broken down into sequential steps. These steps are the same whether you are presenting a handgun from a holster, a holster purse, or a fanny pack.

Initially in the learning phase, each step should be performed separately, in a deliberate manner, to ensure that the important aspects of the step are learned. For safety, your initial practice should be performed with an empty gun. As your skill grows, each step will naturally blend into the next, until you finally achieve presentation with a single smooth movement. This final stage takes place only after many hundreds or thousands of draws; it cannot be rushed (and in the

Fig. 97. Drawing from concealment.

interests of safety, must not be rushed). Always strive to execute each step properly and efficiently; this will produce smoothness.

There are seven steps to handgun presentation.
ACCESS the gun in the holster, holster purse or fanny pack
GRIP the butt of the gun with the strong hand
PULL the gun from the holster, holster purse or fanny pack
ROTATE the muzzle of the gun toward the target
JOIN the weak hand with the strong hand for a two-hand grip
EXTEND the gun toward the target
FIRE the gun if necessary

These steps may be modified depending upon the type of concealment device used: holster, holster purse or fanny pack. Each device will be covered in this chapter.

It is important to remember that firing the gun after it is presented should not be done automatically, but only if a deadly threat still exists. Thus, during the phases of the draw, and before firing a shot, you must continually assess the target to determine if you are still presented with a threat that justifies the use of force.

ACCESS the Gun. In this initial phase, the strong hand gains access to the gun under the clothing or inside the holster purse or fanny pack. This involves clearing any clothing, purse material, etc. out of the way of the hand that will be gripping the gun.

*Fig. 98. Steps in drawing the gun from conceal-
ment. From left, accessing the gun, gripping the gun, pulling the gun from the
holster, and rotating the gun toward the target.*

Fig. 98. (continued). Steps in drawing the gun from concealment. From left to right, joining the hands to form a two-hand grip, extending the handgun toward the target, and firing the handgun if necessary.

GRIP the Gun. Whatever type of handgun concealment device you use, the purpose of this step is the same: to acquire a solid, aligned grip on the gun that does not have to be significantly readjusted for the shooting position that will be used. In this step, the trigger finger is straight alongside the frame of the gun, outside the trigger guard.

PULL the Gun from the Holster, Holster Purse or Fanny Pack. During this movement your trigger finger remains straight alongside the handgun frame. Also, in this step the weak hand is brought to the chest. During the PULL phase you must keep the muzzle of the gun pointed in a safe direction at all times.

ROTATE the Gun Toward the Target. Your handgun is turned toward the general direction of the target without sweeping yourself or others with the muzzle. During the movement the weak hand is kept close to the body so that it is not crossed by the muzzle. The rotated handgun is also kept close to the body. Also, the safety, if any, is deactivated, and the trigger finger can be placed inside the trigger guard once the gun is pointed at the target (except when assuming the kneeling, prone and back positions, as noted in Chapter 19: Presentation and Fire from Different Positions).

If your attacker is at extremely close range, you may fire the gun as soon as it is rotated toward him, if necessary. For this reason, during the ROTATE phase of presentation, you should assess the target to determine if you continue to be faced with a deadly threat.

JOIN the Weak Hand to the Strong Hand. In this step, the hands come together to complete the two hand grip. Care must be taken not to bring the weak hand in front of the muzzle. The handgun is raised somewhat during this movement, so that you effectively assume a two-handed retention ready position; if necessary, as with an arm's-length assailant, the gun can be fired in this position. The JOIN step is omitted in one-handed presentation techniques, such as one-handed point shooting and instinctive shooting. In these techniques, the weak hand is normally kept close to the body, in front of the chest (unless it is used to ward off an attack, grip a flashlight, etc.).

During this phase of presentation, you should assess the target to determine if you continue to be faced with a deadly threat.

EXTEND the Gun Toward the Target. During this step, the gun is extended fully toward the attacker. If an aimed firing technique is to be used, you will also pick up the sights as the gun is extended forward. With a one-handed point shooting technique, the gun will be extended forward below the level of the eyes; with instinctive shooting, this step is deleted altogether, as the gun is fired from a position close to the body.

During this phase of presentation, you should assess the target to determine if you continue to be faced with a deadly threat. If there is insufficient time, or insufficient distance between you and your attacker, for the gun to be fully extended, it may be fired with the arms partially extended, if necessary.

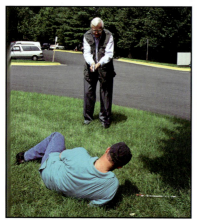

*Fig. 99. Assessing the threat before firing. If an attacker ceases to present a deadly threat, you must **not** fire.*

FIRE the Gun, If Necessary. The handgun can be fired as soon as the gun is aligned with the target, if no other option is available. Alignment can be determined using the gun's sights, as in an aimed fire technique, or simply by feel, as with instinctive shooting.

As has been emphasized before, you must continually assess the threat confronting you. This assessment continues even during the process of aligning the sights and preparing to pull the trigger. If your attacker turns and flees, surrenders or otherwise ceases to present a deadly threat, you must **not** fire.

In addition to these steps, after responding to a threat you should additionally lower the gun below eye level and scan the surrounding area, then, if the threat is completely gone, reholster it.

Although the presentation process is depicted here using a hip holster, the steps are similar for presenting handguns from holster purses, fanny packs and the like.

PRESENTATION FROM A HOLSTER

The specific details of the presentation steps for all types of holstered handguns are very similar. In the discussion below, emphasis will be given primarily to hip holsters, as they represent the safest, fastest, and most secure type of holster for most people. Additional comments will be made regarding other major holster types, where warranted, to point out variations in technique.

As was emphasized earlier, it is important during all the steps of presentation to continue to assess the threat confronting you. You are not justified in firing at an attacker who has ceased to be a threat.

Fig. 100. Accessing the gun. A bladed hand is used to sweep the covering clothing aside (left) to achieve good access to the handgun.

Access the Gun. A holster is almost always concealed under a piece of clothing, such as a jacket, coat, or shirt. A hip, inside-the-pants, or crossdraw holster is usually carried under a jacket or coat, or sometimes a loose shirt, that is long enough to conceal the gun, while shoulder holsters can be carried under short jackets. In all these cases, the article of clothing is usually left open to afford access, or is at most minimally fastened to prevent opening by the wind.

Accessing your handgun involves simply sweeping the covering clothing aside to create a space allowing your firing hand to acquire a grip on the gun butt. If your jacket, coat or other covering clothing is open in the front, you can usually gain access to the gun simply by holding your firing hand with fingers straight, in a knife-blade position, and inserting the fingertips in the slight gap between the clothing and the body. The further movement of the hand toward the gun tends to push or sweep the covering clothing aside.

Sometimes it is helpful to shift the weight away from the holster side of the body as the firing hand reaches toward the gun. This slight, quick movement tends to create a wider gap between the covering clothing and the body, facilitating the acquisition of your firearm. Avoid making this movement before starting the presentation sequence, or you will telegraph your intentions to your attacker. Having keys or some loose change in the holster-side pocket of a jacket used as covering clothing can also assist with access. The inertia of the extra weight in the pocket will create a larger gap when you shift your body to the side, and also will cause the jacket to more widely swing away from the body when your strong hand pushes it aside to access the gun.

In some situations, your weak hand must assist your strong hand to access the gun. For example, if your jacket has been buttoned, the weak hand unbuttons it while the strong hand prepares to reach inside the clothing. Even when your covering clothing is unfastened and open, certain types of holsters (such as shoulder holsters) are more easily accessed when your weak hand pulls the clothing aside. If your garment does not open in the front (such as a polo shirt) use your weak hand to pull the garment clear of the gun. An example is a small-of-the back or inside-the-pants holster.

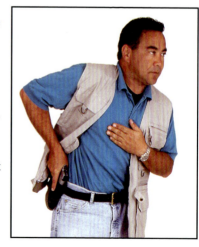

Fig. 101. Gripping the handgun.

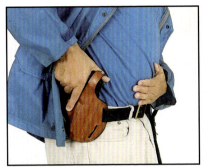

Fig. 102. With some holsters, the GRIP step may also involve releasing a safety strap or thumb snap.

Grip the Gun. As much as is possible, the handgun must be acquired with a normal shooting grip so that, when it is withdrawn from the holster, the hand, wrist and forearm are all in the proper alignment. With a proper grip, the gun, when raised to eye level, will usually have its sights in rough defensive alignment, facilitating a rapid first shot. Correcting a poor grip takes precious time during presentation; and such a grip, uncorrected, will prevent accurate shooting.

With holsters having a safety strap securing the gun, the initial part of the GRIP step is to undo the strap. Most high-quality concealment holsters having safety snaps are designed so that the strap can be disengaged by a finger or thumb during the act of acquiring a normal grip on the gun butt.

When the gun is initially gripped, the trigger finger is located alongside the frame, outside the trigger guard, and the safety lever (if present) remains on. Note that most carry holsters are designed to prevent the trigger finger from contacting the trigger until the gun is drawn.

Learning to quickly acquire the proper grip each and every time requires both considerable practice and a consistent positioning of the gun and holster on the body. Once you have mastered the ACCESS and GRIP steps separately, combine them into one smooth, precise movement. Strive to acquire the gun with the proper grip on the first try, without having to make minor readjustments. Eventually, with much practice, you will be able to feel the gun's location on the body so that you unerringly acquire a proper grip, regardless of your own body position.

Pull the Gun from the Holster. Most holsters require the gun to be withdrawn in a specific way. Usually,

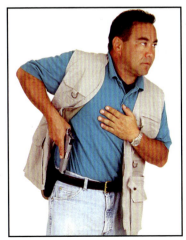

Fig. 103. Pulling the handgun from the holster.

Fig. 104. When drawing from a shoulder holster, the muzzle of the handgun must immediately be turned downward.

the handgun is pulled straight out of the holster; with a few designs, such as spring-clip shoulder holsters, the gun is pulled out of the side or front of the holster against spring tension. Certain holsters may even bind or prevent gun withdrawal if the handgun is not pulled out of the holster in a particular way. Make sure you know how to pull your handgun smoothly from your carry holster; try withdrawing the gun at different angles to see if the holster grabs or binds.

With hip, crossdraw, inside-the pants and small-of-the-back holsters, as well as some shoulder holsters, the gun is pointing roughly at the ground when it is first withdrawn. When the gun is pulled from certain shoulder holsters, most notably horizontal and upside-down shoulder holsters, the gun is initially pointed directly behind you. Learn to direct the muzzle downward, toward the ground, after you pull your handgun from either of these holsters.

During the PULL step, the trigger finger remains outside the trigger guard, and the safety remains on. Furthermore, the weak hand is brought to the chest, keeping it out of the way of the muzzle during the ROTATE step in the process.

Rotate the Gun Toward the Target. In this step, the gun is brought into a position with the muzzle facing roughly toward the target. The weak hand is still held close to the body at the chest, the trigger finger remains outside the trigger guard, and the

Fig. 105. Rotating the handgun toward the target.

Fig. 106. When drawing from a small-of-the-back holster, the gun's muzzle is kept point-ing downward, clear of the body, until it can be rotated straight forward to the target.

safety (if present) is taken off when the gun is fully rotated and pointing toward the target.

With each type of holster, the gun's muzzle takes a different path toward the target during the ROTATE phase, usually dictated by safety concerns. The easiest and safest path is achieved with a typical strong-side hip hol-ster. The handgun is withdrawn with the muzzle pointing down alongside the leg, and is simply rotated forward until it is aligned with the target; the muzzle points at the ground during almost all of the rotation movement.

Great care must be taken when rotating a gun drawn from a crossdraw, shoulder or small-of-the back holster. With a crossdraw or shoulder holster, there is a tendency to sweep the gun across the body with the muzzle held more or less horizontal. On the other hand, a gun withdrawn from a small-of-the-back holster is often rotated toward the target with the muzzle cross-ing part of the body. Either rotation pattern is clearly unsafe. To rotate the gun toward the target safely, first point the gun toward the ground. Then turn the muzzle forward in a straight line. This will ensure that the muzzle

Fig. 107. During rotation from a shoulder holster, the muzzle remains pointed down-ward until it can be rotated directly forward toward the target.

is pointed in a safe direction during the rotation movement, just as with a hip holster.

Be aware, however, that this rotation pattern, though safe, feels awkward to many people. For this reason it is critical to keep the trigger finger out of the trigger guard and the safety on during the ROTATE phase. This technique should be ingrained and reinforced through diligent practice.

At the completion of the ROTATE step, the gun will be in a position from alongside the strong-side hip to slightly in front of the body, depending upon the type of holster the gun was drawn from. When presenting from a hip holster, the gun, at the end of rotation, will be held close to the body on the strong side, just above the hip. A gun drawn from a small-of-the-back holster, properly rotated forward, will also end up in this position. Rotation from either a crossdraw or shoulder holster will usually result in the gun held in the strong hand, slightly forward of the body toward the strong-hand side.

Once the firearm is pointed at the target, the safety may be disengaged and the trigger finger placed inside the trigger guard. If necessary to stop an arm's length assailant, the handgun may be fired at the completion of the ROTATE phase.

Fig. 108. Joining the weak hand to the strong hand.

Join the Weak Hand to the Strong Hand. When a two-handed shooting position is used, the weak hand must be joined to the strong hand to complete the proper grip. To complete the JOIN step, simply take the weak hand from its position in front of the chest, bring it to the strong hand and assume a solid two-hand grip. This presentation step is not required when one-handed shooting techniques, such as the point shooting and instinctive shooting techniques, are used.

Be careful to keep the weak hand from crossing the muzzle as it is brought to the strong hand. Also, the weak hand should move to the strong hand, not vice versa.

Joining the weak hand to the strong hand not only completes the two hand grip; it also helps promote handgun retention. With both hands on your gun, you will better be capable of preventing an assailant from wresting it from you.

Extend the Gun Toward the Target.
During this step the handgun is pushed forward toward the target to complete the desired firing position (Weaver, isosceles, etc.). At the same time, the sights are picked up as the gun comes into the field of view.

Note that the EXTEND step applies to not only two-handed, aimed-fire shooting positions; it is also performed with the one-handed point shooting technique.

Extend the gun in a straight line. Don't jerk the gun forward; extend it with a smooth, controlled movement. Also avoid using a scooping or a rising-and-falling motion: such a motion requires you to

Fig. 109. Extending the handgun toward the target.

overcompensate to bring the gun into alignment. With a straight-line extension into an aimed-fire shooting position, your eyes can pick up the sights as the gun goes forward, allowing you to make small corrections of gun position during the extension. When your gun is extended properly and your body is aligned with your Natural Point of Aim (NPA) in relation to the target, the sights of your gun will be in reasonably good alignment when your arms are fully forward.

Fire the Gun, if Necessary. The FIRE step is normally performed when you have assumed your final firing position and there is no other option available to stop the deadly threat. On those occasions when you are using

Fig. 110. Firing the handgun.

an aimed fire or point shooting technique, the FIRE step follows the achievement of full extension toward the target. When you are using an instinctive shooting technique, you will fire after the gun is rotated up into alignment with the target.

The degree of sight alignment and trigger control you employ will largely depend upon the range and the size of the target. With a full-size target at arm's length, you will likely use instinctive shooting and pull the trigger quickly. With a longer shot on a partially exposed target, on the other hand, you will more carefully align the sights and squeeze the trigger more deliberately.

Be careful in your training not to ingrain the habit of automatically firing at the completion of each presentation; that habit will prevent you from exercising the moment-to-moment judgement that you should use in deciding whether you need to discharge your handgun. Your situation may change in an instant—for example, your attacker may turn to flee—and you need the last-second restraint that enables you to hold your fire when such situations present themselves. Often, firing your gun is not needed. Research by University of Florida criminologist Gary Kleck and others indicates that, in most cases, simply presenting a handgun without firing a shot is sufficient to stop or deter a violent attack. Morally and legally, it is ALWAYS preferable to end an attack without firing a shot, if possible.

Whatever presentation technique you practice, occasionally refrain from taking the final FIRE step to help develop a capacity for restraint. Also, you can structure your training to include shoot/no-shoot situations to simulate real-world decision-making.

Lower, Scan and Reholster. After you have deterred or stopped an attack by effectively presenting your handgun, you must scan the area for additional threats. Remember that you are probably suffering from tunnel vision as a result of being involved in a violent, life-threatening confrontation; you will focus on the immediate threat in front of you, to the exclusion of almost everything else. Visually scanning the area around you breaks tunnel vision, and may

Fig. 111. After firing, lower your gun slightly to break tunnel vision, and then scan left and right, pointing the handgun in the direction of sight.

alert you to other things you need to be aware of, such as additional assailants or an approaching police officer.

Scanning for additional threats when you're outside the home is different from scanning when you're inside the home. The proper technique for scanning the area when you are outside your home is presented in Chapter 8: If You Must Shoot.

Once you have ascertained that there is no further immediate danger to your front, sides or rear, you may do one of two things. If there is a possibility that the threat will return, or that you may face a threat from another direction or assailant, you should lower your firearm to a low ready position (gun pointing downward at a 45 degree angle) and maintain that position until you

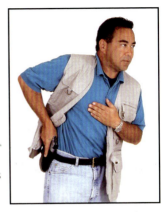

Fig. 112. It is important to be able to reholster without looking at the holster to prevent losing visual contact with a real or potential threat.

are either no longer in danger, or until you must raise the gun to a firing position to protect yourself. Even with the firearm in a low ready position, don't stop scanning for additional threats, and be prepared to seek cover if necessary.

Alternatively, once you establish that you face no further danger, you should reholster your handgun. As was discussed in Chapter 8, you'll want to avoid meeting the responding police officers with a gun in your hand.

To reholster your gun, first take your trigger finger out of the trigger guard and place it alongside the frame. Return the safety, if any, to the "on" position. Release the gun with the weak hand and rotate the gun muzzle downward toward the mouth of the holster. It is preferable to use a holster with a stiff, molded shape that stays open when the gun is withdrawn, as such a holster allows one-handed reholstering. However, if you must use your weak hand to squeeze open the mouth of the holster for handgun insertion, be sure not to cross that hand with the muzzle during the reholstering process. Also, be sure not to drag part of the shirt or jacket into the holster with the gun.

Practice reholstering your empty firearm until you can reholster it by feel, without looking. If you become distracted by focusing on the process of putting your gun back in your holster, you may give a hidden assailant the opportunity to attack you. Some molded leather and synthetic holsters retain their shape even when they are not filled by a gun; with such holsters it is often possible to reinsert the gun with the strong hand only. Other holster types, such as shoulder holsters, usually require both hands.

If you must see what you are doing while you are reholstering, give the holster a quick glance and then immediately return focus to your surroundings; don't look at it for an extended time. It is better to observe what you are doing with a series of rapid glances than with a prolonged gaze.

PRESENTATION FROM A HOLSTER PURSE OR FANNY PACK

The same sequence of steps used when presenting from a holster— ACCESS, GRIP, PULL, ROTATE, JOIN, EXTEND and FIRE—is used when presenting from a holster purse or fanny pack. In fact, the technique for performing most of the steps is virtually identical, whatever type of handgun concealment device is used.

There is only a minor difference in gun position between a front-mounted fanny pack and a holster purse hanging off the weak-side shoulder. With both, the gun hand must reach across the body to access the gun, and the weak hand is used to bring the purse across the body to the same location in which a fanny pack is carried, and then to help open the holster purse and facilitate access to the gun. Also, the body position and handgun movement during presentation is very similar for the two types of devices. For these reasons, it is appropriate to present the technique for both devices together.

As was emphasized earlier, it is important during all the steps of presentation to continue to assess the threat confronting you. You are not justified in firing at an attacker who has ceased to be a threat.

Access the Gun. Holster purses usually have a separate gun compartment that is easily accessed through the forward-facing part of the purse— usually the side. Some holster purses give access to the gun through the top. In either case, access to the dedicated gun compartment is usually achieved by opening a Velcro® or snap closure. Some designs can be opened by the firing hand alone; others require weak-hand assistance.

Practice sharply angling or "blading" the strong side of your body away from the direction of the threat as you begin to access your gun. This accomplishes two objectives. First, as with shoulder holster and crossdraw holsters, you must reach across your body to acquire a grip on the gun—a move that can easily be blocked or interrupted by an arm's-length assailant. Blading yourself away from an assailant makes this harder for him to do, and, in the case of a front-mounted fanny pack, actually increases the distance of the handgun from him. Second, when you are turned away in this fashion, your gun will be pointing more in the direction of the target when it is withdrawn from the purse or pack.

To promote better access to your gun when wearing a shoulder-mounted holster purse, use your weak hand to pull it across your body to a position close to the centerline of your torso. Combined with the blading movement away from the threat, this will have the effect of pointing the gun at the target. With the purse in this position, you can even fire the gun from inside it to stop an arm's-length assailant.

Grip the Gun. The technique for achieving the proper grip inside a holster purse or fanny pack differs little from that used to achieve a grip on a gun in a holster. The handgun must be acquired with a normal shooting grip so that, when it is withdrawn from the purse or pack, the hand, wrist and forearm are all in the proper alignment. With a proper grip, the gun, when raised to eye level, will usually have its sights in rough defensive alignment, facilitating a rapid first shot. Correcting a poor or improper grip takes precious time during presentation; and such a grip, uncorrected, will

Fig. 113. Accessing the handgun in a holster purse. The strong hand fingers are extended, and the weak hand stabilizes the purse and pulls it across the body. Finally, to assist in blading the body away from the threat, the strong-side foot slides rearward..

prevent accurate shooting.

With holster purses or fanny packs having a safety strap securing the gun, the initial part of the GRIP step is to undo the strap. Most high-quality concealment devices having safety snaps are designed so that the strap can be disengaged quickly.

Fig. 114. With the holster purse or fanny pack pulled across the body, the strong hand acquires a firm grip on the handgun inside.

When the gun is initially gripped, the trigger finger is located alongside the frame, outside the trigger guard, and the safety lever (if present) remains on.

Once you have mastered the ACCESS and GRIP steps separately, combine them into one smooth, precise movement. Strive to acquire the gun with the proper grip on the first try, without having to make minor readjustments. With practice, you will be able to feel the gun's location on the body so that you unerringly acquire a proper grip, regardless of your own body position.

Pull the Gun from the Holster Purse or Fanny Pack. During the PULL phase, the handgun is withdrawn from the holster purse or fanny pack. Usually it is pulled out more or less horizontally.

With some purses or packs, the weak hand must open the device, or help hold it open while the firing hand accesses the gun and acquires a grip. Often the weak hand must also hold the the device steady while the gun is being withdrawn; this is particularly true with holster purses hanging by a strap from the weak-side shoulder. Additionally, with some holster purse designs, the weak hand must pull the purse rearward while the strong hand pulls the gun out of its compartment. With all these techniques, you must take care when withdrawing the gun from a purse or pack not to cross your weak hand with the muzzle.

When the gun is pulled from many holster purses and fanny packs—particularly when you are unable to blade your body away from the threat— learn to direct the muzzle downward, toward the ground, immediately after it comes out of a purse or pack.

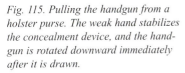

Fig. 115. Pulling the handgun from a holster purse. The weak hand stabilizes the concealment device, and the handgun is rotated downward immediately after it is drawn.

During the PULL step, the trigger finger remains outside the trigger guard, and the safety remains on.

Rotate the Gun Toward the Target. The ROTATE step is perhaps the most critical in terms of safety when you are presenting your handgun from a holster purse or fanny pack. If your strong side is sufficiently bladed away, your gun will be roughly aligned with the target when you withdraw your gun from your purse or pack. The ROTATE step will then involve little more than raising the muzzle of the gun into alignment with the threat.

In the real world, however, under the stress of a violent confrontation, you may not always blade yourself away from the threat before you draw the gun. The attack may happen too suddenly, or your back may be against a wall and you can't easily turn your body away. Whatever the reason, in such a situation your gun will typically be pointing somewhat off to the side when you withdraw it from your holster purse or fanny pack. During your ROTATE step you must learn to direct the muzzle downward, keeping it in a safe direction.

Fig. 116. When rotating the gun, the muzzle must be pointed toward the ground until it is aligned with the target.

To accomplish a safe rotation in this situation, first drop the muzzle so that the gun is pointing to the ground in front of your body. Then turn your wrist and arm so that the path of the muzzle traces a straight line forward, straight to the target.

Fig. 117. Joining the weak hand to the strong hand.

Initially this may seem awkward, but with practice it will become natural and habitual. Moreover, it will help you develop an instinctive awareness of the position of the muzzle at all times. Remember to keep the safety on, and your trigger finger out of the trigger guard, until the gun is ROTATED toward the target.

Join the Weak Hand to the Strong Hand. The JOIN step is performed in essentially the same manner whether you are presenting your handgun from a holster, a handbag, or a fanny pack: the weak hand moves to the strong hand and completes the firing grip. Be careful to keep the weak hand from crossing the muzzle as it joins the strong hand.

Joining the weak hand to the strong hand not only completes the two hand grip; it also helps promote handgun retention. With both hands on your gun, you will better be capable of preventing an assailant from wresting it from you.

Extend the Gun Toward the Target. In this step, the joined hands are thrust forward into a final shooting position. Note that the EXTEND step applies to not only two-handed, aimed-fire shooting positions; it is also performed with the one-handed point shooting technique.

Extend the gun in a straight line. Don't jerk the gun forward; extend it with a smooth, controlled movement. Also avoid using a scooping or a rising-and-falling motion: such a motion requires you to overcompensate to bring the gun into alignment. With a straight-line extension into an aimed-fire shooting position, your eyes can pick up the sights as the gun goes forward, allowing you to make small corrections of gun position during the extension. When your gun is extended properly and your body is aligned with your NPA (natural point of aim) in relation to the target, the sights of your gun will be in reasonably good alignment when your arms are fully forward.

Fig. 118. Extending the gun toward the target.

Fire the Gun if Necessary. The FIRE step is normally performed when you have assumed your final firing position and there is no other option available to stop the deadly threat. On those occasions when you are using an aimed fire or point shooting technique, the FIRE step follows the achievement of full extension toward the target. When you are using an instinctive shooting technique, you will fire after the gun is rotated up into alignment with the target.

The degree of sight alignment and trigger control you employ will largely depend upon the range and the size of the target. With a full-size target at arm's length, you will likely use instinctive shooting and pull the trigger quickly. With a longer shot on a partially exposed target, on the other hand, you will more deliberately align the sights and squeeze the trigger.

In your practice, occasionally refrain from taking the final FIRE step to

Fig. 119. Firing the handgun, if necessary.

help develop a capacity for restraint, and incorporate shoot/no-shoot situations to simulate real-world decision-making. You must be careful in your training not to ingrain the habit of automatically firing at the completion of each presentation; that habit will override the moment-to-moment judgement you should use in deciding whether you need to fire your handgun. In the real world, your situation may change in an instant—for example, your attacker may suddenly turn to flee—and you may need the last-second restraint that enables you to hold your fire. Often, firing your gun is not needed. Research by criminologist Gary Kleck and others shows that simply presenting a handgun without firing a shot is often sufficient to stop or deter an attack. Morally and legally, it is ALWAYS preferable to end an attack without firing a shot, if possible.

Lower, Scan and Reholster. After you have deterred or stopped an attack by effectively presenting your handgun, you must scan the area for additional threats. Remember that you are probably suffering from tunnel vision as a result of being involved in a violent, life-threatening confrontation; you will focus on the immediate threat in front of you, to the exclusion of almost everything else. Visually scanning the area around you breaks tunnel vision, and may alert you to other things you need to be aware of, such as additional assailants or an approaching police officer.

Scanning for additional threats when you're outside the home is different from scanning when you're inside the home. The proper technique for scanning the area when you are outside your home is presented in Chapter 8: If You Must Shoot.

Once you have ascertained that there is no further immediate danger to your front, sides or rear, you may do one of two things. If there is a possibility that the threat will return, or that you may face a threat from another direction or assailant, you should lower your firearm to a ready position (gun pointing downward at a 45 degree angle) and maintain that position until you are either no longer in danger, or until you must raise the gun to

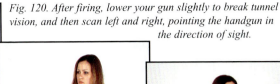

Fig. 120. After firing, lower your gun slightly to break tunnel vision, and then scan left and right, pointing the handgun in the direction of sight.

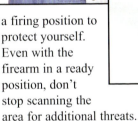

a firing position to protect yourself. Even with the firearm in a ready position, don't stop scanning the area for additional threats.

Alternatively, once you firmly establish that you face no further danger, you should reholster your handgun. As was pointed out in Chapter 8, you will want to avoid meeting the responding police officers with a gun in your hand.

Practice reholstering your empty firearm until you can reinsert it into your holster purse or fanny pack by feel, without looking. If you become distracted by focusing on the process of putting your gun back in your purse or pack, you may give a hidden assailant the opportunity to attack you. Most holster purses or fanny packs usually require both hands to reholster the gun.

Fig. 121. Reholstering without looking at the holster purse/fanny pack.

If you must see what you are doing while you are reholstering, give the holster a quick glance and then immediately return visual focus to your surroundings; don't look at it for an extended time. It is much better to observe what you are doing with a series of rapid glances than with a prolonged gaze.

TRAINING FOR PRESENTATION FROM A HOLSTER, HOLSTER PURSE OR FANNY PACK

Initially, you should practice handgun presentation from a holster using an unloaded gun in your designated dry-fire area. Before commencing dry-firing, always ensure that the gun is unloaded, and that there is no ammunition in the area. Start by performing each step separately as you say the name of the step: ACCESS! GRIP! PULL! ROTATE! JOIN! EXTEND! FIRE! Be sure you know and practice the proper technique for each step, being particularly careful to observe the proper safety precautions associated with each step. For example, it is critical for safety to observe the proper rotation technique when presenting from a crossdraw holster, shoulder holster, holster purse or fanny pack.

Once you have mastered the proper sequence of steps, and the technique for each step, slowly increase your presentation speed. The interval between each step will decrease, and each step will blend naturally into the next. After a while—usually several hundred presentations—you will achieve sufficient proficiency with the technique to begin using live ammunition.

Be aware that some ranges do not allow shooters to draw from the holster, and those that do may only allow such presentation from a strong-side hip holster. Also, some ranges will not permit drawing from a holster under clothing. Discuss your presentation practice with range officials before you start.

At the range, start slow. For the first few presentations, go back to a step-by-step method to review the proper sequence and technique of the necessary steps.

If you are presenting from a holster, begin by presenting the gun without wearing the concealment clothing. As you get more comfortable and proficient with drawing and firing using live ammunition, your control of the firearm will improve and you can carefully reintroduce the ACCESS step at the beginning of the presentation process.

Remember that safety and smoothness are just as important as sheer presentation speed. A slow hit is better than a fast miss; it will do you little good to draw the gun a few tenths of a second faster if you lose control and can't shoot accurately.

HANDGUN PRESENTATION AND CONCEALED CARRY FOR THE DISABLED

The special circumstances of physically disabled persons create unusual challenges for concealed carry. These challenges are complicated by the diversity of physical disabilities with which an individual can be afflicted.

There can be no universal guidelines for the best way for physically challenged persons to carry a concealed firearm. The concealed carry needs of a person who uses a cane likely will differ from those of a person who uses a walker. Many physically challenged persons may need to modify the standard presentation techniques to accommodate their special needs, and to ensure that the handgun's muzzle is always pointed in a safe direction at all times during

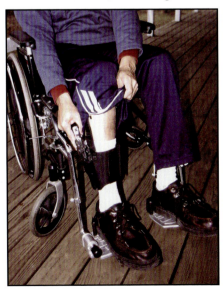

Fig. 122. An ankle or calf holster worn under loose clothing give the wheelchair-bound an effective mode of concealment that also promotes safe handgun presentation.

presentation. Persons with certain physical limitations may also find it difficult or impossible to assume some shooting positions, such as the kneeling or prone positions, or to move quickly to cover. Common sense and an analysis of each individual's capabilities will dictate the carry mode, presentation method and shooting techniques to be used in each case.

One of the more common situations involves an individual in a wheelchair. As a general rule, concealing the gun on the chair itself is not recommended, as the disabled person may be separated from the chair during the struggle of an attack. For the wheelchair-bound, presentation from a hip holster or small-of-the-back holster may be extremely difficult or impossible. Other common modes of carry, such as a shoulder holster, crossdraw holster or fanny pack, are not recommended, as handgun presentation will unavoidably involve sweeping the handgun in an arc, endangering innocent bystanders, or pointing the gun at the legs before it is rotated toward the target.

Many wheelchair users who carry a concealed handgun utilize an ankle or calf holster that positions the gun on the lower leg. With this mode of carry, the handgun's muzzle travels directly toward the target during presentation, providing a safe draw. Ankle or calf holsters for the disabled are especially effective when used in conjunction with loose clothing, such as sweatpants, which can be easily pulled up by the weak hand to allow access to the handgun.

Other modes of carry will be required for other types of disabilities, which are far too numerous to be treated in this book. For advice or information on various concealment options, contact the Manager, Disabled Shooting Services, Competitive Shooting Division, National Rifle Association of America at (703) 267-1495.

CHAPTER 13

SPECIAL CONCEALMENT SITUATIONS

As you go about your various daily activities, you will find that there are situations in which normal carry in a holster, fanny pack or holster purse is inadequate. In addition, there will also be situations relating to concealed carry that may have nothing whatsoever to do with self-defense, but are nonetheless problematical.

The discussion below does not begin to cover all the possible special situations you may encounter; however, it is hoped that you will come away with some general ideas and principles that you can apply to a wide range of circumstances.

CARRY IN A VEHICLE

With the increased number of carjackings in many areas, you may be just as vulnerable in your vehicle as you are while walking on the street. Thus, in your car, you likely will need quick access to your defensive handgun.

However, a holster or holster purse that provides ready access while you are standing or walking may be next to useless when you are seated in a vehicle. Hip holsters and small-of-the-back holsters, for example, are almost impossible to draw from when you are seated in your vehicle. Often, to access your handgun in a hip holster you must lean sharply toward the driver's side window, putting you nearer a carjacker, robber or other threat that is approaching from that side. Similarly, if you carry a gun in a holster purse, you don't normally wear the purse while driving; you put it on the seat next to you or some other convenient location. If you are attacked, however, you may find it hard to access and present the gun quickly from a purse lying two feet away on the seat (or even further if it slides off the seat onto the floor during braking). In addition, a purse lying unguarded on a car seat may be a temptation for a robber when you've stopped at a traffic light.

Ideally, your gun should always be on your person, even when you are in a vehicle, and it should also be readily accessible. Some carry devices, such as fanny packs and shoulder holsters, can satisfy both these require-

Fig. 123. Handgun in vehicle between driver's seat and center console.

ments. If these devices are not your preferred mose of carry, however, you may need to provide an alternative method for carrying your gun in the vehicle so that it is immediately accessible.

Your gun should be in a location that provides easy access, consistent positioning, and concealment from any passing motorist or pedestrian who may happen to look into your vehicle. Some of the more obvious solutions to this problem fail to meet one or more of these requirements. For example, keeping your gun in your vehicle's locking glove box provides concealment, but does not position the gun consistently, makes it difficult to to draw conveniently and quickly, and does not afford quick access.

The same problem exists when you put the gun under your driver's side seat. Concealment is good, but the gun may slide around on the floor, making it hard to access quickly. If the gun slides all the way to the rear, you may not be able to access it at all.

Some personal protection authorities advocate putting your gun on the seat beside you and covering it with a newspaper for concealment. This does provide reasonably quick access; however, under hard braking, the gun may slide forward off the seat, out of reach. The newspaper may also slide off the seat, exposing the gun. The gun may also be exposed in warm weather, if you drive with your windows down and the newspaper blows away.

Specialized gun boxes made for in-car storage are a better alternative, and have the additional benefit of providing safe gun storage in the vehicle when you are not around. However, most models require you to manipulate a combination or Simplex-type lock to open them. Under stress, this may be both difficult and excessively time-consuming.

The center console of your vehicle may be effectively used for gun storage. The console is conveniently reached and provides good concealment. If you use the console for gun storage, however, be sure to not store any other object in the compartment containing the gun.

Many experts recommend the installation of a holster in the space between the driver's seat and the center console. This holster should be attached by adhesives, Velcro® strips or other means, and oriented to position the gun's butt upward for fast access. Properly installed, this holster will provide fast access while adequately concealing the gun.

Do not install the holster on the left side of the driver's seat, even if you are left-handed; it will be exposed whenever the driver's door is opened.

Given the difficulty of quickly presenting a firearm in a vehicle from a hip holster or holster purse (probably the preferred modes of carry for most men and women, respectively), some authorities recommend that a second gun be dedicated to vehicle carry. Such a firearm would be kept permanently in the vehicle in a location allowing both good concealment and immediate access from the driver's seat. Drawbacks of this practice include the possibility of a child or other unauthorized person in the vehicle being able to gain access to the gun, as well as the potential acquisition of the gun by a ciminal if the vehicle was stolen.

CHANGING CARRY LOCATIONS

There will be occasions in which you will find it necessary to change the carry location of your concealed handgun. You must remove your concealed handgun before you enter a United States Post Office, a school, a bar or a government building; and you likely will want to put it back on after you leave. Alternatively, you may have your handgun in a holster next to your seat in your vehicle, as described in the previous section, and you wish to put it back in its holster before you leave your vehicle. In any event, you should do this change both quickly and discreetly.

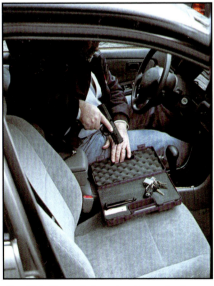

Fig. 124. Concealed carrier discreetly changing handgun location in a vehicle.

Your main concern is to avoid observation by others while you are changing your handgun from one carry location to another. Most of the time, changing handgun location is performed while you are in your vehicle. Be aware of other motorists or pedestrians who are near enough to your vehicle to see inside. If you are in a parking lot, park a little distance away from other vehicles to minimize the likelihood of being observed. Remember that the occupants of many commercial trucks, cargo vans, sport utility vehicles and similar high-riding vehicles can look down into your vehicle, so be aware of such vehicles when they pass. People looking out of the upper-floor windows of nearby houses or office buildings, too, may be able to look down into your vehicle and see you handling a gun.

It is always critical to exercise the utmost discretion whenever you handle your gun in public. Bystanders may become alarmed upon seeing a man with a gun, and may alert the police.

You may also need to change gun carry locations at other times as well. For example, if you carry a small handgun in a coat pocket, you should change the gun's location when you go into an environment, such as your workplace, in which your coat would normally be removed. Change the location of the gun before entering the building, if possible. When that is not practical, change the gun's location in a private area where you will not be observed. A stall in a rest room is ideal for this.

Most situations of this type can be avoided by some simple advance planning. If you know you are going into a business meeting where you will be expected to remove your suit coat, you should not, that day, carry your gun in a shoulder or belt holster, or even in your coat pocket. If the gun is small enough, carry it in your pants pocket; if not, it should be concealed in a day planner, attache case or other object that is appropriate to a business environment.

CONCEALED CARRY IN A REST ROOM

You may not think about being the target of an attack when you are using a rest room at work, in a store or at a gas station. We like to think that others will respect our privacy at such times. However, there have been many cases of people being victimized in public restrooms. Often, the attack occurred when they were most vulnerable—sitting in a toilet stall. Typically, robbers grab the victim's ankles and pull him or her forward off the toilet and under the stall door. Lying on their backs, the victims of these attacks quite naturally feel both helpless and mortified, making them easy prey. Attacks may also come from adjoining stalls, with an assailant peering over the divider and threatening his victim with a weapon.

If you carry a handgun on a belt holster—a crossdraw, small-of-the-back or strong-side hip holster—you must be aware that you can be just as vulnerable to this kind of attack if you leave your gun and holster around your ankles while you are in the stall. Once you are safely locked in the stall, you should remove your gun from its holster and keep it in your lap. This will give you immediate access to the gun if you are attacked. Do the same with a gun carried in a fanny pack. As silly as it may sound, be careful not to let your gun slide off or through your legs into the toilet. Also be aware that even with the gun removed from a belt holster, the holster itself may be visible to anyone glancing at the space under the door to the stall.

A gun in a holster purse need not be removed; however, you should clamp the purse under the weak-side arm so that you can quickly acquire the gun if trouble arises. Never hang the purse on a clothes hook on the inside of the stall door, or place it on the floor next to your feet.

Whatever your mode of carry, you may need to experiment to develop a method of retaining the gun so that it is secure and readily accessible.

Men using a urinal may also be vulnerable, as bathroom etiquette generally discourages them from looking around to observe their environment. Maintaining proper awareness, however, is more important than observing this custom. Also, you can discreetly keep an eye on your surroundings by using the reflections off chrome-plated pipes, shiny fixtures, and tile wall. Finally, whenever possible, choose to stand in a location offering the best view of the bathroom, and the greatest protection against attack.

The scenarios described above are just a few of the many special concealment situations that handgun carriers may encounter. The proper use of visualization can help you recognize other such situations you may be faced with. In many cases, you may be able to anticipate and avoid problematical situations. Simulating these scenarios with dry-fire practice will prepare you to use the specific techniques required in each instance.

DEVELOPING BASIC DEFENSIVE SHOOTING SKILLS

CHAPTER 14

DEFENSIVE SHOOTING CONCEPTS

Mental preparedness—being constantly aware of your environment and having a defensive mindset that promotes confidence, perseverance, and planning—often allows you to avoid a violent encounter. However, on occasion it is impossible to sidestep, evade, flee or otherwise escape an attack. At such times in your life, and the lives of your loved ones, may depend upon your mastery of defensive shooting skills, such as those presented in the NRA Basic Personal Protection in the Home Course.

Before you can begin to master these skills, however, it is important to understand a number of basic defensive shooting concepts. These concepts underlie both your shooting training and practice as well as any actual deadly force encounter you may face in your home.

RESPONSIBILITY

Owning a firearm for personal protection is a right that must be exercised responsibly and ethically. Gun owners owe it to themselves, their families and their communities to always use their firearms in a safe and prudent manner.

No matter what the situation, you must always observe the three primary rules of safe gun handling: **<u>ALWAYS</u> keep the gun pointed in a safe direction, <u>ALWAYS</u> keep your finger off the trigger until ready to shoot,** and **<u>ALWAYS</u> keep the gun unloaded until ready to use.** (Note that you are "ready to use" your defensive handgun whenever you are carrying it.)

Responsible behavior entails more than merely adhering to the rules of safe gun handling, however. On some occasions, it may be more responsible not to use your firearm, even when faced with a deadly threat. Often, the determination of what constitutes responsible behavior is a matter of individual judgment.

IMMINENT DANGER

In most cases, to legally use deadly force, you must be the innocent victim of an attack, and the threat of severe bodily harm must be imminent (about to occur, or immediate). This will be discussed in detail in Part VII: Concealed Carry, Self-Defense and the Law.

TOOL OF LAST RESORT

A firearm is a tool of last resort. It is used only when deadly force is absolutely necessary.

As has been said before, the best way to win a confrontation is to avoid a confrontation. Flight or evasion, if safely possible, is always preferable to the use of lethal force. Legally, in some situations you must do everything in your power to safely flee or evade an encounter before you can resort to your firearm or any other tool of deadly force (see Part VII: Concealed Carry, Self-Defense and the Law.)

SHOOT TO STOP

The purpose of shooting an attacker is to deprive him of the ability to deliver deadly force. Put another way, you shoot an attacker to *stop* his life-threatening attack. Even though a firearm is a tool of last resort, your intent when using it against a violent criminal is not to kill, but simply to stop the attack. This is accomplished when the assailant is incapacitated or no longer presents a deadly threat.

Note that you cannot assume your attacker is incapacitated simply because your shots have hit him. Police reports contain many accounts of felons, high on drugs or possessed of an extreme will to live, who continued their violent depredations even after sustaining lethal wounds. You also cannot assume incapacitation just because the assailant has fallen to the ground; he may still be capable of delivering deadly force.

Be aware, too, that a violent criminal may only feign incapacitation to get you to let down your guard. Additionally, an attacker who was genuinely incapacitated at one moment may subsequently (and unexpectedly) revive and again pose a deadly threat.

Sometimes it is not necessary to incapacitate an attacker; he may flee or surrender, no longer presenting a deadly threat. In general, once an attacker no longer presents a threat, you are no longer legally or ethically justified in employing force against that attacker. Consult Part VII: Concealed Carry, Self-Defense and the Law, for a more thorough discussion of the limitations on the application of deadly force.

VIOLENT ENCOUNTERS: CLOSE, QUICK AND DARK

Contrary to what is portrayed in movies and on television, real-life violent encounters occur at very close range, often in reduced-light conditions, and are over in a matter of seconds. One study of police shootings in a major urban area showed that the majority of encounters took place after dark, at three yards or less, in less than three seconds, and involved the firing of an average of three shots. This compressed time for most deadly encounters requires an acceleration of many of the fundamentals of handgun shooting.

Fig. 125. A typical violent encounter takes place at close range, in reduced light, in a brief period of time.

Furthermore, accounts of defensive and police shootings reveal that it is likely that multiple shots will be required to stop a violent aggressor. Again, the Hollywood depiction of a shooting has little to do with reality. On television and in the movies, it is easy to see bullet impacts, and the attacker is almost always incapacitated with a single shot.

In actuality, it is extremely difficult to perceive bullet strikes during a violent confrontation. Things are happening far too quickly, and the target—the violent attacker—is usually moving rapidly, and is in dim light. Often a person does not even show any immediate reaction to being shot, particularly when under the influence of drugs or when in an excited or enraged state. This is why it is important to keep shooting until a deadly threat is no longer present.

SHOOT AT THE CENTER OF EXPOSED MASS

Under the conditions of the typical deadly force encounter, you may have to shoot quickly, in low light, at a close, rapidly-moving target. Such conditions are not conducive to deliberate pinpoint aiming techniques. The defensive aiming technique taught in NRA courses is called *center of mass of the exposed target*. This simply means that you align your sights not on a specific point, but on the approximate center of the target mass that is presented to you. On a standing target out in the open, the center of exposed mass will be located in the middle of the target. In other cases, such as when an attacker is partially behind cover, the center of exposed mass may be located elsewhere.

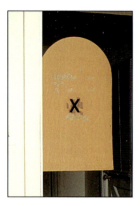  

Fig. 126. These photographs demonstrate the "center of exposed mass" aiming point using targets having different degrees of exposure. The "X" marks the center of mass of the exposed target.

DEFENSIVE ACCURACY

Closely related to the use of a center of exposed mass aiming area is the concept of defensive accuracy. While the ability of both gun and shooter to group shots tightly is critical in the various handgun sports, the characteristics of most defensive encounters make the attainment of pinpoint accuracy both unrealistic and unnecessary. As noted above, defensive shootings generally take place at close range (less than 21 feet) and in dim light, and are concluded in only a few seconds. Often, either the assailant or the defender—or both—are moving rapidly during the encounter. Such conditions do not permit the careful alignment of the sights on a specific aiming point on the target.

Simply put, defensive accuracy is that level of accuracy that allows the shooter to keep all shots in an assailant's vital area. If a center-of-mass hold is used on a fully exposed target, this area is equal to approximately a nine-inch circle—about the size of an average paper plate or sheet of standard typing paper. This minimum level of accuracy (all shots on an 8 1/2" by 11" sheet of paper at 21 feet) is well within the capabilities of virtually anyone with a quality handgun, given sufficient practice.

This discussion of defensive accuracy should not be construed to minimize the importance of accuracy in a defensive shooting situation. Virtually all self-defense authorities agree that accurate shot placement is the key to quickly stopping an aggressive attack. The accuracy standard stated above should be regarded as the minimum level of accuracy that is acceptable for defensive purposes. The responsible defensive-minded

shooter will endeavor to exceed this standard. In any defensive shooting situation, the more accurate the shooter/handgun combination, the greater the likelihood that the shooter will prevail.

Fig. 127. This grouping on an 8 1/2" by 11" piece of papers represents adequate defensive

CHAPTER 15

BASIC DEFENSIVE SHOOTING SKILLS

Like other forms of handgun shooting, defensive shooting is based upon the fundamental principles of pistol marksmanship. These fundamentals are aiming, breath control, hold control, trigger control and follow-through. The special dynamics of aggressive encounters require you to apply these fundamentals in a manner that is more accelerated than when you are relaxed on a range, just plinking at a target.

FIREARM SAFETY

The most basic of all shooting principles deal with gun safety. Whether practicing at the range, cleaning your gun in your workshop, or retrieving your gun from its storage location in your home, the fundamental rules of safe gun handling still apply: **<u>ALWAYS</u> keep the gun pointed in a safe direction; <u>ALWAYS</u> keep your finger off the trigger until ready to shoot;** and **<u>ALWAYS</u> keep the gun unloaded until ready to use.**

Through practice and mindfulness, the basic gun handling techniques will become habits that function regardless of the situation.

AIMING

Aiming is the process of aligning a firearm with a target so that a bullet fired from that firearm will strike the target where desired. In other words, the point of aim will coincide with the point of impact. Aiming is normally accomplished using the gun's sights. Most sights on defensive handguns take the form of a flat-topped front post and a square-cornered rear notch.

Aiming consists of two stages: sight alignment and sight picture. *Sight alignment* refers to the proper positioning of the shooting eye, the rear sight, and the front sight in relation to each other. With the notch-and-post system typically found on defensive firearms, the proper sight alignment for precise shooting occurs when the front post is centered laterally (same amount of space on either side of the front post) in the rear notch, and the tops of both the post and the notch line up. Visual focus is on the front sight. For defensive shooting purposes at close range (9 to 21 feet), however, it is usually sufficient to simply place the front sight post somewhere inside the rear sight notch. This gives an allowable sight deviation that will still keep your shots within the critical aiming area—roughly equivalent to an 8 1/2 inch by 11 inch sheet of paper—at up to about 30 feet, depending upon your gun's sights. Just as in the precision sight alignment used for slower shooting, the visual focus in the sight alignment method used in defensive situations is still on the front sight.

Sight picture refers to the relationship between the gun's properly aligned sights and the target. For defensive shooting purposes, the handgun's aligned sights are placed on the center of exposed mass of the target. That is, the sights are placed in the middle of the target area that is exposed.

During an emergency defensive response, your trigger finger should start in motion automatically when your eye sees that the sights are aligned on the center of target mass. The use of a larger aiming area (the center of target mass) instead of a small aiming point on the target allows you to develop this automatic response to an acceptable sight picture. A larger aiming area also helps you stay focused on the front sight and permits smooth trigger control.

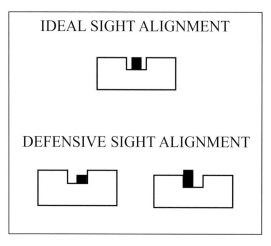

IDEAL SIGHT ALIGNMENT

DEFENSIVE SIGHT ALIGNMENT

Fig. 128. In ideal sight alignment, the front post is centered in the rear notch, and the tops of both sights are exactly even. In defensive sight alignment, you may fire whenever the post is visible somewhere in the notch.

BREATH CONTROL

Breath control is the method used to minimize gun movement due to breathing. With each breath, your ribcage expands and your shoulders rise slightly. This movement is transmitted to your arms, causing your aimed handgun to shift position in relation to the target.

In a defensive confrontation, fear for your life, trying to evade or escape an attack, and attempting to shout a warning to your attacker can all leave you gasping. Your heart will be pounding and your lungs will be demanding air. Breath control under these circumstances involves simply stopping breathing and holding it. Breathing should simply cease momentarily while the shot is being fired. This will steady the position and allow for a quick shot or series of shots. While this method works only for a few seconds, it should be sufficient for the duration of a typical armed response to an attack. In some cases, in fact, the armed defender may have to make a conscious effort to resume breathing after shooting has ended.

HOLD CONTROL

Maximum accuracy is achieved when the firearm is held motionless during the process of aiming and firing. Hold control is the method by which both the body and the gun are held as still as possible for the split second during which the shot is fired.

In a defensive shooting situation, hold control is achieved primarily through a well-balanced, stable shooting position that is naturally aligned with the target. More information on these positions and on target alignment is found in Chapter 16: Shooting Positions.

TRIGGER CONTROL

Trigger control is one of the most important of shooting fundamentals. The term refers to the technique of pulling the trigger without causing any movement of the sight alignment.

In most basic firearm training courses, beginning shooters are taught to apply gradually increasing pressure to the trigger until the shot is fired. The brief duration of a defensive encounter makes such a slow, gradual trigger squeeze impractical. Nonetheless, trigger control is still critical; poor trigger technique can easily cause a shooter to completely miss even a large target at close range.

Trigger control in a defensive shooting environment involves speeding up the process of squeezing the trigger without jerking or flinching. The

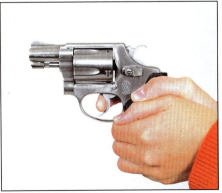

Fig. 129. Proper defensive shooting trigger finger placement on a revolver.

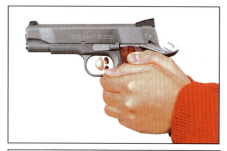

Fig. 130. Proper defensive shooting trigger finger placement on a semi-automatic pistol.

smoother the trigger is pulled, the less the gun's sights will be disturbed during the firing process, even when the time period is compressed.

Good trigger control also involves the proper placement of the trigger finger on the trigger. A properly placed trigger finger allows the force of the pull to be directed straight to the rear, minimizing a tendency to jerk the gun to the right or left. Proper placement also allows the gun to be fired by moving only the trigger finger.

For single-action shooting, the trigger should be pulled using the middle of the last pad of the trigger finger. For double-action shooting, the trigger should be placed approximately on the joint between the last and middle pads of the trigger finger. The ideal trigger finger placement can be achieved through dry-fire practice at a sheet of white paper. Adjust your finger position until there is no movement in sight alignment when the trigger is pulled and the hammer or striker falls. Note that the proper contact point on the trigger finger may change from gun to gun and firing position to firing position.

If possible, you should also leave a small gap between your trigger finger and the frame of the handgun to prevent the finger from contacting or dragging on the frame and thus disturbing sight alignment as the trigger is pulled.

Fig. 131. Photos showing the proper gap between the trigger finger and the frame of a revolver (left) and a semi-automatic pistol.

FOLLOW-THROUGH

The concept of follow-though is common to many sports, such as golf, tennis, baseball, bowling and archery. In shooting, follow-through is the effort made by the shooter to integrate, maintain and continue all shooting fundamentals before, during and immediately after the firing of the shot.

It is true that any alteration in the gun position, stance, sight alignment, and so forth that occurs after the bullet has left the muzzle has no effect whatsoever on accuracy or shot placement. Nonetheless, it is important to consciously maintain the shooting fundamentals for a brief time after the shot has been fired because only by doing so will you be certain that those fundamentals are applied before and during the firing of the shot. Thus, proper follow-through minimizes gun movement as the shot is fired. A shooter who fails to follow through and applies the fundamentals only up to the breaking of the trigger will (in anticipation of the shot) inevitably abandon one or more of the fundamentals just prior to firing, resulting in errant bullet flight.

Fig. 132. Proper follow-through, as well as good recoil control, combine to allow this shooter to fire several accurate shots in rapid succession.

Proper follow-through does more than just ensure adherence to the shooting fundamentals through the firing of the shot. Follow-through also sets up any successive shots that may be necessary. As mentioned above, in defensive encounters it is likely that you will have to fire multiple shots to quickly stop an attacker. By following through, you can maintain your position, alignment with the target, breath control, hold control and sight alignment, allowing easy recovery of the proper sight picture and the fastest possible follow-up shot. During follow-through, you also relax trigger finger pressure, allowing the trigger to reset, but still maintain finger contact with the trigger face.

The follow-through used in defensive shooting is highly compressed to last only a fraction of a second. You can also use this period of time to recover the sights after the shot, assess the effects of the shots fired, and prepare for additional shots if necessary.

All of the basic defensive shooting skills are integrated in the firing of a shot in self defense. The shooter aims (maintaining both sight alignment and a center-of-mass sight picture) while momentarily stopping respiration (breath control) and movement (hold control). Only the trigger finger, properly placed, is moved to fire the shot (trigger control). Before, during and after the shot is fired, the shooter observes all the proper shooting fundamentals, and recovers the sights and aligns them back onto the target immediately after firing the shot (follow-through).

CHAPTER 16

SHOOTING POSITIONS

As presented in the previous chapter, the fundamentals of handgun marksmanship are still observed in a defensive shooting situation, albeit in a modified manner. Effective shooting takes more than just adherence to these fundamentals, however. An effective shooting position is the platform from which the fundamentals are applied.

ELEMENTS OF A SHOOTING POSITION

Although there are many effective shooting positions for different situations, all share a number of common characteristics: consistency, balance, support, natural point of aim and comfort.

Consistency is critical because variations in position produce variations in impact point and/or group size. You must strive to assume each position in the same exact way every time. In the training phase, this is accomplished by conscious attention to each aspect of the position and each step taken to assume it. With repetition, this process of developing a position "by the numbers" will become ingrained in your subconscious, eventually enabling you to flow into the position quickly, effortlessly, naturally and consistently. The "muscle memory" thus developed through rigorous practice will allow the position to be assumed automatically in an emergency situation.

Balance is also an essential component of a proper firing position. Balance is usually best achieved in a stance with the feet spaced at shoulders-width, even weight distribution, and a slightly forward lean with the majority of the weight on the balls of the feet.

A position that is balanced provides the most stable shooting platform, one that absorbs recoil and facilitates both movement and accurate follow-up shots. A balanced position with the head upright and level also is important for controlling body movement. The brain senses body position by a number of mechanisms, including a structure in the inner ear known as the

Fig. 133. A balanced shooting position.

cochlea. An upright, level head position will maximize the ability of the cochlea to promote body equilibrium and efficient body movement.

A good position also offers support to minimize gun movement while aiming. Support can be provided by the skeleton, muscle tension or an external object, such as a table or trash can providing cover or conceal-ment. A two-handed grip, for example, efficiently uses muscle tension to provide more support than a one-handed grip. Generally, standing positions offer less support than kneeling and prone positions. Even the support offered by one-handed positions can be maximized, however, by ensuring that the stance is balanced, the grip is firm,

Fig 134. A good shooting position offers **support**. The shooter above makes use of skeletal support by bracing her support arm on the knee. The position of the left foot directly below the knee relieves the leg muscles of any support role; support is pro-vided only by the rigid bones of the lower leg, ankle and foot. At left, the shooter uses the object providing cover or concealment to support her shooting position. Note that her arms, and not the pistol, rest on the supporting object.

and the shooter is properly aligned with the target.

All effective firing positions incorporate the shooter's natural point of aim (NPA). NPA refers to the natural alignment of the shooter and the gun in any position. To determine your NPA, first assume your position, with your eyes open and your gun aimed at a target. Next, close your eyes. With your eyes still closed, settle into the position that feels most stable and comfortable, and take several breaths. Then, open your eyes and observe where your gun's sights are pointed in relation to the target. The sight pos-ture should be in the middle of the target. Often the sight picture will be

A

Fig. 135. In the NPA (Natural Point of Aim) exercise, the shooter (A) first assumes a position with the gun aimed at a target. Then (B) the eyes are closed, and (C) the shooter settles into the shooting position that feels most stable and comfortable. Note the shift of the gun position from (B) to (C). When the shooter's eyes open (D) and she observes where the gun's sights are pointed in relation to the target, her foot position or some other aspect of her stance can be modified to achieve the proper sight picture while taking advantage of her body's natural point of aim.

B

C

D

aligned to the right or left or slightly high or low, requiring you to modify your foot position or some other aspect of your stance to achieve the proper sight picture while taking full advantage of your body's NPA.

Repeat the NPA exercise until your stance is adjusted for the proper natural alignment. You should make every effort to adopt this same alignment each time the stance is assumed in order to take advantage of your NPA.

Finally, a proper position should be comfortable. A stance that is not comfortable—one that is forced, awkward, strained or painful—is unlikely to be consistent or stable, and thus will not contribute to effective shooting. When practicing shooting positions, you should be conscious of how natural and comfortable each position is. Positions that do not feel comfortable must be modified as necessary. However, in some cases discomfort may be the result of the lack of joint flexibility or muscular strength. In such cases, a minimal amount of physical training is usually all that is needed to allow the shooter to comfortably assume a proper shooting position. Of course, any shooter should consult his or her doctor prior to starting any physical training regimen.

THE TWO-HANDED GRIP

Under most conditions, you will grip the handgun with a two-handed grip. For the vast majority of shooters, such a grip provides more control of the firearm, steadier aiming, better recoil absorption, and stronger gun retention.

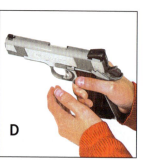

To assume the grip, first grasp the handgun behind the muzzle in your weak (non-firing) hand. Make a "Y" of the thumb and fingers of the strong (firing) hand (A), and place the gun's backstrap firmly in the web of the thumb (B). Then wrap the fingers of the strong hand around the handgun's

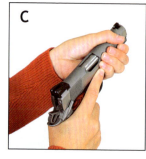

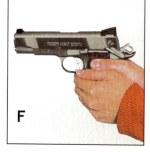

Fig. 136. The steps in assuming a proper two-handed grip on a handgun. Letters refer to steps described in text.

grip (C).

Next, bring the weak hand around the front of the grip (D) so that the weak hand fingers overlie and overlap the strong hand fingers (E). The first joint of the weak hand fingers should be approximately aligned with the knuckles of the strong hand, and the weak hand thumb will lie directly forward of and below the strong hand thumb (F). Gripping the firearm with tension from both the weak and strong hands creates a steadier hold on the pistol, and makes it extremely difficult to take it away from you.

Grip consistency is essential for accurate shooting, whether in bullseye competition or in a defensive encounter. Use dry-fire practice to check and reinforce the correct trigger finger placement (see Appendix C: Opportunities for Skills Enhancement). Note that the proper grip for one specific firearm may not be appropriate for another firearm; your grip may vary depending upon the shape of a gun's grip frame. Also, your grip may vary slightly from position to position.

READY POSITIONS

In some defensive situations, you may not immediately go into a firing position. You may hold your firearm in a ready position for extended periods of time, in anticipation of use. Two ready positions are presented in this course: the low ready position and the retention ready position.

Low Ready Position. To assume the low ready position, take the proper grip on the handgun and extend the arms outward and downward at approximately a 45-degree angle. The firearm will be oriented toward a point on the ground several feet in front of you. Your knees should be slightly bent and the weight slightly forward, in anticipation of either movement or the sudden acquisition of a full firing position. Your foot and shoulder position should reflect the firing position that you plan to assume (e.g., isosceles, Weaver, etc.).

Another way of visualizing the low ready position is to adopt the shooting position and then simply lower the extended arms approximately 45 degree downward.

The simplicity of the low ready position, and the unobstructed view

Fig. 137. The low ready position.

it gives of the target, are two of its primary advantages. The position also permits easy assumption of the shooting position. With the arms already extended, the wrists already locked and the feet and shoulders already aligned, the gun is simply raised to eye level to acquire the sights and fire.

The low ready position puts the firearm away from the body, which can allow a close-range adversary to block the rise of the gun to a firing position. However, in this situation, the defender is usually still able to take shots at the attacker's lower body.

Retention Ready Position. The retention ready position gets its name from the way it places the firearm close to the body, almost tucked into the

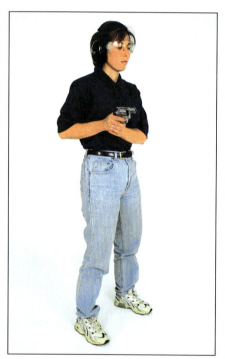

Fig. 138. The retention ready position.

armpit. The retention position can be visualized by assuming the normal shooting position and then simply pulling the firearm to the rear, to the body directly in front of the strong-side armpit. The two-handed grip is retained, and the firearm is pointed forward, toward the target with the barrel parallel to the ground.

The retention ready position has several advantages. First, by keeping the handgun close to the body, it promotes gun retention—physical control of the firearm—and hinders an attacker's efforts to block or grab it. You can easily go from the retention position to the full shooting position by simply extending the arms forward. Additionally, since your firearm is kept pointed at the target in the retention position, a shot may actually be fired from the position if necessary (for example, if an attacker lunges at you at arm's length).

Do not raise the muzzle of your gun or point it upward as it is brought in toward the body. Not only does this negate the advantages of keeping the firearm pointed at the target, but a muzzle-upward orientation can actually be hazardous if you are suddenly startled and reflexively fire the firearm.

TWO-HANDED SHOOTING POSITIONS

Two basic shooting positions are taught in this course: the *isosceles position* and the *Weaver position*. In addition, a modified version of each basic position is also presented.

Isosceles Position. The Isosceles position is so named because in this position your extended arms, when seen from above, resemble an isosceles triangle. In the isosceles position, your feet are placed at about shoulders width, and your feet and shoulders are square with the target. Your knees are slightly bent and your weight is slightly forward, on the balls of the feet. The pistol is grasped in a normal two-handed grip, and is held with both your arms extended fully forward. Your elbows are straight but not locked. Your head is erect, not hunched; your shoulders are at their normal height, not raised; and your firearm is lifted to the level of your eyes for aiming.

The isosceles position is

Fig. 139. The isosceles position, seen from (A) the front, (B) above and (C) side.

a very natural shooting position. Under the stress of an actual defensive shooting situation, many shooters instinctively adopt a modified "instinctive" form of this position. The ease with which you can pivot laterally in the isosceles position facilitates the engagement of multiple targets. The primary limitation of the position is that, at very close range, the arm's length position of the gun may facilitate an attacker's block or grab.

Weaver Position. The Weaver position is named for former San Diego County Sheriff Jack Weaver, who is credited with originating it in the 1950s. To assume the Weaver position, place your body in a rough boxer's stance with your strong hand foot rearward, your weak side shoulder

angled toward the target, your knees slightly flexed and your body weight carried slightly forward, on the balls of your feet. Grasp your gun in a normal two-handed grip, but bend both elbows (the weak- or support-hand elbow pointing downward) to bring the handgun closer to the body than in the isosceles position. The location of the handgun often requires that your head tip slightly to properly view the sights. Tension between the two hands is perhaps the most functionally significant feature of this position: the strong hand is pushed forward into the weak hand, which simultaneously pulls rearward. This push-pull tension creates great stability and steadiness.

Fig. 140. The Weaver position from the front.

The Weaver position gives considerable support to the firearm, and by pulling the gun in closer to the body, affords better gun retention and better maneuverability in tight quarters. Also, the bent elbows and asymmetrical foot position enhance recoil absorption. When a shot is fired, the bent elbows act as springs, bending to absorb recoil forces and then returning the gun to its original position. With heavy-recoiling handguns, the Weaver position affords fast shot-to-shot recovery for many shooters .

Modified Isosceles Position. This position incorporates the natural, fully-extended arm position of the isosceles position with the stability of the asymmetrical boxer's stance foot placement of the Weaver position, which allows better recoil absorption. The head is level and the body leans forward. Often the shoulders rise reflexively, resulting in the instinctive stance referred to above. The modified isosceles position also represents the stance that would result when a shooter in the standard isosceles position pivots sharply to the side.

Modified Weaver Position. The modified Weaver position is very similar to the standard Weaver stance, with the exception that your strong-side arm is almost completely extended toward the target. Your weak-side arm is still bent, however, and your weak hand still pulls rearward against the forward-pushing strong hand. It is important to note that your strong-side arm is not locked but slightly bent, enabling it to flex and absorb recoil. For many shooters, the modified Weaver position offers the same stability as the standard Weaver position, but feels more natural. Some shooters in this position may have to tilt the head slightly to see the gun's sights, but for many the modified Weaver position allows a more upright and level head position than the standard Weaver position.

Fig. 141. The modified Weaver position.

ONE-HANDED SHOOTING POSITIONS

The well-rounded defensive shooter must be as comfortable with one-handed firing positions as with the more familiar two-handed ones. There are many situations in which one-handed firing may be necessary. For example, an injury to a hand or arm might make a two-hand hold impossible to assume. Alternatively, it may be necessary to use one hand to ward off blows or the thrusts of a knife, hold a flashlight or telephone, feel for obstructions in a darkened room, shield a child, and so forth.

The one-handed shooting positions used in defensive situations—the *reverse punch* and *forward punch* positions—are similar to stances used in the martial arts.

Reverse Punch Position. In this position, you assume a boxer's stance, with your foot on the weak-hand (non-firing) side forward, your strong-side foot back, and your upper body bladed away from the target (that is, your upper body does not directly face the target, but is angled away so that your strong-side shoulder is somewhat to the rear). Your non-firing

Fig. 142. The reverse punch position.

arm is drawn in toward the middle of the chest to keep it out of the way of the muzzle, and your non-firing hand is held palm-out to ward off an attacker. With your hand in this palm-out position, you can push an attacker away with the powerful triceps muscle of your upper arm.

Your firing arm is bent slightly at the elbow, and your firing hand is canted inward at a natural angle—the same natural angle created when you form a fist in this position. [Note that, under most firing conditions, canting the firearm is detrimental to accuracy, and thus is generally discouraged. However, at the short distances typical of a violent attack, canting has little detrimental effect.] Your upper body leans slightly forward, with most of your body weight on your forward (weak-side) leg. Your strong-side leg acts as a brace to support an aggressive, forward-leaning stance, with your weight carried on the ball of your strong-side foot.

The reverse-punch position can be easily assumed from the retention ready position, simply by pushing the gun forward. When practicing this position, be careful to keep the weak hand drawn in toward the middle of the chest, clear of the muzzle. Note that it may not always be possible, when struggling with an attacker, to keep the weak hand clear of the muzzle.

The reverse punch position is particularly suited for close-quarters confrontations, as it puts the defensive hand forward to more effectively ward off an assailant, and positions the gun closer to the body, promoting gun retention.

Forward Punch Position. The forward punch position is similar to the reverse punch position, except that the foot, hand and shoulder on the strong (firing) side are now forward, toward the target. Your body

Fig. 143. The forward punch position.

still assumes a forward-leaning stance, and your weak hand is still drawn in toward the middle of your chest, in a defensive, palm-out position. Aside from the defensive position of the non-firing hand and the aggressive body position, there is a degree of similarity between the forward punch position and the one-handed stance used by bullseye shooters.

KNEELING POSITIONS

To take advantage of cover and concealment (see Chapter 18: Utilizing Cover and Concealment Outside the Home) it may be necessary to adopt firing positions other than the standing positions previously presented. The kneeling positions presented in this handbook—the high kneeling, low kneeling, supported kneeling and double kneeling positions—allow the shooter to take advantage of low cover or concealment, such as a car hood, mailbox, fence or trash can.

Kneeling positions have other advantages, too. Even where there is no cover or concealment, a kneeling position makes you a smaller target. Kneeling positions are also generally more stable than standing positions, thus enhancing shooting accuracy.

A kneeling firing position may also allow you to remain undetected by an assailant and thus avoid confrontation altogether. An attacker who expects to see his or her victim at normal standing eye level may be unprepared to respond quickly to a defender below normal eye level. In fact, a defender effectively using low cover or concealment in a kneeling position may not even be seen by an aggressor, especially under low-light conditions.

For most shooters, kneeling positions are quick to move into and out of, and thus are frequently used in defensive shooting situations. The serious defensive shooter should practice the various kneeling positions until they are achieved easily and naturally.

High Kneeling Position. In the high kneeling position, the upper body position is essentially the same as that of a standing two-handed position, the weak-side leg is bent and serves as the support leg, and the strong-side knee is placed on the ground. The body leans slightly forward to counter recoil. For maximum stability, is is important that the strong-side foot rests on the toes and forward part of the ball of the foot, the line between the knee and hip of the strong-side leg is vertical (perpendicular to the ground), and the support-leg knee is directly over the toe. These specific foot and leg placements are essential to ensure that the position is balanced and stable, and to allow you to efficiently move into and out of the position as necessary. It is also important to keep your strong-side lower leg directly behind your thigh.

Fig. 144. The high kneeling position.

The high kneeling position may be assumed in two ways; in either method, the pistol must point in a safe direction at all times. First, you may step forward with your support leg at the same time your strong-side knee is lowered to the ground. In this technique, the strong-side foot remains in place. Alternatively, you may step back with your strong-side foot and then drop your strong-side knee straight down into position. The former procedure may be used when you are approaching cover, or where there is sufficient space to allow the forward step. When you are already close to the object providing cover, or wish to distance yourself from it, the second kneeling technique is used.

A   B   C

Fig. 145. Assuming the high kneeling position. From the low ready position (A), the shooter steps back with the strong-side foot (B) and extends the gun (C).

Fig. 145. (continued). The shooter then drops straight down onto the strong-side knee (D), making sure that the weak-side knee is directly above the foot. Finally, the shooter leans toward the target slightly to provide better balance and to counteract recoil (E).

While assuming a high kneeling position using either technique, the muzzle must be kept pointing in a safe direction. If you go into a kneeling position from a ready position, a retention ready position is preferable to a low ready position. For many shooters, the retention ready position provides better balance while dropping into a kneeling position, and keeps the muzzle pointing toward the target. Your arms are extended forward into a firing position as your knee contacts the ground.

Low Kneeling Position. The low kneeling position allows both a lower shooter position as well as greater stability than the high kneeling position. In terms of leg position it is essentially identical to the high kneeling position, with the exception that the strong-side foot may rest on the ball of the foot or may be placed flat along the ground, for a lower profile. The upper body position differs considerably. Instead of the relatively erect posture of the high kneeling position, the body is bent forward

Fig. 146. The low kneeling position. Note the effective support for the weak hand.

Fig. 147. Two versions of the low kneeling position. The difference is primarily in the position of the strong-side foot. The strong-side foot may contact the ground on the ball of the foot (A) or, alternatively, the foot can be placed flat on the ground under the body (B). The latter position allows a slightly lower profile and may be more comfortable for some shooters.

until the support-side arm rests on the knee of the support leg, with the contact point of the arm located above the elbow. The greater degree of forward lean results in both a lower position as well as better recoil absorption.

The increased stability of the low kneeling position results from both its lower shooter posture as well as its effective use of bone structure to provide support. It is therefore a particularly good position when accuracy is required. However, it is slower to get into and out of than the high kneeling position. The low kneeling position can be assumed either by stepping forward with the support leg or stepping rearward with the strong-side leg.

The low kneeling position is preferred when cover is low, when increased stability is needed to hit a smaller target, or when there is sufficient time to assume the position. Even when cover is sufficiently high to justify a high kneeling position, a low kneeling position may expose less of your body to an attacker, and its recoil-absorbing qualities may allow you faster follow-up shots.

Supported Kneeling Position. In the supported kneeling position, the handgun is supported on the object providing cover or concealment, such as a trash can lid, car hood, or mailbox. In this position, your lower-body positioning is similar to that used in the high kneeling and low kneeling positions. Your upper body leans forward, both to absorb recoil and to enable you to get as low as possible.

Note that only your hands, wrists or arms, and not the handgun itself, make direct contact with the object providing cover or concealment. A handgun that is fired when its grip is resting on a solid surface likely will place its shots in a different location than when fired from an unsupported or *offhand* position, and may also produce larger groups. Furthermore, supporting some semi-automatic pistols on their magazine baseplates can cause a stoppage. In addition, allowing your handgun to contact a hard object may produce a sound that gives away your position.

If the supporting object is very low, it is preferable to sit back into the position slightly rather than bend too far forward at the waist. By sitting back, the weight of your upper body is still centered over your lower body, giving better balance and allowing rapid movement if necessary. Excessively bending the upper body forward shifts your balance too far to the front to allow quick changes in position.

Fig. 148. The supported kneeling position. Only the shooter's arms contact the support object, and the shooter has achieved a balanced position by sitting back on her heels.

Double Kneeling Position. The double kneeling position is probably the quickest of all the kneeling positions to get into. Simply bend both knees simultaneously, dropping them to the ground. Your body leans slightly forward to absorb recoil and the line between your hip and knee is not perpendicular to the ground but angled slightly to the rear, for better balance.

Fig. 149. The low (left) and high double kneeling positions.

The lower your position, the more you will have to sit back in the position to keep the body weight centered.

While the double kneeling position is fast and simple to assume, it may not be appropriate for older, less flexible shooters, or those with knee problems. Also, there is a possibility of knee injury if the knees are driven hard into an unyielding concrete or asphalt surface. In addition, for heavier or older shooters, the double kneeling position may present more of a challenge to move from.

SQUATTING POSITION

In some situations it may be necessary to quickly minimize exposure to an adversary, but it may not be possible or desirable to assume a kneeling position. This might be the case when the surface underfoot is uneven, strewn with broken glass, poorly seen (as in very low light) or likely to make a telltale sound that would give away your position. Under these conditions,you can simply squat straight down behind any convenient object providing cover or concealment.

The primary advantages of the squatting position are simplicity, quickness and silence. Some people may have difficulty maintaining balance while in this position; stability may be improved by widening the stance and placing the strong-side foot slightly to the rear of the weak-side foot. Additional stability may be acquired by supporting the extended arms on the object providing cover or concealment. Even with such support, the squatting position is not as stable as any of the kneeling positions. Also, older persons or those with knee problems or weak leg muscles may find the squatting position taxing to maintain or move from. Even

Fig. 150. The squatting shooting position is perhaps the quickest position to assume from a standing position, and is achieved by simply squatting straight down.

young and fit persons will likely experience leg muscle tremor after a minute or so in this position; the squatting position should thus be considered a temporary position.

ROLLOVER PRONE POSITION

A prone firing position may be preferred in situations in which there is no ready cover, or only very low cover, such as a curb, and you must present as small a target as possible. Prone positions also generally allow very stable gun support, and thus may be used when greater accuracy is desired.

The prone position that is universally taught by defensive shooting instructors is called the rollover prone position. To assume this position, first face toward the target. The shoulders may be square to the target, or the strong side may be angled slightly rearward. With the strong hand, the gun is drawn from the holster and rotated and extended toward the target, and the trigger finger is located alongside the frame, out of the trigger

Fig. 151. Steps in assuming the prone position. Note use of weak hand to support the body as it is lowered to the ground.

Fig. 152. Rollover prone position showing body weight rotated to strong side, and weak-side foot crossed over strong-side leg.

guard. The weak hand is held to the chest, clear of the muzzle. When the muzzle is rotated toward the target and the gun is well out in front of the body, drop to both knees. From a kneeling position, go forward and down, supporting the weight of your upper body with your extended weak hand. During this movement, keep the gun's muzzle pointing at the target and out in front of your weak hand. If this movement is performed smoothly, you should be able to see the sights as you go forward, achieving a rough sight picture that requires only minimal refinement after you have completed the position. You should come to rest on the strong side of your body, with your strong-side arm supported by the ground. Finally, join your weak hand to the strong hand to complete the two-hand grip, bring your weak-side leg up toward your abdomen to shift more weight onto the strong side of your body, and rest your face on your strong-side shoulder. Your strong-side arm will be extended straight out, and both arms, as well as the strong hand, will be supported by the ground.

Rolling the body onto the strong-hand side accomplishes two things. First, it takes weight off the diaphragm, making it easier to breathe and reducing the amount of sight disturbance that occurs with each breath. Second, it creates a steadier platform for accurate shooting than would be afforded by a flat prone position. Note that some people gain additional stability in this position by crossing the weak-side foot over the strong-side leg.

Avoid dropping heavily to the ground when assuming the rollover prone position. In addition to potentially causing injury, a hard impact with the ground will disrupt your view of the sights. The additional time it will take you to regain sight alignment will more than offset any time you save by dropping to the ground a fraction of a second more quickly.

Also, avoid supporting the handgun on the ground. Contact of the magazine basepad with hard ground can cause erratic accuracy, and can, in some pistols, increase the likelihood of a stoppage.

While the rollover prone position minimizes the exposure of the body when there is no cover, and allows accurate extended-range shooting, it may be difficult for persons with certain physical limitations to get into and out of. Also, with this position it may be difficult to obtain an unobstructed sight picture on terrain that is uneven, strewn with debris or overgrown with tall grass.

It is impossible to predict how an attack may occur, or what shooting position may have to be used to counter it. For this reason, it is important for the citizen who carries a concealed handgun to know how to assume, and fire effectively from, a variety of shooting positions.

CHAPTER 17

AIMING AND FIRING TECHNIQUES

Mastering the fundamentals of handgun shooting and the various defensive shooting positions only partially prepares you to use a handgun effectively to protect your life. It is also essential to understand and apply other defense-related skills and concepts, such as defensive accuracy, flash sight picture, point shooting, firing multiple shots, facing multiple assailants, and breaking tunnel vision to assess for additional threats.

DEFENSIVE ACCURACY

Violent encounters typically take place at a distance of only a few feet and are completed in a few seconds. Thus, a high level of pinpoint accuracy is not required of the individual, the gun or the ammunition. A good general estimate is that the ability to keep all shots on a standard 8 1/2" by 11" sheet of paper at 21 feet, hitting in the center of exposed mass, is sufficient for most defensive purposes.

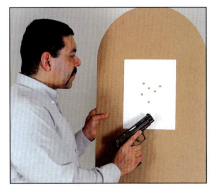

Experienced shooters will recognize that this is an extremely modest level of accuracy, well within the capabilities of virtually any handgun even in only moderately skilled hands. However, what can be easily attained in a well-lit practice range, firing at a stationary target using a stable two-hand grip, is

Fig. 153. Adequate defensive accuracy as reflected by this group fired on an 8 1/2" by 11" sheet of paper at seven yards.

far different than what can be expected during the stress of a sudden attack.

In the vast majority of defensive encounters, once the need to shoot becomes unavoidable, it is essential to fire as fast as you accurately can. Both a proper shooting position and good execution of the shooting fundamentals are essential to accurate, rapid fire.

Inevitably, there will be a certain degree of shot dispersion around the center of mass. This is not the result of deliberately aiming at different spots. All shots are aimed at the same area—the center of exposed mass.

The shots are spread out due to the speed with which shots are fired and the less-than-perfect alignment of the sights.

Note that if you are shooting ragged one-hole groups in the center of the exposed target mass during practice, you should probably be shooting faster. If your shots are spreading to the edge of a large target, beyond the

maximum allowable group size (an 8 1/2" by 11" sheet of paper) at 21 feet, you should slow down.

Probably more than any other factor, the effects of stress are responsible for the deterioration in accuracy often observed during defensive shooting situations. Studies of shooting incidents involving law enforcement officers, which typically take place at relatively close range, show that police officers achieve hits less than 20 percent of the time. In other words, four out of five shots fired by trained law enforcement officers miss the target completely. Even under the relatively modest level of stress imposed by activities such as practical shooting competition, it is not uncommon for shooters to completely miss a large, close target.

Fig. 154. If you are shooting tight 21-foot groups, as in the upper target (above), you should speed up your shooting. If some of the shots in your group are almost off the paper, slow down. The group shown at right represents good accuracy for defensive purposes.

Poor shooting is not inevitable under the extreme stress of a defensive encounter, however. Your actual shooting performance during such an encounter can be improved by incorporating stress and realism in your practice, and by always striving for a higher level of accuracy. A shooter who can keep his or her shots within three inches at 21 feet has much more of a margin for stress-induced error than one who can do no better than eight inches at the same distance.

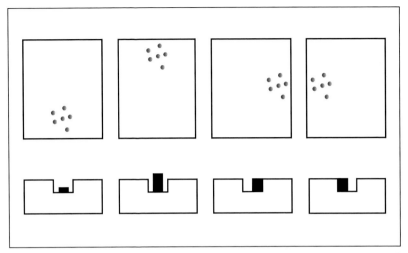

Fig. 155. Acceptable defensive or "flash" sight pictures, with the expected placement of the group on an 8 1/2" by 11" sheet of paper at 21 feet in relation to a central aiming point.

FLASH SIGHT PICTURE

The aiming technique most often used to produce quick yet acceptably accurate hits with a defensive handgun is known as flash sight picture. In this technique, the shot is fired as soon as the front sight is roughly lined up somewhere within the rear sight notch. The front sight blade may be slightly off to the right or left, or may be slightly high or low. As long as it is visible somewhere in the rear sight notch, your shots will fall within an 8 1/2" by 11" piece of paper at 21 feet.

For those using very short-barreled handguns, the precision of sight alignment—even with a flash sight picture—is more critical than for longer-barreled models. This is because the closer the front and rear sights are, the greater the inaccuracy resulting from any misalignment of the sights.

A flash sight picture is used for the first shot fired when that shot is delivered at close range, and must be taken quickly. The technique is also used to deliver rapid follow-up shots, or to quickly engage several threats at the same time.

With practice, it will become possible for you to acquire a flash sight picture within a fraction of a second of bringing the sights onto the target at close range. Extensive dry-fire and live-fire training will enable you to go from a ready position to a shooting position with the sights seemingly pre-aligned on the target. This can be achieved most readily if your shooting position is consistent and you use proper grip alignment, correct trigger finger placement, and your Natural Point of Aim (NPA).

Remember, too, that distance equals time. In general, the farther away a threat is, the more time you will have to acquire proper sight alignment before shooting. At the same time, as the distance to your target increases, the more critical proper sight alignment becomes in achieving a hit.

POINT SHOOTING

Sometimes an attack occurs so fast and so close that any reference to sight alignment becomes unnecessary or impossible. *Point shooting* is the technique used in such circumstances.

Point shooting involves simply raising or extending the handgun in a one-handed or two-handed firing stance, with the muzzle pointed toward the center of mass of the target, and firing as soon as you are in the shoot-

Fig. 156. The two-handed point shooting position, viewed from the side. Note that the shooter's line of sight is above the sights of the handgun.

ing position. There is no attempt whatsoever to visually align the front and rear sights, or the sights with the target. You are focused on the target instead of the sights; specifically, you are focused on the precise area—the center of exposed mass—you want the bullet to strike. Although you are not actively using the sights, the handgun will be just below eye level and you likely will be aware of at least the rear sight in your peripheral vision. Also, you will perceive (in your peripheral vision) the general outline of the firearm, and use that outline as a visual reference to roughly align the gun with the target. Additionally, your kinesthetic sense--your ability to sense the position of your limbs and body--will aid in properly aligning the gun with the target.

The use of a thumb-forward two-handed grip aids in point shooting by allowing you to "point" with the support hand thumb, which is held parallel to the barrel.

For more information on the point shooting technique, see Chapter 23: Point Shooting.

INSTINCTIVE SHOOTING

On occasion, an attack may occur at such close range, and with such unexpected suddenness, that the armed citizen lacks the time to employ either aimed fire or point shooting techniques. In such a circumstance, instinctive shooting is used.

In the instinctive shooting technique, the handgun is not extended toward the target, but is simply pointed at the target and fired, usually at the hip (as when the gun has just been drawn from a holster). Firing occurs when the handgun is "felt" to be aligned with the target. Unlike point shooting, there is no peripheral visual reference to assist in aligning the handgun.

The development of the ability to hit a target reliably with this technique takes a great deal of practice, and even when proficiency has been achieved, instinctive shooting is typically limited to distances of only a few feet. Instinctive shooting will be presented in greater detail in Chapter 24: Instinctive Shooting.

Fig. 157. Your practice should regularly include multiple-shot drills that build recoil control and contribute to both speed and accuracy.

MULTIPLE SHOTS

Several shots may be required to end a violent assault. Thus, you must learn techniques for delivering multiple shots accurately and rapidly.

Defensive shooting instructors recommend that the armed citizen shoot until the assailant no longer presents a deadly threat. In training drills, two rapid initial hits on the target are often required, not because there is any special magic about the number two, but because two-shot drills allow the simulation of multiple shot firing sequences. This focus on firing multiple shots gives rise to specific shooting techniques designed to maximize the hit probability of rounds fired in quick succession.

Effective multiple-shot shooting involves techniques that may be modified depending upon the speed of shooting required by the situation. When great accuracy is required—such as when a target is located at longer ranges (generally 10-15 yards or more) or when only a small target is exposed—good sight alignment is required, and shots are fired in succession as quickly as you can recover the proper sight alignment. The speed with which you can fire such shots depends upon your ability to recover from recoil, re-establish proper sight alignment, breath control, hold control and NPA, and execute the shot using proper trigger control and follow-through. Remember, all the shooting fundamentals still apply; they are simply compressed to allow faster shooting.

To engage targets at closer range (such as three to seven yards), multiple shots may be fired more quickly. To execute such shots, a flash sight picture is used instead of refined sight alignment and the sequence of trigger pull, firing and follow-through for each shot is accelerated. The speed with which such accelerated shots can be fired varies with individual skill and experience; most people execute these shots more quickly than the aimed shots required at longer ranges. However, the shot dispersion of accelerated shots is generally greater than with aimed shots, making the multiple-shot technique more difficult, for most people, when the target is distant or only slightly exposed.

When a violent attack occurs quickly, at extremely close range, the multiple-shot technique can be further accelerated to allow successive hits on the target in the least possible time.

At extremely close range (five to 10 feet or less), shots can be fired once you have established a flash sight picture, or, in situations essentially at arm's length, can be fired as a variation of point shooting. In both cases, the second and successive shots are fired in rapid succession without any conscious attempt to align the sights. "Aiming" of successive shots is done by feel, using muscle memory; these shots are fired as soon as you sense that the gun has returned from the recoil of the preceding shot and is again pointed at the target. With most defensive handguns having moderate recoil, successive shots can be fired as quickly as you can pull the trigger.

Note that the various shooting fundamentals are either modified or substantially compressed as the speed with which multiple shots are fired increases. However, good trigger control is still essential. Even though the trigger pull is accelerated, there should still be little or no gun movement or misalignment of the sights if the trigger finger is properly located on the trigger.

With considerable practice, these accelerated shots can be fired quickly and with surprising accuracy. Skilled practical pistol shooters can trigger two shots with an interval of .20 second or less, and place them only a couple of inches apart on a target five to seven yards away. Such ability is the result of the development of a high level of coordination and the mastery of both the shooting fundamentals and the elements of a proper shooting position, allowing successive shots to be fired immediately as the gun returns to its original firing position. Frequent, focused practice—both live- and dry-fire—is the only way to achieve this level of skill.

This technique of firing quick, accurate multiple shots should be reserved for encounters occurring at very close range—from arm's length to not more than 10 to 20 feet.

When practicing, experiment with different cadences for each multiple-shot technique and distance, and note which produces the best groups.

MULTIPLE ASSAILANTS

Crime statistics indicate the growing prevalence of attacks involving more than one assailant. Although the same basic defensive shooting skills are used whether you are facing one violent criminal or several, successfully defeating multiple adversaries involves a slightly different kind of threat assessment.

When confronted with multiple assailants, the primary rule is to engage the targets in the order of the greatest threat. For example, if you encounter two intruders in a parking garage, one armed with a gun and one with a

Fig. 158. In the case of multiple assailants, you may have to assess the relative threat posed by each assailant, and respond accordingly. Here, the closer of the two attackers is wielding a knife, while the other attacker has a handgun. In this case, the attacker closest to you may represent the greater threat, even though he is armed with a seemingly less effective weapon than his partner.

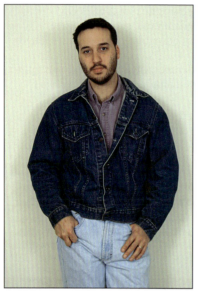

Fig. 159. A casual pose can conceal a deadly threat. At left, the individual lounges against a wall, his hands seemingly empty. However, when his right hand is rotated forward (right), a large folding knife is shown to be concealed in his palm.

piece of pipe, you would normally engage the gun-wielding criminal first. Factors involved in threat assessment include:

- the distance of each attacker;
- the type of weapon possessed by each attacker; and
- the mobility of each attacker.

The attacker armed with a gun may not always represent the greatest threat, however. An intruder with a baseball bat, running at you from only a few feet away, may be more of an immediate threat than his accomplice, 20 feet away with his gun stuck in his waistband.

In assessing any threat, whether single or multiple assailants, train yourself to always look at the hands of your attackers; that is where the threat will come from. Be suspicious of hands kept where you cannot see them, such as in pockets, alongside the thigh or behind the back. For example, an attacker armed with a knife may hide his weapon by hanging the hand down naturally, just out of sight behind the thigh. In this fashion it does not appear that he is hiding anything, but the knife can be brought up in a deadly thrust before you can react to it. Always assume that hands that are out of sight may hold a weapon.

When visualizing a multiple-adversary attack, or when practicing at the range using multiple targets, keep both the target distance and your gun's magazine capacity in mind. Both affect how you decide to engage the targets. If all targets are close, it may be preferable to engage each target with one round and then assess the remaining threats, rather than put two shots on each threat. If you try to engage each of three targets with two shots, for example, you may be vulnerable to the last threat while you are firing at the first two. Also, if your firearm has a very limited capacity, you may run out of ammunition before engaging all targets if you choose to fire two shots at each threat.

BREAKING TUNNEL VISION

During a life-threatening confrontation, you likely will be affected by tunnel vision—the tendency to concentrate on the target to the exclusion of everything else around you. This phenomenon is made worse by high stress levels. Tunnel vision can persist for several moments even after the encounter has been resolved, whether that resolution involves the assailant fleeing, surrendering, or being shot. In all of these circumstances, you will tend to keep focused on the area from which the threat came. While you are experiencing tunnel vision, you are vulnerable to attack by additional, unseen assailants.

To maintain maximum alertness and readiness, you must train to break tunnel vision after an attack is stopped. To do so, first lower the handgun and then scan the area to the left and right of the direction of the threat. The scanning technique used depends upon the situation you find yourself

 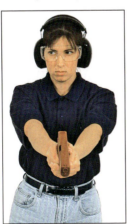 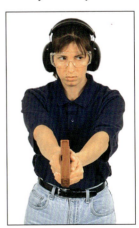

Fig.160. Breaking tunnel vision after an attack is accomplished by first lowering the handgun and then scanning to the left and right. If your attacker is incapacitated or has surrendered, the gun remains pointed at him and the eyes scan quicly left and right, keeping him in the peripheral vision, as shown above.

in. If your attacker is down on the ground in front of you, either as the result of your shots or because he has simply surrendered, keep the gun pointed at him and scan by moving your eyes and head only slightly to the left and right with rapid movements, quickly returning to a forward-looking position. Keep your attacker in your peripheral vision at all times.

On the other hand, if your assailant has fled, you may scan the area using a wider arc, moving your entire upper torso with the head so that your eyes and the gun's muzzle track together as a unit. This ensures that your defensive firearm always points in the direction in which you are looking. However, be aware of your muzzle when scanning the area to avoid pointing your firearm in an unsafe direction. You need to visually locate any persons in the vicinity, but without sweeping them with your gun's muzzle.

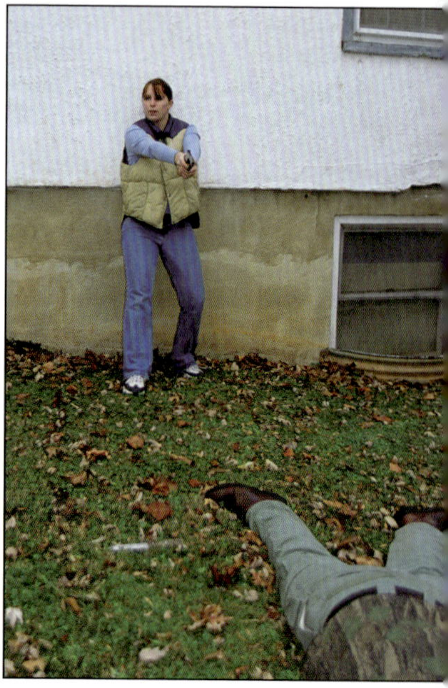

In situations in which your attacker has surrendered, you should minimize

Fig. 161. When you are covering a surrendered or downed attacker and are waiting for police assistance, back up against a wall and be sure to keep your assailant in view at all times.

the period of time your eyes are off him. Removing your eyes from the surrendered assailant to scan the area behind you may give him the opportunity to resume the attack on you. When you are covering a surrendered attacker, back up against a wall to eliminate the possibility of being attacked directly from the rear by an unseen assailant, and then scan as far left and right as possible without losing sight of the surrendered criminal in your peripheral vision. In this way, you will be aware of any movement the attacker makes. If it is not possible to back up to a wall, you must scan the area behind you. This scan should be performed as quickly as possible to minimize the time the surrendered assailant is out of your view.

PART V

DEVELOPING CONCEALED CARRY SHOOTING SKILLS FOR USE OUTSIDE THE HOME

CHAPTER 18

UTILIZING COVER AND CONCEALMENT OUTSIDE THE HOME

Shooting skill is only one of the factors that determine whether you prevail in a violent encounter. Of equal importance are the strategies you use to minimize the threat posed by your attacker and maximize the effectiveness of the response you make.

When you anticipate being confronted by an armed attacker, the most immediate tactical response you should make is to attempt to leave the area; avoiding or escaping from a threat is always the best course of action. If avoidance or escape is not possible, you should retreat and seek cover or concealment. In motion pictures and on television, people often seek cover or concealment only after they have been shot at. In the real world, however, you should seek cover or concealment whenever you encounter an aggressor, before he attacks. A protected position allows you to more safely assess the situation and decide upon your course of action.

Fig. 162. Armed defender behind cover.

The concepts of cover and concealment are sometimes used interchangeably, but actually are very different. *Cover* is anything that will protect all or part of your body when you are behind it. *Concealment,* on the other hand, is anything that will hide all or part of your body from observation. An object that provides concealment may not protect your body. By definition, objects that provide concealment do not necessarily provide cover. Objects affording cover, however, usually provide some level of concealment.

The importance of cover lies in its ability to prevent injury during a violent confrontation. Avoiding injury during an attack is critical. Anything you can do to minimize your risk of injury during an encounter with an attacker will increase the chance that you and your loved ones will prevail.

Cover provides protection not only from an assailant armed with a gun, but also from one using other weapons or even bare hands. At close range, a knife or baseball bat can be as deadly as a firearm. By putting a hard object between you and your assailant, you may be able to avoid injury while gaining time to escape or, as a last resort, to employ your firearm.

Concealment can help prevent an assailant from locating you or directing accurate fire at you. Proper utilization of concealment may also allow you to avoid or escape an attacker completely. Even when your assailant knows you are somewhere in the vicinity—in a nearby alley, for example—your use of concealment can give you an advantage.

It is almost always preferable to seek cover rather than concealment. Items providing cover usually afford some level of concealment as well, so the choice between cover and concealment is usually not an "either-or" proposition. In defensive shooting situations, however, there are few absolute rules, and there may be occasions when it is preferable to choose a position offering concealment rather than one offering cover. For example, if a concealment position affords a better escape route, less exposure to a second attacker, or a better firing position than a position behind cover, you should choose the concealment position.

OBJECTS PROVIDING COVER AND CONCEALMENT

Every environment contains objects that can provide either cover or concealment, or both. Items providing concealment don't necessarily need to be large enough to hide your entire body. In a pinch, even relatively small things—such as a trash can, a fire hydrant, or a discarded cardboard box—can disguise your outline, preventing an attacker from immediately detecting you. This is particularly true under low-light conditions. In general, larger objects, such as trees and bushes, mailboxes, freestanding telephone booths and so forth are preferred for concealment purposes.

Fig. 163. Defender (arrow) taking cover behind a telephone pole.

NRA Guide to Personal Protection Outside the Home

Fig. 164. Objects providing concealment.

Whether a given object can provide cover depends upon a number of factors. For example, the more material that must be penetrated by the bullet, the better cover is afforded. An empty trash can made of thin-gauge steel provides little or no protection from even low-powered cartridges; filled with household refuse, however, it may completely defeat many handgun rounds.

Objects that most people might intuitively think of as providing cover may, in fact, provide little protection. For example, a sheetrock wall in a store or office may not stop even a .22 bullet. Grocery shelves, office

Fig. 165. Objects providing cover.

furniture, public toilet stalls, car doors and the like are also capable of penetration by typical handgun rounds. Even a thick hardwood door may be penetrated by a jacketed bullet from a moderate-power cartridge, such as a .38 Special or 9mm Parabellum.

Though most environments contain many things capable of providing concealment or partial cover, there are relatively few objects capable of providing complete cover. On the street, such cover is usually provided by cars and other vehicles, U.S. Postal Service mailboxes, steel dumpsters, and the walls of brick or concrete buildings.

Fig. 166. Defender making good use of shadows and cover.

Even if they are unable to provide complete protection from incoming fire, many objects can nonetheless provide limited cover—that is, they are capable of deflecting or slowing a bullet and decreasing its injury-causing potential. A degree of cover may also be provided by objects that are capable of stopping a bullet but are not large enough to completely shield your body, such as a fire hydrant or telephone pole. While it is always preferable to seek cover behind items affording complete protection, this may

Fig. 167. Defender minimizing his exposure behind cover.

not always be possible. Limited cover is better than no cover at all.

The degree of protection an object provides from bullet penetration may depend upon the angle of the bullet strike in relation to the object. A shotgun blast directed straight against a windshield will penetrate it; fired at an oblique angle, shotgun pellets may be deflected. Similarly, in an office, a bookcase full of books, shot front to back, provides little protection. Shot from side to side (lengthwise), however, with the bullet traversing several feet of books, the bookcase may provide more cover, though less concealment.

Even when no adequate cover is available, you should still endeavor to conceal yourself behind any available object. The less of you an attacker sees, the less of you there is to aim at—and the harder you are to hit. Furthermore, your assailant may not have the presence of mind to realize that you are still vulnerable behind an empty trash can, a bush or a thin-gauge car body.

Fig. 168. Defender taking cover behind fire hydrant.

IDENTIFYING LOCATIONS FOR COVER AND CONCEALMENT

On the street, in your car, in a store and in your workplace, you should survey your immediate environment to determine which objects may provide cover or concealment. Assess each item for the level of protection it may afford and its placement in relation to possible lines of attack and retreat.

Look for cover in locations affording a good firing position, as well as an escape route allowing you to retreat to a position of safety. Avoid seeking cover in locations in which you would be vulnerable from attack by a second assailant.

Make use of natural shadows and less-illuminated areas when selecting locations for your cover and concealment. Select spots having a background that tends to break up your outline; avoid rear illumination that can clearly silhouette you.

Fig. 169. Defender (arrow) using low light to hide behind trash can used for concealment.

Fig. 170. Defender using quick peek technique to scan for threats around corner. The defender employs only the absolute minimum degree of exposure, and chooses a vantage point that is unlikely to attract attention (arrow).

TECHNIQUES FOR USING COVER AND CONCEALMENT

Minimizing your exposure in a defensive encounter is critical.

At times you may not be able to see around the corner of a building, the hood of a car, etc. Rather than slowly peering around the obstruction (which would allow an attacker time to detect you), use a quick peek to scan the area. Rapidly bob your head to the side just enough to get a "snapshot" of the area and just as quickly tuck it back behind cover. Your total exposure should be less than a second—too little time for an armed adversary to see you and react with an accurate shot. Also, if you peek more than once, vary the location you peek from. If you take several quick peeks from the same location, an assailant may aim at that spot and be ready to fire at your next appearance.

On those occasions when it is essential to avoid being spotted behind cover or concealment, it is important to keep still. The eye is very sensitive

to motion; a slight bob of the head or movement of the gun may draw an attacker's attention and give away your location.

When you must fire from cover, there are several important techniques you should utilize. To minimize exposure while firing from behind cover in a standing two-handed position, use the leaning out technique. First, assume the proper two-handed stance behind cover. Then, simply tilt or lean your upper body to the right or left (as necessary) just enough to acquire the target. Note that when leaning out to the weak-hand side, you should not grip the firearm in your weak hand. The strong-hand grip is maintained, and you simply lean out as needed to acquire the target. The gun may be canted slightly, and your body will be slightly more exposed than when shooting from the strong side. When practicing the "leaning out"

Fig. 171. Defender leaning out around wall that provides cover.

technique, be conscious of the amount of body mass that is exposed from each side, and adjust your position so as to keep as much of your body as possible behind cover.

When shooting multiple shots from cover, avoid emerging from the same point every time you fire. Typically, as with the quick peek technique used to observe an area from behind cover, you should emerge only long enough to acquire the target and fire accurately (in most cases with a single assailant, a rapid pair of shots) and then duck back behind cover. When you re-

Fig. 172. Gun's muzzle clear of cover.

emerge for subsequent shots, vary the point from which you fire. This may necessitate using different shooting positions (kneeling, standing, etc.) from behind cover.

You must also ensure that your gun's muzzle is clear of the object providing cover. Whether shooting over an object, such as a trash can lid or a concrete wall, or around the side of a building or mailbox, it is critical to ensure that the muzzle is clear of the cover. This is particularly necessary when the shooter cants the gun to minimize exposure from behind cover.

Moreover, you should avoid resting or bracing the handgun on or against cover. Contact with cover can impede the rotation of the cylinder of a revolver or the operation of the slide of a semi-automatic; both conditions can cause gun stoppages. Even when contact with cover does not cause gun malfunctions, that contact can degrade accuracy.

Take care to prevent the firearm from banging against cover during recoil. This is particularly important when firing through a narrow horizontal space, such as under a cross-member of a fence or the body of a car. If the muzzle is placed too close to the cover, recoil can smash the front sight against the cover object, possibly damaging the sight or preventing normal slide travel, or both. You can avoid the problems caused by gun contact with cover by staying back from the cover at least far enough to

Fig. 173. Defender canting handgun when firing from left side of barricade to prevent brass from going back into ejection port.

prevent the gun's muzzle from protruding beyond it. Maintaining this distance will often provide you with better mobility, as well as greater concealment and protection.

Since most semi-automatic pistols eject to the right, special care must be taken when firing a semi-automatic pistol from the left side of cover. With the pistol held vertically close to cover, an ejected case can bounce off the object providing cover and into the ejection port, jamming the pistol. To prevent this, a semi-automatic pistol fired from the left side of a solid wall, mailbox or other cover should be canted to move the ejection port away from the cover and to produce an ejection trajectory that will minimize the chance of case bounce-back.

Keep in mind that the various positions used for shooting from cover share the same basic characteristics as other shooting positions:

- Consistency
- Balance
- Support
- Natural Point of Aim (NPA)
- Comfort

MOVEMENT TO COVER AND CONCEALMENT

In any defensive encounter, try to keep as much distance as possible between you and your assailant. When your assailant is unarmed or armed only with a club, knife, tire iron or the like, increasing your distance from him may remove you from immediate harm and give you the opportunity to escape the encounter or, if that is impossible, to take appropriate measures to stop the attack. An unarmed attacker who is allowed to approach too closely may succeed in blocking your firearm or taking it from you. Even when your attacker has a firearm, it still makes sense to move away as far and as quickly as possible.

During an encounter with an aggressor, try to move not only away from that person, but also toward a source of cover. Again, remember that you should not wait until you are shot at or otherwise attacked to seek cover. Also, always seek cover after you have fired shots, even if your shots seem to have stopped the attack. Just because an assailant has gone down and appears incapacitated does not mean he or she is no longer dangerous. Your attacker may be stunned or shamming, or may suddenly "come around" with a burst of violent energy.

Practice moving backward and laterally toward cover. There are specific techniques for both types of movement, which allow you to maintain your:

- View of your assailant or of an area (a doorway, alley, etc.) where that assailant may appear.
- Firearm in a ready position or shooting position for the quickest possible shot if necessary.
- Balance while moving, preventing stumbling on obstacles or making unnecessary sound.

Movement—either backward or lateral—is a good idea after firing shots, even if the distance moved is only a few feet. As noted previously, many violent attacks occur in low light, and an assailant may be able to pinpoint your position primarily through your muzzle flashes. Changing position will make it more difficult for an assailant to locate you.

Moving Backward. The proper technique for moving backward is relatively easy to master with practice. The knees are bent and the hips are lowered, making your center of gravity lower and increasing stability during movement. Your eyes are kept focused on the attacker or on the area from which danger may come.

There are two methods for moving backward. With both, movement is commenced by extending your lead foot rearward with the toe down and the heel high to feel for obstacles. This is necessary because you may be required to move in darkness or low light, and in any event must not look away from the attacker or danger zone to check for obstructions or debris. When the toe contacts the floor, the rest of the sole of the foot rolls down until the heel touches the floor. Your weight should not shift to the rear foot until that foot is fully flat on the ground. In this way, if the foot encounters an obstacle or an uneven surface, you can move it to a different location that is clear of debris without causing a loss of balance.

The difference in the two methods lies in the way steps are alternated. In the first method, the same foot always serves as the lead foot, with the trailing foot brought in line with the lead foot but never behind it. This is a technique that may be used when you are unsure of your footing, and retention of balance is more important than speed. In the second technique, both feet alternate as the lead and trailing foot. After

Fig. 174. Defender moving rearward to cover.
Note that the foot moving rearward (arrow) is lowerd to the ground with the toe touching first to feel for obstacles.

Fig. 174. (continued). Defender completing rearward movement to cover, extending gun to fire if necessary (left) and then moving laterally to move directly behind object providing cover.

the lead foot has been placed firmly on the ground, the other foot becomes the lead foot, and the same procedure is repeated. This technique allows faster, if less stable, rearward movement.

Avoid shooting while moving. The proper procedure is to shoot, move, shoot, then move again.

Moving Laterally. When cover is located to one side, rather than to the rear, or when you find yourself backed up against a wall, only lateral movement may be possible. To move laterally, first bend your knees and drop your hips (though not as much as when moving rearward). Then extend the lead foot to the side with the outside edge held high in order to feel for obstacles. The inside edge of the lead foot plants in

Fig. 175. Defender moving laterally to cover. The feet do not cross each other when stepping to the side.

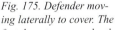

Fig. 175. (continued). Defender completing lateral movement to cover. The body is lowered to minimize exposure behind the object used for cover.

position first, and the foot rolls to the outside edge as the weight is shifted to the foot. Do not shift your weight to the lead foot until that foot is fully flat on the ground. In this way, if your foot encounters an obstacle or an uneven surface, you can move it to a different location that is clear of debris without causing a loss of balance.

Note that the feet do not cross during this lateral movement. Once the lead foot is planted, the trailing foot is brought inward only until it can be planted alongside the extended lead foot. The lead foot extends again,

Fig. 176. Sequence of foot movement when moving to the left to cover. (A) Right foot is brought into left foot, but does not cross it; (B) left foot is extended to the side; (C) edge of left foot is turned down as foot is lowerd to feel for obstacles.

repeating the process. As with backward movement, avoid shooting while moving. The proper procedure is to shoot, move, shoot, then move again.

Learning to use, and move to, cover and concealment can be as important in a defensive encounter as the ability to use a firearm effectively. The proper use of cover and concealment should be included in your dry-fire practice, and, if possible, your live-fire drills as well.

CHAPTER 19

PRESENTATION AND FIRE FROM DIFFERENT POSITIONS

In many different shooting disciplines, the firing positions are prescribed by the rules, making each stage predictable and consistent. Real-world situations are never predictable, however; no two are ever the same. In one case, you may be standing right next to cover—a mailbox or concrete wall; in another, you may be in the middle of a parking lot with no cover for 50 yards in any direction.

The ability to respond to the wide variety of confrontational situations that may occur requires the use of a variety of techniques, including the varied shooting positions presented in Chapter 16: Shooting Positions. In this chapter those positions are revisited and integrated with the presentation of a handgun from concealment and with the effective use of cover. In addition, three new techniques—presentation starting from a seated position, presentation from standing to prone, and presentation from standing to lying on the back—are introduced.

PRESENTATION FROM STANDING TO KNEELING BEHIND LOW COVER

The various kneeling positions presented in Chapter 16: Shooting Positions, allow you to fire effectively while taking full advantage of low cover. In addition, a kneeling position may be used to present a smaller target when there is no cover, or to give more support and thus greater accuracy. You should develop the ability to quickly assume a covered kneeling position as an automatic response to a deadly threat.

Whatever kneeling position is to be assumed, the presentation sequence is the same. Your handgun is presented from the holster, holster purse or fanny pack in the usual manner, as when you are in a standing shooting position; the kneeling position is assumed only after the handgun is pointed forward, to minimize the chance of crossing the body with the muzzle.

After this movement is safely mastered, you may overlap the final phase of handgun presentation with the start of the kneeling movement. That is,

Fig. 177. Presentation from standing to kneeling behind low cover. Starting behind cover (A), the gun is accessed, pulled from the concealment device and rotated toward the target (B,C), the hands join and extend the gun as the knees begin to bend and the weak-side foot slides forward (D) and the strong-side knee is placed on the ground to complete the position (E). The gun may be fired if necessary. The same procedure can be utilized to go from a standing to a squatting position behind low cover (F).

you may begin to lower yourself into a kneeling position only after you have rotated your pistol's muzzle toward the threat. Don't wait until you are fully kneeling to draw your gun; that can be awkward and time-consuming.

Also, do not put your trigger finger inside the trigger guard when you rotate the gun toward the target; wait until you have completed the kneeling movement. This will prevent an inadvertent discharge should you be jarred when your knee hits the ground.

Practice going from a standing position to the different kneeling positions, with first dry-fire drills and, after considerable practice, with live ammunition. Use kneepads to protect your knees. Experiment with cover of different heights, at different distances. This will allow you to develop a feel for the best kneeling position to be used with a particular type of cover, as well as the best technique—stepping forward, stepping back, or dropping straight down—for going into a stable kneeling position.

PRESENTATION FROM STANDING TO SQUATTING BEHIND LOW COVER

When there simply isn't enough time to go into a kneeling position, or when you want to have the ability to move instantly after firing, a squatting shooting position can be adopted. Although faster to get into and out of than the kneeling positions, the squatting position is not quite as stable, and it is difficult to maintain for extended periods of time.

When presenting your handgun from a standing position and assuming a squatting position, you must complete the presentation sequence before you drop down into a squat. As with the process from going from a standing to a kneeling position, you can accelerate the process slightly by beginning the squatting movement right after the pistol is rotated toward the threat and the gun is being fully extended.

With first dry-fire and later live-fire practice, go into a squatting position behind cover of different heights; on the street you cannot count on finding cover that is conveniently the same height as that you practiced with. Also, experiment with varied foot positions in the squat. Depending upon their flexibility, strength or balance, or their particular shooting position, some shooters find it more comfortable or stable to put one foot or the other slightly forward, or to have a slightly wider or narrower stance.

PRESENTATION FROM SITTING TO STANDING

Few people practice shooting from a sitting starting position; nonetheless, in real life, the first hint of an attack may occur while you are sitting in a chair in your workplace, in a fast-food restaurant or on a park bench.

A

B

C

Fig. 178. Presentation from sitting to standing. Starting from a sitting position (A), the strong hand begins to access the handgun as the body weight is shifted forward in preparation to stand. As the defender stands, the strong hand accesses the gun, but does not pull it from the concealment device until he is fully erect.

To present your handgun starting from a sitting position, first rise to a standing position, then begin the presentation sequence. Do not attempt to draw your handgun from a sitting position.

To speed the presentation process somewhat, you may wish to access and grip the firearm with the strong hand before standing. This will help stabilize the gun as the body rises. Do not, however, pull the gun from the holster until you are standing.

Practice this technique using dry-fire; few ranges have facilities for you to start from a sitting position. In your dry-fire area, position your chair in front of a table and practice standing and presenting your handgun.

PRESENTATION FROM STANDING BEHIND COVER

In the street, the nearest cover may be immediately to your front or side—a brick wall, a door or door frame, a telephone pole or tree trunk, a car, and so forth. You must be able to quickly present your firearm while using the available cover to protect as much of your body as possible.

When you present your gun from behind cover, you must allow enough distance—about an arm's length—to keep the gun or your hands from hitting it. With both dry- and live-fire, practice presenting the gun from both

Fig. 179. Presentation from standing behind cover. The process is similar to simply presenting the handgun from standing, except that the defender must begin presentation at a sufficient distance from the object providing cover to allow the gun to be rotated and extended toward the target. The defender should minimize his exposure past cover.

sides of a barricade. Use the lean-out technique to expose only the minimum amount of your body. Whichever side you elect to shoot from, you will normally extend the firearm forward only after you are leaning out sufficiently to prevent the gun from contacting the cover.

Avoid resting or touching the gun on the cover object; brace your hands against it instead, or don't contact it at all. When shooting a semiautomatic pistol, don't forget to cant its ejection port away from the cover object to prevent a spent case from bouncing back in the port and jamming the gun.

PRESENTATION FROM STANDING TO PRONE

When there is only very low cover, such as a curb or fire hydrant, or no cover at all, a prone position may be the better choice to minimize your exposure. Either the standard or rollover prone positions, described in Chapter 16: Shooting Positions, may be used.

As with many of the other techniques in this chapter, the proper technique is to complete much of the presentation before assuming the prone position. Specifically, the handgun is accessed, gripped, pulled from the holster and rotated toward the target with the strong hand prior to beginning the descent to the prone position. The trigger finger is kept out of the trigger guard during the rotation of the gun toward the target, and contacts

*Fig. 180.
Presentation
from standing
to prone. The
gun is ac-
cessed (A) and
rotated toward
the target (B),
and the knees
are bent with
the weak hand
extended for-
ward (C). The
body is low-
ered until the
weak hand
touches the
ground (D)
and then the
legs are
extended rear-
ward while the
gun is extend-
ed forward
(E). Both
hands join to
form a firing
position with
the elbows on
the ground
(F).*

Fig. 181. An alterma-tive prone position is the rollover prone position, in which the body is rolled to put its weight on the strong side, with the weak-side leg crossed over the strong-side leg. The rollover prone position allows a somewhat lower body position.

the trigger only after the full prone position is achieved, to prevent an inadvertent discharge should you be jarred as you descend to the ground.

To get into the prone position, the knees are bent and the weak hand is extended forward to brace the body against the ground. At the same time, the strong hand holding the gun, pointed toward the threat, is also extended forward. When the knees are bent almost to a squatting position, the weak hand touches the ground and the upper body weight is transferred to that hand. The legs are then extended rearward, the body comes to rest on the ground, the hands join together in a two-hand grip and the body assumes the final position of the prone position. During the entire process of lowering the body to the ground, it is critical to keep the handgun extended out forward in the strong hand, rotated toward the threat. Also, the trigger finger is kept out of the trigger guard until the full prone position is achieved, to prevent unintentional firing if you are jarred as you lower to the ground.

Use knee pads or a padded mat during dry-fire or live-fire practice of this technique. Initially strive for precision and smoothness in the technique, not speed, and always be aware of the position of the handgun in relation to the weak hand and the rest of the body. Also, be extremely careful to maintain the trigger finger outside the trigger guard and alongside the frame until the prone position is assumed and you are ready to fire.

PRESENTATION FROM STANDING TO LYING ON BACK

If you are violently attacked, there is a good chance that you will end up on the ground on your back, either as the result of a shove or trip by your

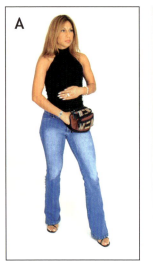

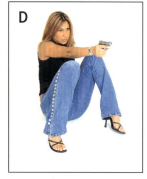

Fig. 182. Presentation from standing to lying on back. The handgun is accessed (A), and withdrawn from the concealment device and rotated toward the target (B). The body assumes a squatting position with the weak hand extended (C), the buttocks are lowered to the gound (D) and the upper body leans back while the legs extend forward with the knees apart to keep them out of the line of fire (E). Finally, the hands join and the handgun is raised to point at the center of mass of the target (F).

attacker or because you lose your footing while retreating rearward. There may also be occasions when you would deliberately go to the ground, such as when your attacker is advancing so quickly toward you that you cannot back up quickly enough to escape, and there's not even enough time to draw your defensive firearm. In this situation, getting on the ground, on your back, creates distance between you and your attacker, and allows you to use your feet to kick him or ward off his. assault. This action can also give you additional time to present your defensive firearm.

Whether you go to the ground accidentally or intentionally, your ability to deliver effective fire from a position in which you are lying on your back may be critical in surviving a violent assault.

When practicing or using this technique, the key is to remain in control as you go from a standing position to a position on your back. Rather than a falling movement, you should employ a controlled rearward roll. Begin the technique by accessing, gripping, and pulling the handgun from the holster in the standing position. Rotate the handgun forward toward the target, but do not join the weak hand to the strong hand. Be sure to keep the trigger finger outside of the trigger guard and alongside the handgun frame. Bend the knees to lower the buttocks to the ground, and at the same time extend the weak hand to the side and slightly behind you in anticipation of using it to feel for the ground. When your buttocks touch or nearly touch the ground, roll rearward onto your back. Keep your back curved forward to produce more of a rolling movement and to prevent your back from hitting the ground all at one time. Use the weak hand to help stabilize this roll. You should end up with your back on the ground, feet wide apart and knees slightly bent, your shoulders off the ground and your head up, and the handgun gripped with both hands, pointing toward the target.

Be aware of the position of the gun's muzzle during every phase of this technique. Also, your knees, although slightly bent, should be kept as low to the ground as possible to prevent the gun from crossing them.

Practice the technique initially without a handgun to get accustomed to the body control required to execute the roll properly. Use a padded mat to prevent injury or discomfort. After the movement becomes smooth and natural, incorporate your unloaded gun or a training simulator into the movement. Maintain an awareness of the muzzle position in relation to your knees or other parts of your body; drop your knees if necessary to keep them from being crossed by the muzzle.

It may be difficult to find a range allowing you to practice this technique with live ammunition. Rigorous dry-fire practice, however, should prepare you to use this technique effectively should the need arise.

CHAPTER 20

PRESENTATION, MOVEMENT AND FIRE FROM DIFFERENT POSITIONS

The previous two chapters covered specific techniques for integrating handgun presentation with different shooting positions. In each of these techniques, the shooter remains more or less stationary.

In real life, however, you may encounter many situations in which presentation must be coupled with movement. For example, as has been stated in other chapters, one of the first things you should do when faced with an actual threat in any environment is to move to cover (assuming you cannot avoid or escape the threat). Cover may be in front of you, to your side or to your rear, and it may be high or low; you must be able to move to it quickly.

As was presented in Chapter 18: Utilizing Cover and Concealment Outside the Home, there are occasions when there is insufficient time to move to cover safely. For instance, in a close range confrontation with an assailant who has already produced a weapon, turning to run for distant cover may simply give your attacker the opportunity to shoot, club or stab you in the back. Under such conditions, you may be better off firing at the criminal before, or as, you move to cover.

Movement of another sort is required when you must quickly engage attackers from your side or rear. You must develop the ability to quickly turn, assume a stable firing position, and fire accurately if necessary.

PRESENTATION AND MOVEMENT

There are three basic techniques of presentation and movement that you should master: presentation and moving forward to cover (both high and low); presentation and moving laterally to cover (both high and low); and presentation and moving rearward.

Presentation and Moving Forward to Cover

Although you should generally try to move away from a threat that is in front of you, there are times when the best cover—or the only cover—is

Fig. 183. Presentation and moving forward to cover. Starting some distance from cover (A), the handgun is presented (B, C), and the defender moves forward with the gun at the ready position (D, E). When approaching cover, the gun is extended, and may be fired if necessary (F, G). Finally (H), the defender uses the cover for support.

located forward of your position.

When you move to cover, keep your knees bent and your hips lowered, increasing your stability and making you a smaller target. Keep your eyes facing forward, toward the attacker.

Whether you wear the gun in a holster, fanny pack or holster purse, the gun should be drawn as you initiate movement, and held in a ready position as you move. This allows the gun to be extended forward and fired if necessary before cover has been reached. The gun may be held in two hands or in one hand, if the weak hand is needed to keep your balance, feel for obstacles, or fend off an attack.

In darkness or reduced light, particularly in an unfamiliar site providing questionable footing, you should modify your movement technique to reduce the chance of tripping over obstacles. With most of your weight on your rear foot, advance your lead foot with the toes pointing forward and slightly down, feeling for obstacles. Carefully lower your lead foot, toes first, while feeling for any objects that would interfere with solid foot placement. Your toes will touch the ground first, followed by the rest of your foot. When your lead foot is firmly planted on the ground, your weight is shifted to that foot, and your rear foot is lifted and brought forward in a straight line to become the new lead foot, and the process is repeated.

This technique allows you to move confidently on uncertain terrain, such as a gravel road, or a lawn, and additionally allows you to move in stealth and silence when necessary. With practice, you will be able to move with surprising speed, even in darkness.

Presentation and Moving Laterally to Cover

When cover is located off to one side, rather than to the rear, when you find yourself backed up against a wall, or when there are multiple threats arrayed to your front and side, only lateral movement may be possible.

To move laterally, first bend your knees and drop your hips (though not as much as when moving rearward). Then extend the lead foot to the side with the outside edge held down in order to feel for obstacles. The inside edge of the lead foot plants in position first, and the foot rolls to the outside edge as the weight is shifted to the foot. Do not shift your weight to the lead foot until that foot is fully flat on the ground. In this way, if your foot encounters an obstacle or an uneven surface, you can move it to a different location that is clear of debris without causing a loss of balance.

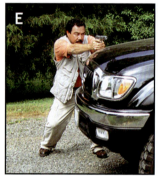

Fig. 184. Presentation and movement laterally to cover. Starting away from cover (A), the defender extends the lead foot laterally as the gun is drawn (B), and brings the trailing foot in, without crossing the lead foot (C). This is repeated until the defender is behind cover (D, E). During movement, the gun is extended and may be fired if necessary.

Note that the feet do not cross during this lateral movement. Once the lead foot is planted, the trailing foot is brought inward only until it can be planted alongside the lead foot. The lead foot extends again, repeating the process. The trailing foot never crosses or passes the lead foot.

Again, whether you wear the gun in a holster, fanny pack or holster

Fig. 185. When moving laterally, the lead foot is extended, the trailing foot is brought into the lead foot without crossing it (middle), and the process is repeated as necessary. The lead foot is extended with the edge of the foot down, to feel for obstacles (right).

purse, the gun should be drawn as you initiate movement, and held in a ready position as you move. This allows the gun to be extended forward and fired if necessary before cover has been reached. The gun may be held in two hands or in one hand, if the weak hand is needed to keep your balance, feel for obstacles, or fend off an attack.

Presentation and Moving Rearward

The movement used in moving rearward is similar to that used to move forward—an exaggerated walk with knees bent and the hips lowered. Your lead foot is

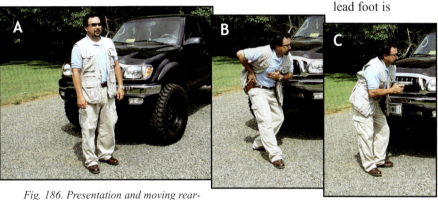

Fig. 186. Presentation and moving rear-
ward to cover. Starting some distance from cover (A), the body is
lowered as the gun is drawn, and the lead foot extended rearward, toe pointed down to
feel for obstacles (B). The trailing foot is brought alongside the lead foot (C), and the
process is repeated as necessary. During movement, the gun is extended toward the tar-
get and may be fired if required (D, E). Finally, a lateral step may be taken to place the
body fully behind the object used for cover, and the gun may be fired (F).

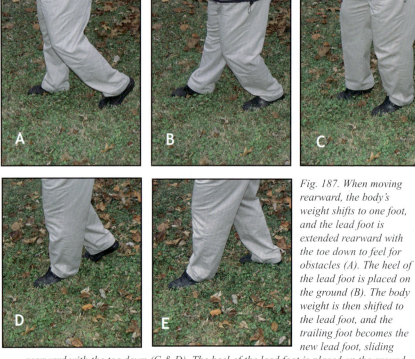

Fig. 187. When moving rearward, the body's weight shifts to one foot, and the lead foot is extended rearward with the toe down to feel for obstacles (A). The heel of the lead foot is placed on the ground (B). The body weight is then shifted to the lead foot, and the trailing foot becomes the new lead foot, sliding rearward with the toe down (C & D). The heel of the lead foot is placed on the ground (E), allowing the weight to be shifted and the process to be repeated.

extended rearward with your toe pointing down and just barely above the ground; in this way your foot can feel for obstacles or debris. The toe of your lead foot touches the ground first, and the rest of your foot rolls down to plant the sole flat on the ground. When your lead foot is solidly on the ground, your weight shifts to that foot, the other foot becomes the lead foot and the whole process is repeated.

PRESENTATION AND TURNING

Threats to your safety do not appear only from the front; they may also come from the side or the rear. You must develop the ability to swiftly engage threats from any direction.

Presentation and Turning 90 Degrees to the Strong or Weak Side

In all presentation techniques that involve turning, the first step is to acquire a grip on the handgun in the holster, holster purse or fanny pack and bring the weak hand to the chest before the turning movement begins. This is done to locate and stabilize the gun during body rotation.

The turning motion must be completed, and the body facing the threat, before the handgun is withdrawn from the holster; this prevents the gun from swinging in a wide arc. Whether you are turning toward the strong-hand or weak-hand side, you can accomplish the turn in either of two ways. Toward the strong-hand side, you can rotate your body by pulling your strong-side leg rearward, or advancing your weak-side leg forward. Turning toward the weak-hand side is performed in the opposite fashion: the strong-side leg can be moved forward, or the weak-side leg pulled rearward. As a general rule, because techniques in which you step forward give you greater visibility for stable foot placement, they are preferred to those in which you step backward.

In a real-life encounter, you may be on unfamiliar or uneven ground, or a surface covered in debris. You may also be in dim light. Under these conditions, stepping either forward or rearward without looking may cause your foot to hit or stumble upon an unseen obstacle. To promote stable footing, keep your foot close to the ground as you move it, and feel for debris with your toe.

In some situations, it may

Fig. 188. Presentation and turning 90 degrees to the strong side. From a starting position (A), the defender turns toward the threat and accesses the gun (B), slides the weak-side foot forward (C), and faces the target to present the firearm in the normal manner (D).

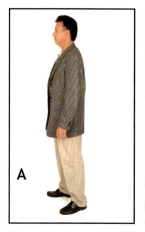 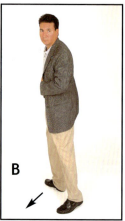 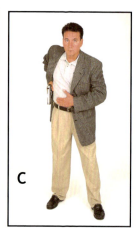

Fig. 189. Presentation and turning 90 degrees to the weak side. From a starting position (A), the defender turns toward the threat and accesses the gun (B), slides the strong-side foot around to face the target (C), and presents the firearm in the normal manner.

not be practical or possible to move your feet to face a target. This may be the case when a threat must be engaged suddenly, or when the ground you are standing on does not allow you to move your feet without the risk of stumbling or falling. Under such circumstances, you can use a "turret turn" to quickly engage targets to either side. With this turn, your feet stay in place, and the shoulders and upper body are rotated as a turret to bring the

gun into alignment with the target. For many people, an isosceles shooting position gives the greatest flexibility to turn in either direction.

Fig. 190. When there is not time to execute a complete turn to the weak or strong side, a turret turn may be used to address a threat to the side.

Presentation and Turning 180 Degrees to the Strong or Weak Side

As when you are turning 90 degrees to the strong side or weak side, you must first acquire a grip on the gun in the holster, holster purse or fanny pack before the turning movement begins. Also, your gun is not withdrawn until your turning motion is completed, and your body faces the target.

To turn 180 degrees to your left, you can either step forward and around with your right foot, pivoting on your left, or step rearward and around with your left foot, pivoting on your right, before rotating your body to the left. To rotate 180 degrees to the right, reverse the movement: step forward and around with your left foot or rearward and around with your right foot. As was pointed out earlier, techniques in which you step forward give you better visibility for stable foot placement, and are thus generally preferred to techniques in which you must step rearward.

The particular technique you choose will depend upon your immediate surroundings. For example, it is usually better to increase your distance from your attacker rather than move toward him; thus it would seem that your turning movement should always begin by stepping forward with the foot opposite the direction of the turn. Stepping forward might not always be possible, however, so you must learn to complete the turn by stepping rearward as well.

When you are attacked from the rear at very close range, execute your 180 degree turn to leave the non-gun side of your body facing toward

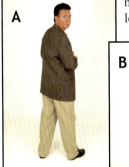

Fig. 191.
Presentation and turning 180 degrees to the strong side. From a starting position (A), the defender looks over his shoulder toward the threat as he accesses the gun (B), slides the weak-side foot forward in an arc (C),and pivots on the strong-side foot until he faces the target and can present the firearm (D).

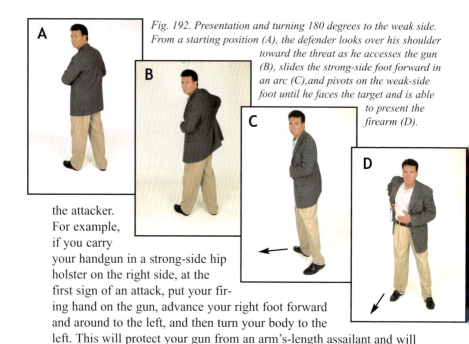

Fig. 192. Presentation and turning 180 degrees to the weak side. From a starting position (A), the defender looks over his shoulder toward the threat as he accesses the gun (B), slides the strong-side foot forward in an arc (C), and pivots on the weak-side foot until he faces the target and is able to present the firearm (D).

the attacker. For example, if you carry your handgun in a strong-side hip holster on the right side, at the first sign of an attack, put your firing hand on the gun, advance your right foot forward and around to the left, and then turn your body to the left. This will protect your gun from an arm's-length assailant and will allow you to fend off his attack with your weak hand.

The exact shooting position you end up in depends upon your final foot position. In the example above, if your right foot swings around until it is on the same line, perpendicular to the target, as your left foot, you can employ an isosceles stance. Swinging the right foot only part of the way around will put you into more of a Weaver stance.

PRACTICING PRESENTATION, MOVEMENT AND TURNING

Your goal in all your practice should be to simulate realistic situations as much as possible. Rather than simply repeat the same drills over and over, try to combine the various skills in new and challenging combinations. For example, try a drill in which you begin in a seated position, then rise to your feet, turn 180 degrees, fire two shots and then move to low cover in a kneeling position and fire two more shots. The number of such combinations is virtually infinite, and is limited only by your own imagination.

If your local range does not allow such drills, you can at least try them in your designated dry-fire area. Also, many practical shooting matches give you the opportunity to test your skills under the pressure of competition and tight time constraints. See Appendix C: Opportunities for Skills Enhancement for more information on this form of competition.

CHAPTER 21

HANDGUN RETENTION

If you carry a handgun on your person in public, you must make every effort to ensure that you retain control of that handgun under any and all circumstances. During an encounter, of course, you must retain your handgun in order to use it for self-defense. However, you must retain possession of your gun at other times as well.

Three factors contribute to handgun retention: the design and use of your holster, holster purse or fanny pack; your ability to recognize and avoid situations in which handgun retention is threatened; and your mastery of handgun retention techniques.

DESIGN AND USE OF YOUR HOLSTER, HOLSTER PURSE OR FANNY PACK

The way a holster, holster purse or fanny pack is made and used has a large effect on the degree of handgun retention it provides. In general, better quality devices provide better retention. Top quality molded leather or synthetic holsters, for example, will usually better retain a handgun than lightly-constructed fabric holsters in which the gun fits loosely.

Holster purses and fanny packs, too, vary in their retention properties. Some purses and packs have retention straps, often fastened with Velcro®, inside the gun compartment; these will retain the gun even when the compartment's zipper or snap closure opens.

Better holsters, holster purses and fanny packs often incorporate features that promote retention. For example, retention is improved in double-stitched, snugly-molded holsters that only allow handgun withdrawal in a specific direction, and which resist an attacker's efforts to rip

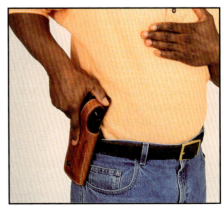

Fig. 193. Holster affording good retention by way of features such as safety strap, belt loops and gun-specific molded fit.

the gun out of the holster. There have been cases of attackers under the influence of drugs who have literally pulled a holster apart while pulling away the handgun inside.

Note, too, that there are several types of holsters that simply, by their design, limit your ability to retain the handgun. For instance, crossdraw holsters and many shoulder holsters hold the handgun with the grip frame toward the front—a poor location for retention. Small-of-the-back holsters, too, can present a retention problem.

Fig. 194. This holster purse has several features giving good retention, including a robust shoulder strap and secure gun compartment closure.

Guns in holster purses, on the other hand, may be lost if the purse itself is stolen. Often a purse-snatcher will come up behind a woman carrying a purse on a shoulder strap, cut the strap, and yank the purse away. To foil this, some high-security purses have straps reinforced with steel mesh that resist cutting.

The ability of even the best handgun concealment device to retain your handgun can be compromised if you don't use the device properly. Always use the correct holster for your gun, and if you use a hip holster, also select a sturdy belt of the proper width. With fanny packs, proper positioning in the front is also critical.

RECOGNIZING AND AVOIDING SITUATIONS IN WHICH HANDGUN RETENTION IS THREATENED

The absolute best way to promote handgun retention is to recognize and avoid those situations in which retention is threatened. In general, this also means avoiding situations in which your life or limb could be threatened, for one threat to retention is that posed by assailants who want to take your gun.

In Chapter 4: Awareness you learned about the different levels of awareness. Always be conscious of what is going on in your environment. Being

Fig. 195. Careless handling of your handgun, such as hanging your holster purse on your chair while visiting the restroom at a restaurant, can lead to loss of retention.

in an Aware condition may allow you to recognize many threats to retention, such as a pickpocket bumping into you in a crowd or in an elevator.

You must also recognize that there are areas and activities you should avoid altogether to ensure handgun retention. In reality, when you are armed, you should take even greater care to avoid potential trouble when you're out in public. Think ahead. Suggestions for avoiding threatening situations are in Chapter 6: Avoiding Confrontations Outside the Home.

HANDGUN RETENTION TECHNIQUES

Beyond secure concealment and avoiding risky situations, certain physical techniques may also help you retain your firearm.

Be aware that this book contains only a sample of the many available handgun retention techniques. You are urged to review materials that deal specifically with this subject, or to take advantage of courses on handgun retention offered at many firearm training centers.

There are four basic methods to prevent an attacker from taking away your firearm: *be aware of any attempt to disarm you*; *block your attacker from touching your gun*; *block an attacker from withdrawing your gun from its concealment device*; and *control your gun by maintaining contact with it*.

Fig. 196. In an arm's-length physical confrontation, an assailant may easily grab a defender's holstered gun.

Be Aware of Any Attempt to Disarm You. Always maintain an awareness of the location of strangers or potential threats in relation to you and your firearm. Be especially wary of persons exhibiting suspicious behavior, such as those who try to approach too close or who seem, by their body language, to be positioning themselves for a lunge or a grab. Be alert to the most subtle clues, such as a stranger's repeated glances at your holster purse or at the slight bulge caused by your hip holster.

Also develop an awareness of any physical contact, no matter how slight or innocent, in the area of your gun. In a crowded corridor, you may mentally dismiss such a touch as incidental contact; but it actually may represent a criminal's effort to determine if you are wearing a gun or just a pager. Sometimes that slight contact will be all that you feel.

Train yourself to sense even the slightest contact with the clothes or body in the vicinity of your gun, and to regard it as suspicious.

Block an Attacker from Touching Your Gun. Anytime you sense a criminal's attempt to disarm you, you must instantly take steps to prevent him from touching your gun.

The exact response you make will depend upon the nature of the attempt your assailant makes. With an assailant coming at you from the front, you may be able to blade your body so that the gun in its concealment device is on the side

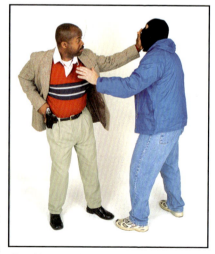

Fig. 197. Armed citizen warding off assailant with weak hand while retaining handgun with strong hand

of your body opposite from him. The attacker will find it more difficult to acquire your gun if he has to reach all the way across your body.

Any attempt to grab your gun should be blocked or parried with the weak hand, if possible. At the same time, access and grip your gun with your strong hand. With your hand on the gun your assailant will be unable to touch it (or touch enough of it to wrest it away from you). This position also allows you to quickly draw your gun if the circumstances dictate.

If you are carrying your gun in a hip holster or shoulder-strap holster purse, you may be able to block an assailant's grab by simply clamping the gun or holster purse to your body using your elbow. This move may work especially well when an attacker tries to get to your gun from behind. After securing the gun against the body, you may turn that side of your body sharply away from the assailant and get a grip on your gun with your firing hand.

Block an Attacker from Withdrawing Your Gun from its Concealment Device. If your attacker succeeds in getting a grip on your gun, you must keep him from withdrawing it from the concealment device

at all costs. One method of preventing him from acquiring your gun is to simply put your hand over his and apply pressure to prevent gun withdrawal. For example, if an assailant acquires a grip on your gun in your hip holster, simply grab his hand with your strong hand and push downward to prevent the gun from being withdrawn. Strike at his throat or eyes with your free hand, stomp on his instep, and kick at his knees and groin. This may distract, startle or incapacitate him, and his grip may weaken, allowing you to pull your gun away.

If your attacker is larger or stronger than you, or if your concealment device makes gun retention difficult, use both of your hands to keep him from acquiring your gun, and keep kicking at his knees, groin and shins.

Yell for help. Also, yell at your assailant: LET GO OF MY GUN! This

Fig. 198. Defender blocking assailant's attempt to remove gun from hip holster by clamping gun with the strong-side elbow.

has several effects. First, it may startle or distract him. Second, it will increase the power of your efforts, in the same way that a sharp yell gives a martial artist additional strength and power when breaking boards or executing a kick. And finally, it will draw attention to your attack, which may panic your attacker and cause him to flee.

Control Your Gun by Retaining Your Grip. Despite your efforts, your attacker may succeed in withdrawing your gun from its concealment device. Try to maintain your grip on his hand(s). Even against a larger, stronger attacker, you will often be able to control the direction of the muzzle. Avoid letting go at all costs. Use your feet to kick at vulnerable areas, such as his knees, groin, instep and shins.

At the same time, yell loudly: LET GO! LET GO! The more noise you make, the more likely a police officer or bystander will notice your predicament and come to your aid.

Keep in mind that the vast majority of criminals are not interested in getting into a prolonged struggle with a victim; they would prefer to complete their criminal activity quickly and quietly, without attracting attention. By maintaining control of your gun, you are buying time for yourself. He will be afraid that your yells have attracted the attention of the police, or of someone who will call the police. Eventually he may get tired of your kicks bruising his legs and your screams hurting his eardrums, and he may simply give up and flee.

Fig. 199. Armed citizen holding onto gun with both hands while yelling and kicking at attacker.

Retaining Your Drawn Gun. Occasionally, you will hear a person state that he or she is afraid to have a gun for self-defense because, in the event of an attack, "the criminal will probably just take it from me." In reality, that almost never happens. Studies by University of Florida criminologist Gary Kleck and University of Chicago economist John Lott show that guns are used for self-defense up to 2.5 million times a year—hardly an indicator that guns are being used against their law-abiding owners. If you are properly trained, and willing to use your handgun to protect your life, that should virtually never happen.

Most criminals will simply flee when you present your handgun. A criminal who does not must be regarded with special caution. He may be under the influence of drugs, and in his chemically distorted view of reality may believe himself to be invulnerable. He may think that you are unwilling to pull the trigger, and he may talk to you while working his way close enough to deflect and grab your gun: "You're not going to shoot me." He may also use this line of talk to distract you while his accomplice sneaks up behind you.

Fig. 200. Defender with gun pulled back to retention position using both hands.

To prevent your gun from being taken away in such a situation, you should first maintain (and if possible, increase) your distance from your assailant. Pay no attention to his words; order him to STAY BACK! or GO AWAY! in a loud and determined voice. If he is very close, pull your gun back from your extended firing position to a retention position with both hands on the gun: this will put the gun a couple of feet further away from the attacker.

Also, be aware of other assailants. Your attacker's posturing may simply be a ruse to buy time for his partner in crime to approach you, unseen, from the rear. While keeping your gun on your attacker, turn your head slightly to the right and left to pick up movement to your side and rear in your peripheral vision, without losing visual contact with your primary attacker. If possible, back up to a wall or other solid object.

Finally, be ready and willing to shoot if necessary. Remember that an unarmed attacker who intends to take your gun away can be a deadly threat. You have retreated; you have warned him: if he persists with an effort to cause you serious bodily harm, you must shoot until he stops the attack, either by fleeing, giving up or becoming incapacitated by his injuries.

TRAINING FOR HANDGUN RETENTION

To improve your handgun retention skills, you will need a training partner and a training gun. Never use a real gun for handgun retention training. Several brands of non-firing plastic training guns are available, in versions that are identical in size and weight to most common handguns. These training guns should be used for all your retention activities.

Have your partner try to take your training gun from varied positions; experiment with different techniques for thwarting the takeaway attempts to see what works best for you. Make your training realistic; your partner should make a serious effort to take your gun. Don't forget to yell, and don't give up.

Also, don't focus exclusively upon the physical techniques for blocking or resisting an assailant's attempt to take your gun. It is always easier to retain your gun by preventing an assailant from grabbing it. Simulate situations in which an attacker tries to acquire your drawn training gun; experiment to determine how far away he must be kept to prevent him from lunging and touching it. Remember that distance; in a real-life encounter, an attacker who comes closer than that poses a deadly threat.

In addition to the techniques described above, there are many handgun retention techniques based on the joint locking and joint manipulation

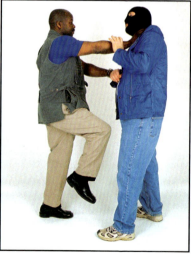

Fig. 201. Many martial arts contain techniques that can be used to promote gun retention; these can be mastered through diligent study at a martial arts studio.

techniques taught in martial arts such as aikido. These techniques can be used to promote gun retention at each stage of an attempt to take your gun. Though these techniques are beyond the scope of this book, when properly applied they can be extremely effective in both thwarting an assailant's attempt to obtain your gun and in disabling him. Consult a martial arts instructor conversant with street self-defense, or a training facility offering gun retention classes.

PART VI

SPECIAL DEFENSIVE SHOOTING TECHNIQUES

CHAPTER 22

STRONG- AND WEAK-HAND PRESENTATION

In a real-life defensive encounter, you may not always have the ability to use two hands to present and grip your handgun. You may need one hand to hold a flashlight, support a child, use your cell phone to call for help, or maintain your balance in dark and unfamiliar surroundings. In all of these situations, you may have to use your handgun with one hand only.

PRESENTING THE HANDGUN WITH THE STRONG HAND ONLY

The procedure for presenting your handgun from a concealment device using your strong hand only is basically the same as that for presenting the handgun with two hands, except that the JOIN step is omitted. When practicing one-handed presentation, keep the weak hand close to the the middle of the chest. In an actual encounter, of course, the weak hand may be used for a variety of purposes.

Fig. 202. Shooter demonstrating strong-hand-only presentation technique.

With some concealed carry devices, such as certain fanny packs and holster purses, two hands are desirable or even necessary to gain access to the gun. If you use such a device, experiment to determine if one-handed access is possible, as well as to formulate the proper technique for doing so. If you cannot under any circumstance acquire the gun with one hand only, you might consider replacing that handgun concealment device with one that does permit one-handed gun access.

Your selection of the Reverse Punch or Forward Punch one-handed shooting positions—or any other such shooting position—will be determined by the immediate circumstances. The appropriateness of any position will be judged on the basis of the extent to which the position is balanced, stable and safe.

PRESENTING THE HANDGUN WITH THE WEAK HAND

Weak-hand presentation skills are potentially useful in the event of an incapacitating injury to your firing hand or arm. In this technique, the weak hand, unaided by the strong hand, withdraws the handgun from the holster, holster purse or fanny pack.

Most handgun concealment devices do not permit easy withdrawal of the handgun by the weak hand. Many snug-fitting molded holsters only allow the handgun to be pulled out in one direction; and some designs by their very nature (such as small-of-the-back holsters) are virtually impossible for the weak hand to use.

Other handgun concealment devices can, in theory, allow weak hand only access. Crossdraw holsters, for example, place the handgun with the grip frame conveniently positioned for weak hand withdrawal. Some shoulder holsters, as well as certain holster purses and fanny packs, also

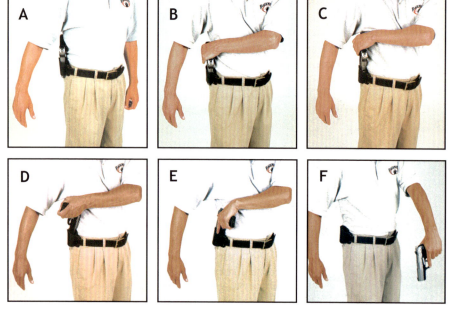

Fig. 203. Weak hand only technique from a hip holster. (A) Gun in holster, (B) accessing the gun with the weak hand, (C) pulling the gun partway out of the holster, (D) turning the gun with the muzzle still in the holster so that the butt is forward, (E) getting a final grip on the gun, and (F) removing the gun completely from the holster, muzzle down.

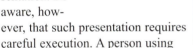

Fig. 204. *Presenting the handgun from a crossdraw holster with the weak hand only. (A), Accessing the gun, (B) pulling the gun from the holster, (C & D) rotating the gun toward the target, being careful not to cross the body or sweep the muzzle laterally. At (D) the gun may be fired instinctively, or extended toward the target and fired using the sights.*

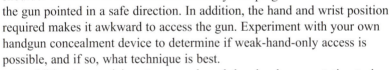

permit weak hand only presentation. Be aware, however, that such presentation requires careful execution. A person using his or her weak hand alone to draw from a crossdraw holster or holster purse mounted on the weak-side shoulder will have to be conscious of always keeping the gun pointed in a safe direction. In addition, the hand and wrist position required makes it awkward to access the gun. Experiment with your own handgun concealment device to determine if weak-hand-only access is possible, and if so, what technique is best.

In addition to practicing strong- and weak-hand-only presentation techniques, you should also familiarize yourself with one-handed techniques for reloading and clearing stoppages. Such advanced techniques are beyond the scope of the current work, but are taught at some shooting schools, and described in many works on defensive shooting (see Appendix D, Information and Training Resources). Such techniques should be practiced only with an empty gun, and with dummy ammunition.

CHAPTER 23

POINT SHOOTING

Much of this book is devoted to aimed-fire shooting techniques in which the sights are aligned to achieve a hit. Aimed fire is the best overall technique to use in most instances, as it is the surest way of making an accurate shot. Aimed fire is not the only defensive shooting technique you should know, however. An attack can occur so quickly and at such close range that you must shoot before sight alignment can be achieved. In such a situation, point shooting may be preferred.

Fig. 205. Shooter demonstrating point shooting technique

Point shooting is a defensive shooting technique used at close range in which you extend the firearm forward below the level of the eyes, align the body with the target, and aim the gun using your body's own kinesthetic sense as well as the position of the gun in your peripheral vision. Your kinesthetic sense is your awareness of the position of every part of your body in relation to every other part. This sense enables you to point your finger accurately at an object even though you cannot see your hand, or to touch your fingertips to your nose with your eyes closed. With practice, your kinesthetic sense will allow you to point your handgun accurately at a target.

Your peripheral vision also contributes to accurate point shooting. One of the major differences between aimed fire and point shooting is that, in the latter technique, your visual focus is on the target, not the sights. Nonetheless, your extended gun is visible in your peripheral vision, and you are thus aware of its alignment with the target.

ADVANTAGES AND LIMITATIONS OF POINT SHOOTING

The major advantage of the point shooting technique is speed of presentation. It takes precious time to raise the gun to your eye level, acquire the sights, align them with each other and then finally align them with the target. With a close-range attacker, you will not have that much time. Simply extending the gun forward and pointing it at the target is much faster. Remember that the gun is held below the level of your eyes when you're employing point shooting.

Point shooting's only major limitation is simply that it is a less accurate firing technique than aimed fire. This, in turn, restricts its use to close-range confrontations, usually of 15 feet or less.

THE POINT SHOOTING TECHNIQUE

Point shooting can be performed using a one-handed or two-handed grip; each technique has strengths and limitations. The one-handed point shooting technique is generally faster than the technique requiring a two hand hold. Furthermore, it allows the weak hand to remain free to ward off a weapon wielded by an arm's length attacker, to employ a flashlight, or to steady your balance when you're on uncertain ground. In addition, the one-handed technique can be used with virtually any body position. The two-handed point shooting technique, on the other hand, has the advantages of greater recoil control, decreased arm fatigue when holding the gun for extended periods, and better handgun retention.

To perform the one-handed point shooting technique from the holster, start by facing the target with the feet approximately shoulder width apart. The knees are slightly bent and the feet are roughly on a line perpendicular to the direction of the target. The feet may be somewhat staggered, however, if this is more comfortable.

With the handgun in the holster and the body facing the target, the strong hand first sweeps aside the covering clothing to access the gun, and achieves a proper grip on the grip frame. Simultaneously the weak hand is brought to the chest.

The handgun is next withdrawn from the holster, rotated toward the target, and extended forward. Ideally, the gun hand, wrist and arm should all be fairly straight and aligned with the target, and the gun should be situated roughly at the center of the body below eye level. Positioned at the center of the body, the gun is directly in front of the face, and its alignment with the target can be easily seen in the peripheral vision. The gun is fired as soon as you sense you are aligned with the target.

The two-handed point shooting technique from a holster is performed in much the same way as the one-handed techniques, with the exception that

Fig. 206. Two-handed point shooting technique with a hip holster. The handgun is accessed (A), gripped (B) and pulled from the holster and rotated toward the target (C) in the normal manner. The weak hand joins the strong hand (D) and the handgun is extended toward the target with the sights just below eye level (E). The shooter's kinesthetic sense and peripheral vision are used to align the handgun with the target.

the weak hand joins the strong hand before the gun is extended toward the target.

The point shooting technique can be adapted for use with other carry modes as well. From a front-mounted fanny pack or a shoulder purse hung over the weak-side shoulder, the handgun is withdrawn from the pack or purse in the usual way, and is extended forward and fired as soon as it is aligned with the target. Care must be taken during rotation to keep the muzzle pointed in a safe direction. The handgun will still be extended from the center of the body toward the target. A similar technique is used when the handgun is worn in the crossdraw position, or in a shoulder holster.

Whether the handgun is presented from a holster, holster purse or fanny pack, the one-handed point shooting technique has the additional advantage of allowing effective shooting even when the body and feet are not square to the target. Whether the

Fig. 207. View from front, showing how gun is below line of sight in point shooting technique.

Fig. 208. Two-handed point shooting technique from a fanny pack. With the body strongly bladed away from the target, the handgun is first accessed (A) and then pulled and rotated toward the target (B). The hands join and extend the gun toward the target with the sights below eye level (C).

strong side of the body is bladed either away from or toward the target, the technique is the same: the gun is extended with the strong hand toward the target, positioned below eye level and directly in front of the face. With this positioning, the head does not have to be tilted to see the gun clearly in the peripheral vision.

DEVELOPING THE POINT SHOOTING TECHNIQUE

To learn point shooting, first start with an empty gun in the holster in your prescribed dry-fire practice area. As you practice presentation, start slowly to ensure your mastery of the proper sequence of events. As with all presentation techniques, always make sure that your trigger finger does not contact the trigger, and the gun's safety is on, until the gun is pointing at your target.

When practicing point shooting with live ammunition, safety must always be your first priority. Go slowly at first, making sure that each step is properly executed.

Even when you can execute a fast, smooth, safe draw from the holster to a point firing position, you may still have difficulty in hitting even a close-range target consistently. Trigger control is often the problem in such circumstances, so make sure you are not flinching, jerking the trigger or dipping the gun in anticipation of recoil. Also review the basics of a shooting stance and shooting position, focusing on aspects having the most relevance for point shooting, such as grip and body alignment. In practice, try point shooting without first drawing the gun. Start from a one-handed low ready position and quickly raise the gun to the proper position. With enough practice, your body and brain will learn the hand, wrist and arm position that produces hits when point shooting, and will coordinate that with the draw movement.

Also practice point shooting with the strong side of the body turned both toward and away from the target. In a sudden close-range confrontation, the threat may come from any direction; you will not always have the time to align your feet and body so that they are square with the target. For most people, the most awkward position is with the strong side turned away from the target and the gun brought across the chest to assume the proper position. Just as you can accurately point your finger at an object regardless of your body alignment, so, too, can you learn to point shoot accurately in different positions.

To build accuracy, start with the target at a distance of about six feet. When you can keep all your shots on an 8 1/2" X 11" sheet of typing paper at that distance, move the target back a bit. Your groups will open up; slow down until all your shots again are contained on the sheet of paper. Repeat this process until you can use the point shooting technique quickly and accurately.

The proper gun position for accurate point shooting can also be learned through the use of laser training and sighting devices. Some of these are cartridge-shaped devices that fit in the handgun's chamber and emit a beam of laser light along the axis of the bore when they are struck by the gun's firing pin. Others are used for sighting the gun, and consist of a switchable laser that is mounted in the handgun's grip or guide rod, or in a unit that affixes to the trigger guard. Properly adjusted, all of these units will put a dot of laser light where the gun's bullet will strike, helping you to improve point shooting accuracy without expending live ammunition.

CHAPTER 24

INSTINCTIVE SHOOTING

Some violent confrontations take place so suddenly and at such close range that there is neither time nor space to use either the aimed fire or point shooting techniques. Under these conditions, the instinctive shooting technique is employed.

Instinctive shooting is a one-handed shooting technique that allows the fastest possible response to a threat at arm's distance. Instinctive shooting is a technique specially geared to hip holster carry, though it can be adapted for use by those using holster purses, fanny packs, and even crossdraw and shoulder holsters.

THE INSTINCTIVE SHOOTING TECHNIQUE

Unlike either aimed fire or point shooting, in instinctive shooting the gun is not extended in front of the body, and is not seen in the peripheral visual field. It is fired from a position alongside the hip, after the gun is rotated toward the target just after clearing the holster. With practice, it is possible to use instinctive shooting to hit a target roughly 8 1/2 by 11 inches at two to six feet.

The instinctive shooting technique involves most of the same basic steps as are used to perform other presentation techniques. (NOTE: The following detailed description is based on carry of the handgun in a hip holster. Modifications of the technique to accommodate other carry modes will be described later.) With the handgun in the holster and the strong side bladed away from the assailant, the strong hand first sweeps aside the covering clothing to access the gun, and achieves a proper grip on the gun. Simultaneously, the weak hand is brought to the chest. During an actual close-range defensive

Fig. 209. Shooter demonstrating instinctive shooting technique.

Fig. 210. Defender using instinctive shooting against arm's length assailant.

encounter, the weak hand may be employed to block a knife or club.

The handgun is next withdrawn from the holster, rotated toward the target, and fired just as soon as you feel that it is aligned with the target. This sequence of motions should take only a fraction of a second. The handgun may be kept at the hip for immediate follow-up shots, or may be extended forward into a ready position or a shooting position suitable for aimed fire.

Special consideration must be taken when using the instinctive shooting technique with a semiautomatic pistol against a close-range attacker. If the pistol is held at the hip, it should be angled slightly outward to prevent the slide from contacting the body and causing a gun stoppage. Also, the muzzle of the gun should not contact the assailant's body; this may push the slide out of battery, preventing the gun from firing.

The instinctive shooting technique may be adapted for use with other carry modes as well. When the gun is drawn from a front-mounted fanny pack or a shoulder purse hung over the weak-side shoulder, the

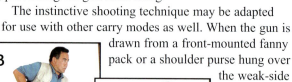

Fig. 211. Instinctive presentation technique: A, accessing the gun, weak hand on chest; B, pulling gun from holster; C, clearing the holster; and D, full rotation toward target, at which point the gun may be fired if necessary.

handgun is withdrawn from the pack or purse in the usual way, with the strong side sharply bladed away from the threat. Once the handgun is withdrawn from the pack or purse, it is rotated forward and fired as soon as it is aligned with the target. This will usually place the handgun in front of the abdomen instead of alongside the hip. With this firing position, special care must be taken during practice sessions to always keep the muzzle pointed in a safe direction.

Fig. 212. Left, defender bladed away from threat with fanny pack brought across body. Right, defender with gun withdrawn from holster purse and aimed at target.

Fig. 213. Defender with handgun in instinctive shooting position, using weak hand to ward off assailant.

A similar technique is used when the handgun is worn in the crossdraw position. The body should be turned almost 90 degrees away from the target; this puts the handgun in a position in which it is almost pointing at the attacker as soon as it is drawn from the holster. As with the other variations on the instinctive shooting technique, the gun may be fired as soon as it is rotated into alignment with the target.

The instinctive shooting technique offers the advantage of a speedy first shot—important when your attacker may only be an arm's length away. Additionally, when you are shooting instinctively, the weak hand is free to ward off a knife or club, hold a flash-

light and so on.

Note that when the strong side of the body is sharply bladed away from the assailant, the handgun may be presented from a fanny pack, holster purse or even a crossdraw holster so that it is pointing at the attacker almost as soon as it is drawn.

Fig. 214. When holding a semi-automatic pistol at the hip, cant the gun outward to prevent it from contacting the body and jamming the gun.

DEVELOPING THE INSTINCTIVE SHOOTING TECHNIQUE

Use dry-firing to develop the basic instinctive shooting technique. Start with an an unloaded gun in the holster in your prescribed dry-fire practice area. Go slowly initially to ensure your mastery of the proper sequence of events, then slowly increase your speed. As with all presentation techniques, always make sure that your trigger finger does not contact the trigger, and the gun's safety is on, until the gun is pointing in the direction of the target.

When practicing instinctive shooting with live ammunition, safety must always be your first priority, so you

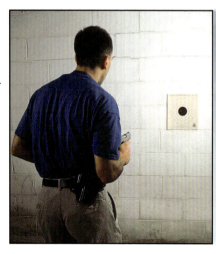

Fig. 215. Dry-fire instinctive shooting practice.

should again go very slowly initially. To promote accuracy, start by firing from the hip without first drawing the gun. With enough practice, your body and brain will learn the hand, wrist and arm position that produces hits when shooting from the hip.

Once you can reliably hit an 8 1/2" by 11" sheet of paper at three feet by shooting from the hip, you can then move to the next level: starting with the gun holstered. Again, you should seek to keep all your hits on an 8 1/2" by 11" target at three feet. When you achieve this, move the target back a bit. Your groups will open up; slow down until all your shots again are contained on the sheet of paper, then gradually increase the speed. Repeat this process until you can use the instinctive shooting technique quickly and accurately at three yards.

As with point shooting, laser training and sighting devices can help you to learn the proper gun position for accurate fire from the hip. See Chapter 23: Point Shooting for a more detailed description of these devices and how they can be used for handgun marksmanship training.

CHAPTER 25

ENGAGING MULTIPLE TARGETS

Studies of contemporary patterns of criminal behavior have revealed an increasing trend for criminals to work in groups rather than alone. In some cases, this may be related to the growing prevalence of criminal street gangs. Whatever the reason, citizens should be prepared to deal with two or more assailants.

DEFENDING AGAINST MULTIPLE ATTACKERS

There are many scenarios in which you may be threatened by multiple attackers. The most clear-cut is when you are directly confronted by two or more persons. Unfortunately, criminals don't always operate in such a straightforward manner. For example, it is not uncommon for a pair of muggers to split up, one distracting you from the front while the other sneaks up on you from the rear to strong-arm you.

Often the way in which multiple assailants will choose to attack depends upon their criminal intent. As was just described, some muggers or purse-snatchers split up to better take advantage of stealth or surprise. On the other hand, a gang may confront you directly as a group. In any life-threatening situation, however, you need to be aware that there may be additional attackers outside your immediate field of view.

This reality re-emphasizes the importance of a high level of awareness outside your home. The greater your level of awareness, the more readily you will perceive real or potential threats to your safety. And the earlier such threats are

Fig. 216. Multiple assailants.

identified, the more time you have to both plan an appropriate course of action and to scan the area for potential trouble.

Controlling the Encounter

The importance of controlling an encounter is even more critical when dealing with multiple attackers. In situations in which a single assailant will be deterred by the presentation of a firearm and flee, multiple assailants may be encouraged by each other's presence or incited by peer pressure to attack even when they know you are armed.

As with a single attacker, the best way to deal with a violent encounter with multiple attackers is to avoid it altogether by being aware of the threat far enough in advance to evade it or flee from it. When this is not possible, however, you can take steps to control an encounter with multiple assailants by employing several common-sense principles.

Don't Let Your Attackers Get Too Close. Keeping a threat at a distance is even more important when you're dealing with several attackers. The closer your assailants are, the more easily they can distract you and make it harder for you to defend yourself. Even when two or more individuals represent only a potential threat, as a group of young men loitering in a mall parking lot, you should compensate by extending your threshhold distance for the *Alert* stage of awareness. For example, if you have estab-

Fig. 217. Armed defender attempting to keep multiple assailants at a distance.

lished that a single stranger approaching you within 20 feet constitutes a potential threat, you should extend that range to 30 feet for a group of strangers.

Don't Get Distracted By One Attacker. One tactic used by two or more attackers is for one of them to distract you in some way while the other attacks from another direction.

Avoid focusing exclusively on one member of any group that confronts you. Develop the habit of shifting your focus briefly from one member of the group to the next, and use your peripheral vision to remain alert to the position of each person in the group.

Once you have identified a group that constitutes a potential or real threat, keep track of the members of the group; anyone who quietly disappears may be circling around behind you. If escape from the situation is not possible, back up against a wall, vehicle, etc. to prevent a rear attack.

Fig. 218. Defender distracted by one assailant while a second approaches from the rear.

Keep Your Assailants in a Line. When two or more criminals are preparing to mount an attack, they will often approach you somewhat spread apart. This spreads your visual focus over a wide arc, diluting it,

and makes it easier for all your assailants to attack at once. If possible, move so that two or more of the aggressors are in line with each other relative to your line of sight. In this way, the aggressor in front will block the attack of the one behind him.

Fig. 219. Defender keeping two attackers in line relative to his line of sight.

Determining the Order of Engagement

Successfully engaging multiple targets is not just a mechanical shooting skill: it also involves split-second decision-making. Remember that most attacks occur very quickly, and often with little or no warning. Thus, you may only have a heartbeat in which to decide which assailant presents the greatest threat to you.

As with many other aspects of defensive handgun use, determining the proper order of engagement of multiple assailants is a matter of subjective judgement. Each situation will be different. In some confrontations, all your assailants may be armed; in others, only one may hold a weapon.

Fig. 220. Two assailants at different distances and with different weapons--which to engage first?

Sometimes your attackers will be close together; at other times, they will be separated and at different distances.

In general, the assailant who represents the greatest immediate threat to you should be engaged first. This may not always be the assailant who is armed with a gun. A criminal rapidly approaching you with a knife at a distance of 15 feet is more of a threat to you than one 30 feet away with a gun in his waistband, and a man at arm's length with an upraised baseball bat is more dangerous than either.

In most instances, the closest armed assailant represents the greatest danger to your safety.

Armed and Unarmed Assailants

Not every attack will involve armed assailants. You may encounter a group consisting of both armed and unarmed aggressors, or you may be confronted by two or more persons lacking weapons altogether. Whether or not you use deadly force in such situations will depend upon a realistic assessment of the threat that these persons represent.

It is often difficult to legally justify the use of a deadly weapon against an unarmed person; such a person is not usually considered a threat to life or limb. In the case of multiple assailants, however, the potential danger is greatly increased, particularly if the attackers are larger, younger or stronger than you. For example, a frail, elderly person could easily succumb to an assault by several unarmed young men. The legal standard is the "Reasonable Man" standard: if an imminent attack by unarmed persons is likely, in the eyes of a reasonable person, to result in death or serious injury, the intended victim may be justified in using deadly force in self-defense.

Number of Rounds Required to Stop the Threat

It has been stated previously in this book that you should engage an attacker with as many rounds as necessary to stop the threat. However, during an attack by multiple assailants, you do not have the luxury of waiting to see if one attacker is stopped before turning to the others.

The number of shots you take at each target is a judgement call that depends upon many factors, including the caliber and capacity of your defensive handgun, your level of skill with your handgun, the number of attackers, and the distance to each.

Fig. 221. Defender with five-shot revolver facing five assailants--no margin for error!

Defensive shooting experts frequently recommend firing two quick shots (often called an "accelerated pair") at each target, on the theory that two hits are more likely to stop a threat than one. This is a particularly important consideration if your defensive handgun is chambered for a relatively low-powered cartridge, such as the .22 LR or .25 ACP, which is not likely to rapidly stop an aggressor with a single shot. More shots may also be required when the danger to life or limb is even more immediate and extreme, such as with an armed assailant at arm's length; two or more well-placed shots will usually stop such a threat faster than a single shot, regardless of caliber.

Accelerated-pair proponents point out that it takes virtually no longer to achieve two hits than one. With practice, just about any shooter can learn to hit the target twice at 21 feet with an interval of less than a quarter of a second between the two shots.

Firing a rapid pair at each assailant is not always advisable, however. With four assailants and a two-shot interval of .25 second, firing rapid pairs delays your engagement of the fourth target by .75 second. This may not sound like much time, but it is enough for an attacker standing 10 feet away to reach you with a knife blade, or to go from a ready position to a firing position with a handgun.

Furthermore, accelerated pairs may be impractical with a low-capacity handgun. If you carry a five-shot revolver and you are assaulted by four criminals, an attempt to engage each with two shots will cause you to run out of ammunition before you engage all the targets.

It is impossible to come up with an absolute rule regarding the number of shots that should be fired at each of several assailants. However, a general guideline might be to put a single hit on each target as quickly as possible, with those targets representing a greater, more immediate threat receiving two hits. Then quickly observe the targets and direct your fire at those targets that still constitute a deadly threat.

ENGAGING MULTIPLE TARGETS

Probably the single most important factor in effectively engaging multiple targets is the ability to swiftly achieve a hit on each identified threat. Most criminals do not begin their attack from across the street; they will usually get as close to you as they can before exhibiting overt signs of aggression. Thus, you will have a very brief period of time in which to try to stop each of several deadly threats. You must be able to draw quickly to engage the aggressor posing the greatest immediate danger, and then immediately shift your fire to the remaining attackers.

Fig. 222. When confronted with these attackers, it is easy to focus on the club-wielding assailant on the right and ignore the gun-carrying criminal on the left.

When engaging multiple targets, you should generally try to align your natural point of aim (NPA) with a spot roughly midway between the left- and right-most targets. This allows you to engage the targets in either direction with the least possible disturbance of the NPA.

Reducing your target-to-target time will come only with practice. There are, however, a few techniques that can help you gain speed and accuracy more quickly.

First, visualize the order in which you will engage the targets. For example, if you are approached by three threatening, aggressive persons, determine the danger each one represents and mentally establish the sequence in which you would engage them.

Second, when you have fired your last shot at a target, immediately go to the next target. This may seem obvious, but many shooters will wait to see the sights settle back into alignment, or will look for bullet strikes, before switching to the next target. You are not likely to see bullet strikes in any event, so don't bother to look for them. Trust your own shooting ability.

Finally, don't go too fast. Remember to stop the gun at each target; it is next to impossible to hit anything with the gun's sights moving through the target area. (The only exception to this is a situation in which the target is moving, and you must swing the gun laterally to track the target.)

One final thought. Sometimes your first shot will cause some or all of the attackers to turn and flee. You must develop the ability to recognize when an attacker is still a threat and when he has given up or is trying to run away, as well as the target discipline to hold your fire when deadly force is no longer warranted.

PRACTICING TO ENGAGE MULTIPLE TARGETS

The first requirement for developing skill in engaging multiple targets is to have access to a shooting range where multiple target arrays can be set up. Ideally, you should be able to set up targets from around three feet to as much as 50-75 feet.

Vary the target setups to build real-world shooting scenarios. Don't just put out three targets of the same size at the same height and distance; your attackers probably won't space themselves out so evenly. Put one at 10 feet, one at 15 feet and one at 25 feet, at different heights. Use partial targets to represent assailants behind cover. Try mixing different types of targets—for example, using 10" paper plates, 6" red fluorescent dots, NRA Action Pistol (Bianchi Cup) targets, and IPSC targets—in the same array.

Fig.223. Target array for practicing the engagement of multiple targets.

This will add an element of visual confusion, and will improve both your shooting and your power of concentration.

Learn to use the firing technique that is most appropriate to the target size and distance. While aimed fire should be used for shots on partial or relatively distant targets, there are faster techniques for engaging close-range threats. For example, a full-size Bianchi Cup target at four feet can be engaged by instinctive shooting, while a similar target at six to 12 feet should be shot with a point shooting technique.

Don't establish set patterns of target engagement. For example, don't get in the habit of always engaging multiple targets in left-to-right or right-to-left order; vary the selection of the first target to be shot. Also, vary the number of rounds that you fire at each.

More realistic training can be achieved by incorporating an element of surprise in your practice. For this you will need a shooting partner; a shooting timer is a desirable but not essential tool. Use at least three NRA Action Pistol targets, each with its own stand. With your handgun holstered and unloaded, face 180 degrees away from the target area while your partner moves the targets to different distances and positions. To add the element of decision-making to this type of practice, he or she can affix a life-size cutout of a knife or gun to one or more of the targets; this will indicate the level of threat that each target represents. After positioning the targets, your partner returns to a position behind the firing line. Load your gun and, on signal, turn 180 degrees and engage the targets. Just as in real life, you will face targets in a new and unfamiliar situation, and you will be forced to make decisions regarding the order of engagement, the shooting technique used, and the number of rounds you fire at each.

CHAPTER 26

ENGAGING TARGETS AT EXTENDED RANGE

Police statistics show that most attacks, whether unarmed or armed, take place at very close range (21 feet or less). Common sense bears this out; even the most inexperienced criminal understands that starting his attack from a distance gives his victim time to flee, call for help, or take other defensive measures. Thus, the bulk of your defensive shooting training should take place at a range of around 21 feet or less. There may be occasions, however, when you could face a deadly threat at 10, 15 or 25 yards, or an even greater distance. Your training and practice should prepare you for these occasions.

LEGAL CONSIDERATIONS

Under some conditions, using deadly force to defend yourself against a distant attacker can become a legal issue.

In any court proceeding that may follow your use of deadly force in self-

Fig. 224. To shoot or not to shoot? You may not always be justified in using deadly force against a distant threat, even if they are brandishing a weapon.

Fig. 225. Use of deadly force in self-defense at a distance may be justified when the assailant is armed with a rifle or shotgun.

defense, it may be difficult to justify shooting a criminal who attacks you from a distance. Remember that you may use deadly force against an attacker only when two conditions are met: he must represent an imminent threat to life or limb, and he must be capable of causing death or serious injury. The more distant your attacker, the harder it can be to satisfy both these conditions in the eyes of a judge or jury.

For example, when a person at arm's length pulls a knife from his waistband and screams, "I'm going to kill you!," there is little doubt that the danger is immediate and real; your use of deadly force in self-defense is clearly justified. Move that same attacker 50 feet away, and the situation becomes much less clear-cut. A knife-wielding attacker that distant, it could be argued, does not constitute an imminent threat, as you may be able to flee and avoid a confrontation altogether. Even when your assailant is armed with a handgun, he likely will be seen as constituting less of an actual threat if he is distant than if he is close.

Generally, you would be justified in using deadly force against a distant assailant under two conditions: first, if he constituted an imminent threat to your life or limb (or that of some other innocent victim); or, second, if failing to engage the assailant at that distance would substantially increase the likelihood that he would cause death or serious bodily injury.

Fig. 226. A fit, determined attacker even 30 feet away may be able to reach his victim before a shot can be fired in self-defense.

The first condition is fairly obvious and intuitive. An attacker firing at you with, say, a carbine at a distance of 50 yards constitutes a real and immediate threat that would likely justify your use of deadly force (if flight or seeking cover was not safely possible). The second condition applies only in certain specific situations; determining which situations apply requires a real-world understanding of how attacks unfold.

For example, an armed attacker some 30 feet away may not seem, at first look, to constitute an imminent threat. Some people might question your response if you engaged such an assailant with your handgun. They may claim that you had plenty of time to flee, or that you should have waited until the assailant was closer before deciding to use deadly force. While these claims may seem reasonable, they do not hold up under scrutiny.

A 30-foot distance between you and a person armed with a knife or club may indeed give you the opportunity to retreat in safety—but not always. If you are confronted by a person who is merely posturing with a weapon, your retreat may be interpreted as the gesture of fear or submission that he was seeking, and an attack will not ensue. On the other hand, if that person is actually intent upon harming you, 30 feet probably isn't enough space to guarantee a safe retreat. Keep in mind that most violent crimes are committed by young males, who as a group are generally more physically fit than the rest of the population. Even with a 30-foot head start, it is unlikely you could outrun a young, fit, armed criminal who was truly intent upon inflicting harm. In that kind of situation, flight can actually increase your chances of injury or death.

Fig. 227. Defender utilizing cover.

The assertion that you should wait until your assailant approaches before choosing to use deadly force is also unrealistic. Many people can easily cover 30 feet in two seconds or less, which is uncomfortably close to the time required for the average person to present a defensive handgun and fire a shot. Remember, too, that a single shot may not stop the threat.

Deciding to employ deadly force against an attacker at extended range is thus a judgement call that is based upon the ability of your attacker, the type of weapon he is armed with, the distance between you, the likelihood of being able to retreat or flee in safety, your own shooting ability and many other factors.

FIRING AT EXTENDED RANGE

Once you have determined that retreat is not an option, use aimed fire to engage a distant threat. The technique for firing at extended range does not differ significantly from any other aimed fire technique. There are, however, additional techniques to maximize your survival in an actual violent encounter.

Fig. 228. Defender seeking cover.

Seek cover. If you're dealing with a distant attacker who is armed with a firearm, you should take the time to seek cover, as was discussed in Chapter 18: Utilizing Cover and Concealment Outside the Home.

Make yourself small. Your attacker may also take more deliberate aim; don't make it easy for him to see you by presenting a large target. Protect as much of your body as possible with the available cover; don't leave arms, legs, or shoulders protruding.

Fig. 229. Arned defender making himself small behind low cover.

If cover is not available, use a prone position. This will have two benefits: it will give you the smallest possible profile, and it will allow you to support your firing hand on the ground for greater accuracy.

Use available support. Whether or not you are able to seek cover, try to take advantage of all available support to steady your aim. Even objects that don't provide cover, such as a fence or car hood, can be used to provide support.

Take your time. This is the most important factor in shooting effectively at extended range. You must be more careful to observe the shooting fundamentals, particularly sight alignment, sight picture and trigger control. Concentrate on sight alignment and on trigger control.

Retreat to safety at the first opportunity. Fortunately, most encounters, both at close range and far, don't turn into gun battles. An attacker who comes under your return fire usually flees. If, upon being fired on, you take cover and carefully return fire, the attack will usually stop. You should always take any safe opportunity to flee yourself, either when you are first attacked or at any time thereafter.

PRACTICE AT EXTENDED RANGE

The two most important skills you should practice to prepare for extended-range confrontations are slowing down to make good shots and utilizing cover and support.

To develop the ability to slow down and shoot accurately, try placing two targets, one at very short range—no more than about 10 feet—and one at 60 to 75 feet. Engage the close target first. Then, switch your focus to the distant target; this will require a conscious effort to slow down. Misses or poor hits will indicate that you are still going too fast. When you can use the proper speed to get a single good hit on each target, fire accelerated pairs at both. Not only will you require more time to fire the first accurate shot at the distant target; you will also find that the interval between

Fig. 230. Proper use of the handgun's sights is essential for extended-range accuracy.

Fig. 231. Shooter bracing weak-hand arm against cover for support in extended-range shooting.

each shot of the pair will also lengthen.

Develop the habit of immediately seeking cover or support when you are shooting at a distant target. Employ the techniques presented in Chapter 19: Presentation and Fire from Different Positions, and Chapter 20: Presentation, Movement and Fire from Different Positions. Make use of objects of various types, such as a trash can or standing barricade, to simulate both high and low cover.

Don't forget to also do some drills with no cover available at all. In such drills, you should practice quickly assuming a prone firing position. Be sure to take advantage of the natural support that the ground provides.

Fig. 232. Prone shooting is a critical extended-range skill.

CHAPTER 27

ENGAGING TARGETS IN LOW LIGHT CONDITIONS

As has been pointed out earlier, most criminal attacks occur in low light. Even during daylight hours, criminals prefer to practice their predations in dark areas such as unlit parking garages and shadowy walkways between buildings.

It is therefore likely that if you are involved in a violent attack, it will probably take place under conditions of reduced light. As a consequence, you need to be able to shoot accurately and effectively under such conditions.

PRESERVE YOUR NIGHT VISION

When your eyes are in no or low light for an extended period of time, your visual sense will accommodate to the absence of light. This accommodation is called night vision, and it allows you to detect objects you would be unable to see under ordinary conditions. You experience this kind of vision just about every night, when you go to bed and your lights go out. At first everything is dark and indistinct; but after a few moments you begin to pick out the shapes of objects.

If you face a defensive encounter under reduced-light conditions, especially at night, you must take steps to preserve your night vision. First and foremost, avoid looking at bright sources of light. Shield your eyes from car headlights, streetlights and so forth. Exposing your eyes to such light sources will reduce your night vision—and once it is gone, it takes several minutes to get it back.

Among the bright sources of light you should avoid is the flash of your own ammunition. Exposure to bright muzzle flash is just as detrimental to preserving

Fig. 233. At night, a bright muzzle flash can reduce your low-light accommodation, or night vision.

night vision as bright sunlight. Many manufacturer's produce defensive ammunition utilizing low-flash powders; your local gun shop should be able to recommend a variety of brands.

AVOID LOW-LIGHT SITUATIONS

Fig. 234. Attacks are much more likely to occur under low-light conditions, such as this empty parking lot at night..

One of the best ways of avoiding the problems associated with low-light shooting is to simply keep to well-lit areas, whether walking or driving. Avoid low-light situations whenever possible. Stay out of dark alleys and streets; at night, park your car under, or near to, a streetlamp; and avoid taking shortcuts through poorly-lit areas. Not only will you escape being faced with a low-light situation; you will also be more likely to avoid an attack altogether.

SIGHTS FOR LOW-LIGHT SITUATIONS

Several types of handgun sights are available to improve sight visibility in low light. The simplest type incorporates high-

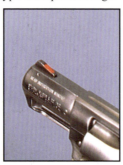

Fig. 235. The visibility of the sights in low-light conditions can be improved by with tritium night sights (A), fluorescent orange paint (B), or a white dot on the front sight and a white outline around the rear notch (C).

visibility white, yellow or red painted dots, bars or sight outlines. Many shooters apply these colors to their sights themselves, using commonly available paint (often paint used for model airplanes). These improvements tend to work best in normal or only slightly reduced light.

Another type of high-visibility handgun sight utilizes short lengths of colored fiber-optic plastic. Each fiber-optic piece picks up light and concentrates it along its axis; this makes the cut end of each piece glow brightly. As with colored paint, fiber-optic sights work best in normal-to slightly low-light.

The most effective type of sight for low light is the "night sight," which incorporates small capsules of luminous tritium (a substance that emits a low level of harmless radiation) into the front blade and rear sighting plane, typically in three-dot, straight eight or bar-dot patterns. Night sights are usually available in light green and amber colors; the front dot in a three-dot pattern is often given a different color to allow quicker centering between the rear dots. Tritium has a half-life of about 12 years, so tritium sights will typically need to be replaced about once a decade, or whenever the loss of luminosity becomes noticeable.

Unlike other types of high-visibility sights, night sights are visible in total darkness. Thus, in addition to aiding low-light aiming, tritium sights can also be used to locate the gun on a nightstand or in a drawer in conditions of total darkness.

When shooting in extreme darkness, it is usually impossible to use any but tritium night sights. Sometimes it is possible, however, to pick up the outline of both front and rear sights during the instantaneous light of the muzzle flash. This will allow you to check the alignment of even plain iron sights in total darkness. Note that none of the sights described in this section will help with target illumination or target identification.

LASER SIGHTS

Lasers (an acronym from Light Amplification through Stimulated Emission of Radiation) generate a beam of coherent light (usually red) that can be focused into a thin, non-diverging beam. Sights employing laser light are commonly mounted on handguns in one of three ways: contained in a special pair of grips, incorporated into a full-length guide rod, or mounted in a separate unit that attaches to the frame or trigger guard. Grip-mounted lasers are available for just about all semi-automatic pistols or revolvers, can be focused to align the beam with the iron sights, and are

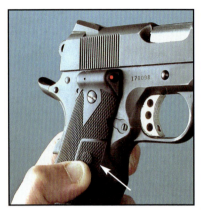

Fig. 236. Grip-mounted laser sight on an M1911-type handgun. Laser is activated by a pressure switch (arrow) embedded on either side of the grip.

usually turned on using a pressure switch that is integral with the grip. Lasers mounted in a guide rod are probably the least obtrusive, but are limited to semi-automatic handguns only. Least practical for the concealed carrier are "add-on" units that attach to some part of the gun, as such sights are bulky, easily knocked or nudged out of alignment, and prevent the gun from being carried in most standard concealment holsters. Such sights do have the benefit of low cost, however.

Laser lights allow the visual focus to be on the target, and, when properly aligned with the gun's sights, provide an accurate visible reference for where the gun is aimed. Thus, lasers can be especially effective when non-sighted shooting techniques (such as point and instinctive shooting) are employed. Additionally, some defensive shooting authorities claim that the distinctive glowing red dot from a laser beam, when seen by an assailant on his person, can act to stop or deter an attack.

Laser sights have potential disadvantages, however. When they are on, they can help an attacker pinpoint the location of the handgun and the person holding it; thus, laser sights can provide aiming assistance to both an armed citizen and a gun-wielding assailant. Also, some laser units may become misaligned or damaged if the gun is dropped, or disabled by exposure to moisture or solvents; and laser sights of all types are useless when the batteries are exhausted.

As noted in Chapter 24, Instinctive Shooting, laser sights can also be used as a dry-fire training aid to improve the accuracy of the kinesthetic feel used to achieve hits in the instinctive shooting technique.

FLASHLIGHTS

Flashlights are not utlized as sights, but are extremely useful in reduced-light situations in at least four ways. First, the illumination of a flashlight can be used to improve your low-light target identification. Before you

Fig. 237. Defensive flashlights come in a variety of styles and sizes.

consider using your firearm, you must determine whether an indistinct shape in the darkness is a potential attacker or merely an innocent bystander. Second, when moving at night, or even in poorly-lit areas in the daytime, a flashlight can help you discern obstacles and other hazards in your path. Third, the sudden burst of light from a powerful flashlight can disorient or even temporarily blind an assailant, and will neutralize his low-light visual accommodation. And finally, if you must shoot, a flashlight will give you a better view of both the target and your sights.

There is currently a wide variety of flashlights that can be used in conjunction with a handgun. Some are expressly designed for that purpose. Models vary in size and power. Older designs powered by alkaline batteries generally have the lowest light output, with lights using

Fig. 238. Defensive flashlights are generally activated by pushbutton switches on either the side (left) or end of the light body.

rechargeable nickel-cadmium (Ni-Cd) batteries being somewhat brighter. The highest light output in small lights is usually provided by modern models with lithium batteries.

As important as beam intensity intensity is beam uniformity. The best flashlights create a circle of light that is even and uniformly bright, with no dark spots. Some models allow for beam focus.

Light output is measured in lumens. As a broad generalization, lights that are to be used with your defensive handgun should generate at least 50 lumens. Some new designs generate as much as 500 lumens, a level of light intensity that can be effective in visually disabling an assailant.

Flashlight bodies are usually made of aluminum or a tough polymer, allowing them to be employed as a weapon in a close-range emergency situation. Defensive flashlights have pushbutton on-off switches on the side or end of the body, to accommodate the various methods of holding these lights when used in a shooting grip. Often these switches can be turned on momentarily by only partially depressing the button, producing a quick burst of light. This feature is important in a situation in which a prolonged beam may allow an assailant to easily target the armed citizen holding the light.

Fig. 239. A flashlight to be used in defensive situations can be carried in a pocket or in a belt-mounted holster. The latter allows easier and more consistent access.

Defensive flashlights can be carried in a pocket or, for better and more consistent access, in a holder that attaches to the belt on the weak side.

Any flashlight shares two of the disadvantages of laser lights: it depends upon batteries, and in total darkness, it can give away a defender's location and provide an aiming point for an armed assailant. Flashlights also have a single unique drawback, in that the additional complexity of carrying and using them in conjunction with a handgun is often simply not practical for many people, including knowledgeable and dedicated concealed carriers. Even a small flashlight creates additional concealment issues, and in the stress of a high-speed attack, it may simply be unrealistic to expect the average armed citizen to present his or her concealed firearm with one hand while acquiring a flashlight with the other, and then assume an effective firing stance utilizing both tools together.

This is not to say that a flashlight cannot be useful, even essential. When the armed citizen negotiates unfamiliar terrain at night, scans for threats after an attack has been stopped, or has advance warning of an attack, a flashlight can often be produced and used in a timely and effective manner.

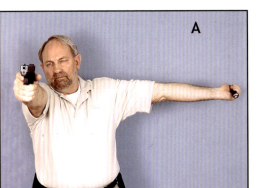
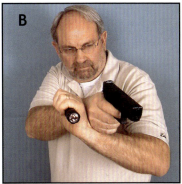

Fig. 240. Some of the best-known techniques for using a flashlight with a defensive handgun. The FBI method (A) places the flashlight out to the side, minimizing an assailant's opportunity to injure the defender by firing at the light. In the Harries method (B), the back of the weak hand pushes against the back of the strong hand, stabilizing the gun. A light with a switch mounted on its end works best with this technique. The Ayoob technique (C) places the strong and weak hands side by side, with the thumbs in alignment; a light with a side-mounted switch is preferred. The Rogers/Surefire technique (D) places the light between the first and second fingers of the weak hand, with its end-mounted button operated by squeezing the light against the palm. The weak hand joins the strong hand in a conventional two-hand hold. This technique was originally designed to be used with a Surefire flashlight, but can be used with any small light with an end-mounted pushbutton switch.

There are several widely-taught methods of incorporating a small flashlight into a one-handed or two-handed shooting stance, including the Ayoob, FBI, Harries and Rogers/Surefire methods. While the Harries and Rogers/Surefire are probably the most widely used, all have advantages under certain conditions. The choice of technique depends upon a number of factors, including the size and type of light, the situation in which it is used, and the type of shooting stance with which the armed citizen is most comfortable. For example, the Rogers/Surefire technique generally works only with a small light having an end-mounted pushbutton switch, while the Ayoob technique can be employed with both small and large flashlights having a side-mounted switch.

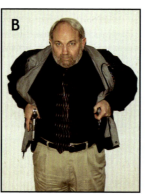

Fig. 241. To perform the Rogers/Surefire technique, access the light and gun simultaneously (A). Draw the gun (B) and rotate it toward the target while withdrawing the light and grasping it between the first and second fingers (C). Keep the light-carrying hand close to the chest. As the strong hand extends toward the target (D), it is joined by the weak hand (E) and extension is completed (F).

Whatever type of light, concealment method and firing stance you use, proper training and frequent practice are both critical, especially to prevent crossing the weak (flashlight) hand in front of the muzzle during presentation. The proper techniques of employing defensive flashlights are taught at many shooting schools.

TRAINING TO SHOOT ACCURATELY IN LOW LIGHT

The best way to learn to shoot in low light is simply to practice in low light. In some areas it may be possible to darken an indoor range for that purpose, or to shoot at an outdoor range past sundown.

Often, neither of these options is practical. It is possible to reasonably simulate low-light conditions by shooting while wearing sunglasses or, for a deeper darkness, welder's goggles.

Don't focus all your low-light training on simply shooting; also practice reloading and clearing stoppages. Since most defensive situation will take place under reduced-light conditions, most gun problems will, too.

When practicing low-light shooting, be especially conscious of gun safety. While wearing sunglasses or welder's goggles, or shooting in a darkened range, it can be easy to miss visual cues that would be seen otherwise.

Fig. 242. Welder's glasses may be used to safely simulate low-light conditions during practice.

PART VII

CONCEALED CARRY, SELF-DEFENSE AND THE LAW

CHAPTER 28

FIREARMS, SELF-DEFENSE AND THE LAW

We live in a society of laws—laws that impact on most areas of our lives. Gun ownership is one of the most heavily regulated of those areas. It is critical for the defensive gun owner to have at least a working knowledge of the local, state, and federal laws that govern the purchase, possession, transportation and transfer of firearms, as well as their use in defensive situations. Also essential is an understanding of the basic legal principles surrounding the use of deadly force in self-defense.

LEGAL REQUIREMENTS GOVERNING THE PURCHASE AND OWNERSHIP OF HANDGUNS

Nationwide, there are more than 20,000 federal, state and local laws regulating gun purchase and ownership. Many of these apply specifically to handguns. Outlined below are some of the provisions of the major gun laws currently in effect. It is the gun owner's responsibility to know, understand and obey all laws relating to firearm ownership and use that are in force in his or her jurisdiction.

Gun Control Act of 1968. This law, passed partially in response to the tragic assassinations of Martin Luther King, Jr. and Robert F. Kennedy, Jr., eliminated the mail order purchase of modern firearms (those made after 1898) and established a variety of classes of persons prohibited from owning or possessing a firearm. These prohibited persons include felons, those who use illegal drugs, those who have been committed to a mental institution, those who are not U.S. citizens and those who have renounced their U.S. citizenship.

Bureau of Alcohol, Tobacco, Firearms and Explosives (BATFE) Form 4473. All persons purchasing a firearm—whether it is a rifle, shotgun or handgun—from a federally licensed gun dealer must complete a BATFE Form 4473. This form contains information on the buyer, the serial number and description of the firearm or firearms purchased, and the name and address of the Federal Firearms License holder. Additionally, the Form

4473 has a section in which the prospective purchaser attests to whether he or she falls into any of the classes of persons prohibited from owning a firearm. Giving a false answer to any item on Form 4473 is a felony punishable by a fine or imprisonment.

Brady Law. This 1994 law was named for gun-control advocates James and Sarah Brady, who were instrumental in its adoption. In its initial form the law mandated a number of provisions for gun buyers, several of which have since expired. As of this writing, the Brady Law now requires a national computerized instant background check of all persons purchasing a firearm from a Federal Firearms License holder.

Violent Crime Control and Law Enforcement Act. This law, also known as the 1994 Crime Bill, prohibited the sale, transfer or possession of magazines for semi-automatic firearms having a capacity of more than 10 rounds. The law also contained a list of banned semi-automatic firearms (erroneously labeled as "assault weapons"), and established certain combinations of features (including, among others, pistol grips, flash suppressors and folding stocks) that may also make other firearms fall into the "assault weapon" category.

With the expiration of the 1994 Crime Bill in 2005, the abovementioned federal prohibitions against "assault weapons" and high-capacity magazines are no longer in effect. Nonetheless, some of the Crime Bill's provisions have been incorporated into the laws of several states, but there are still many other federal laws in effect such as those that govern the assembly of semiautomatic firearms from imported parts.

Lautenburg Amendment. This law, named for New Jersey Senator Ed Lautenburg, expands the list of persons prohibited from possessing firearms or ammunition to include anyone who has been found guilty of a misdemeanor crime of domestic violence. The prohibition also applies to persons under certain restraining orders. This far-reaching law is retroactive—that is, anyone who has ever been found guilty of, or who has pleaded guilty to such a crime, is subject to firearm forfeiture. The law also makes it a felony for anyone in the prohibited category to possess any firearms or ammunition.

State and Local Laws. In addition to federal laws, further restrictions are imposed by numerous state and local laws. For example, in some states a permit to purchase must first be obtained before a firearm can be bought.

Successful completion of the permit process may result in the issuance of a gun owner identification card.

Many states and municipalities also have enacted laws that prohibit or restrict certain classes of firearms based on type (such as semi-automatic pistols or so-called Saturday Night Specials), magazine capacity or other characteristics, sometimes resulting in a list of state-approved guns. Waiting periods and background checks prior to purchase, and registration of guns owned, are also required by law in some jurisdictions. And, of course, there are almost always fees accompanying the permits, background checks and registration applications. Specific legal requirements will vary for each different state, and also may vary among the counties and municipalities within a state.

Intrastate and Interstate Acquisition and Transfer. Generally speaking, there are two ways to acquire a firearm: from a federally licensed dealer, or from a private individual. Federally licensed dealers include gun shops, professional gunsmiths, and other businesses, such as hardware stores and pawn shops. Whenever you purchase a firearm through a federally-licensed dealer, you must meet the requirements of BATFE Form 4473, plus any additional restrictions imposed by state or local law.

In many states, the transfer of a firearm by a resident of that state to a resident of that state—whether as the result of sale, gift, loan, or bequest— is considered a simple property transaction between two private individuals, and need not go through a federally licensed dealer. In other states, some or all firearms transfers between individuals must go through a federally licensed dealer. Note that even in those states in which transfers between private citizens do not go through FFL holders, the seller still may not transfer a gun to an individual falling into any of the classes of persons prohibited by law from possessing a firearm.

Note also that, for legal purposes, transfer does not necessarily mean selling. Anytime you allow a person to possess one of your firearms—that is, have it under their physical or constructive control—you have, for that period of time, transferred the firearm to that person. Thus, depending upon your state's laws, allowing a person in a prohibited class to simply hold one of your guns in his or her hands (whether the gun is loaded or not) may constitute a transfer of possession, and thus may be illegal.

Interstate transfers of handguns always must go through federally licensed gun dealers, whether the transfer is between an individual and a gun shop, or between two individuals, in different states. If the transfer is between two individuals, the one transferring the gun may send it directly to the FFL holder in the recipient's state of residence, who will transfer it to the recipient. Alternatively, the person transferring the handgun may take it to an FFL holder in his or her state of residence, who will arrange to ship the gun to the FFL holder in the recipient's state of residence. In either case, the recipient will have to observe all the legal requirements, such as Form 4473 and Brady Law instant check provisions, that apply to a handgun sale.

Various jurisdictions may have additional laws regarding firearms sales and non-sale firearms transfers, such as gifts or bequests, as well as transfers to certain classes of people, such as minors.

Handgun Possession and Transportation. Legally, possession is defined as the holding or occupancy of a thing such that physical control can be exerted over it. Legal ownership, or title, is not a requirement for possession. Many different federal, state and local laws relate to handgun possession under various circumstances.

At the present time, federal law imposes few if any restrictions on possession in one's home, business or vehicle, or in public places. However, federal law does prohibit possession of a firearm in federal government offices or buildings, such as post offices, IRS offices and the like. Possession may also be prohibited or restricted in other areas, including (but not limited to) military bases, some federal lands (such as national parks), and school zones. Note that a state or local carry permit does not abrogate federal restrictions on gun possession on federal property.

Virtually all states and local jurisdictions have laws regulating firearm possession. The restrictions imposed by these laws vary considerably from jurisdiction to jurisdiction, and situation from situation. Your rights and obligations likely will vary depending upon whether you possess the firearm in your home, a temporary residence (such as a hotel or campground), or a vehicle. Even in your home or business, your specific rights may be contingent upon whether you are physically inside the structure, or outside on your own lawn or grounds. Moreover, your rights regarding possession on your person in public places will vary. Some states allow you to carry your handgun openly, without a permit; many others have a permit process if you wish to carry a concealed handgun, and other jurisdictions permit you to have your firearm on your person only if it is unloaded and locked in a case.

Many states, counties and municipalities also have laws prohibiting the possession of firearms in schools or government offices or buildings, similar to the federal laws previously mentioned.

Transporting a handgun within a jurisdiction is generally subject to that jurisdiction's laws regarding possession in public. If you hold a state concealed-carry permit, for example, you can usually carry a firearm in the passenger compartment of a vehicle without having to lock it up or otherwise make it inaccessible. Some states have specific laws regarding the transportation of hunting firearms to and from a game area. In other jurisdictions, you may legally transport your firearm in your vehicle only if it is unloaded, locked in a case and secured in a locked trunk or other inaccessible part of your vehicle, with ammunition in a separate inaccessible locked container. This is also the recommended method for carrying firearms in your vehicle on interstate (federal) highways.

Some states and other jurisdictions require the registration of any firearm located within their boundaries, even temporarily, or totally prohibit the possession of certain types of guns. The 1986 McClure-Volkmer Gun Owner's Protection Act exempts firearm owners who are transporting their arms interstate from the laws of such jurisdictions (as long as the gun owner is merely passing through the jurisdiction). The firearm should be locked in an inaccessible part of the vehicle as described above. Although the federal Gun Owner's Protection Act overrides state and local law, in practice a gun owner may still be harassed or arrested by overzealous local law enforcement officials who don't know about the federal law.

Fig. 243. Gun owner putting cased handgun into trunk of car to transport it.

Transporting a firearm on public transportation—a bus, train, subway or aircraft—is regulated both by applicable local, state and federal law, as well as any specific requirements of the transportation company or authority. If you are transporting the firearm within the boundaries of a state and have a state-issued concealed carry permit, you may be able to carry your gun on any mode of public transportation. The most notable exception to this is an airline flight. Only sky marshals and certain other types of law enforcement or security officers are allowed to carry firearms on their persons aboard commercial aircraft.

When transporting a firearm across state lines via public transportation, the firearm usually must be unloaded and locked in an approved case, and you must give the carrier written notice that a firearm or ammunition is being transported. This is also the procedure for transporting a firearm aboard any commercial airline. Other restrictions and procedures (such as a special check-in procedure) may also apply.

THE USE OF DEADLY FORCE IN SELF-DEFENSE

There are many legal definitions, theories and principles surrounding the use of deadly force for self-protection. It is beyond the scope of this chapter to discuss these in detail; only a brief outline of the major concepts can be presented. You are strongly advised to consult an attorney for a more thorough explanation of your rights and responsibilities in relation to armed self-defense in your jurisdiction.

The "Reasonable Man" Standard. In judging the legality of a person's conduct, it is often necessary to determine whether a party acted in a way that was appropriate or reasonable. This determination is often made by judging whether a hypothetical "reasonable man" would act in a similar way under the same conditions. By such a "reasonable man" standard, for example, shooting an intruder who approached you with a weapon despite your verbal warnings likely would be deemed justifiable, because the reasonable man would consider the intruder's actions to be immediately life-threatening.

Be aware that a judge or jury, in applying the "reasonable man" standard to an action, is making a judgment about a chain of events that occurred under stress and over the course of a few seconds or less. What may seem reasonable to you or to most people under the conditions of an immediate violent attack might be unreasonable to a jury sitting in the comfort and safety of a courtroom.

Use of Reasonable Force. The degree or amount of force you can use in defending yourself must be reasonable—that is, proportional to the level of threat presented. In rough terms, you can't use a gun to defend yourself from a slap in the face. A 300-pound, 30-year-old professional football player attacked by an unarmed 135-pound, 70-year-old man would not be justified in using deadly force to defend himself, due to the relatively low level of threat the smaller, older man represented to him. On the other hand, if the 70-year-old attacker was armed with a knife or gun, the football player might then be justified in using deadly force to defend himself (if certain other conditions are also met).

By law, you can sometimes use force in other circumstances—to protect your property from theft or vandalism, for example, or to remove a trespasser from your property. The amount of force you may legally use, however, must be only that which is required to obtain the desired result.

Use of Deadly Force. The justifiable use of deadly force is limited only to situations in which certain requirements are met. Although those requirements may vary somewhat in different jurisdictions, there are some fairly universal guidelines. Deadly force can only be used by an innocent victim of an attack, and only when that attack represents a threat of serious bodily harm or death; it cannot be used to defend property rights. This threat of serious bodily harm or death must be imminent (about to happen immediately) and within the ability of the attacker. In addition, in some situations, the victim of an attacker must first retreat (or attempt to do so if safely possible) before being able to utilize deadly force in self-defense.

Ability of an Attacker. An attacker is considered to represent a threat to life or limb only if they are actually capable of causing death or serious injury. In the sample situation presented earlier, a small, elderly, unarmed man generally would not be considered to have the ability to threaten the life or limb of a large, young, muscular man. Even if the elderly man

demonstrated the intent to kill the younger man (as by screaming, "I'll kill you!"), deadly force would generally not be justified in repelling his attack, as the hypothetical "reasonable man" would not consider him capable of following through on that intent.

Presence of an Imminent Threat. Another requirement for the use of deadly defensive force is that the threat of death or seri-

Fig. 244. This distant threat does not represent an imminent threat, and the use of deadly force is not justified.

ous bodily harm must be imminent—that is, about to occur immediately. A future threat to your life and limb does not generally justify the present use of deadly force. For example, if a person threatens, "Someday soon I'm going to catch you alone and blow you away," you cannot respond by immediately using deadly force against him—even if he is, say, a paroled murderer whom you know is fully capable of making good on his threat. You will be legally able to defend yourself with a deadly weapon only at the point that his threat becomes real and imminent.

Innocent Victim of Attack. For you to claim justifiable self-defense in your use of deadly force, you must not yourself have caused or incited your assailant's attack. For example, you cannot provoke a person into attacking you and then shoot him or her in self-defense. Nor can you respond to an attacker in a way that further incites or inflames him or her. For example, if you were to innocently step on another person's shoes, he might react by shoving you. You are not entitled to escalate the situation to the level of deadly force by using your firearm.

Duty to Retreat. In many self-defense situations, you have a duty to retreat from a confrontation before you can legally use deadly force to defend yourself. Duty to retreat simply means that you must attempt to

Fig. 245. In most jurisdictions, an armed citizen is required to retreat from an attack, if this can be done safely, before deadly force may be used. When facing a potential threat, you should be aware of available pathways to retreat (arrow).

physically escape or evade a confrontation if you can do so safely. You are not obligated to retreat if doing so will expose you to greater danger.

Most states require you to retreat from confrontations occurring in public. In many jurisdictions, however, you may not be obligated to retreat from an attacker in your own home or on your own property. Consult an attorney for the laws applicable in your area.

Brandishing. In many if not most jurisdictions, brandishing, or displaying your firearm in a threatening or aggressive manner, is illegal and may undermine your claim of legitimate self-defense. As a practical matter, if you brandish your firearm to deter an attacker, it may be unclear to both witnesses and law enforcement authorities exactly who is the aggressor and who is the victim.

Cessation of Threat. You are entitled to use deadly force against an attacker only as long as he presents a threat. Once the threat has ceased—

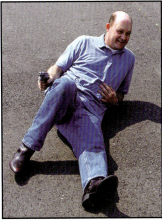

Fig. 246. When a threat or an attack has ceased (left), you are no longer permitted to use deadly force in self-defense. Deadly force may continue to be used, however, against an assailant who, though down, continues his attack (right).

as by their flight, surrender, or inability to continue the attack—so must your use of lethal force.

Castle Doctrine. This doctrine, derived from English common law and expressed in the familiar saying, "A man's home is his castle," gives you special rights in your own home that you may enjoy nowhere else. For example, in many jurisdictions you have no duty to retreat from an attacker in your own home. Also, in some jurisdictions, the very presence of an intruder in your home may allow you to treat him as a threat. Some jurisdictions also allow you to extend the Castle Doctrine beyond your home to include any place you might be domiciled for the night, such as a friend's house, hotel room, campground and so on. Other rights may also derive from the Castle Doctrine, depending upon the laws in your jurisdiction.

The above material is merely a partial overview of some of the many complex legal issues concerning firearm ownership, firearm use, and the employment of deadly force in self-defense. Every gun owner should seek additional information from an attorney familiar with the firearm and self-defense laws in his or her jurisdiction.

CHAPTER 29

LEGAL ASPECTS OF CONCEALED CARRY

In addition to the information presented in Chapter 28: Firearms, Self-Defense and the Law, you should also be familiar with certain other legal aspects relating to concealed handgun carry. Note that the information presented in this chapter is not meant to take the place of competent legal advice from an attorney familiar with the laws in your jurisdiction. You should consult such an attorney to learn the specific legal obligations that apply in your area.

Concealed Carry Permits. In almost all states allowing any type of concealed handgun carry, a carry permit is required. At the time of this writing, only Vermont allows its residents to legally carry a concealed firearm without first obtaining a permit to do so.

Concealed carry permits can be divided into two types: discretionary permits and shall-issue permits. Discretionary permits are so called because they are issued to certain persons at the individual discretion of a judge, police chief or other high public official.

State shall-issue concealed carry permits are required by state law to be issued to any resident meeting certain objective criteria (hence the name "shall-issue permits"). Although the specific criteria vary from state to state, shall-issue permits are typically issued to persons at least 21 years of age who have no criminal or mental health record. Often, applicants are also required to show evidence of firearm training and/or experience, such as a record of military service, a hunting license, or a certificate of completion from certain NRA firearm courses. It is also common in many but not all states to require fingerprints and/or a photograph from the applicant. A nominal fee must be submitted with the application, and several weeks normally elapse before the permit is issued.

Restrictions on Concealed Carry. A concealed carry permit does not give you an absolute right to carry a firearm anywhere and anytime you please. The concealed carry laws of almost all states contain restrictions on concealed carry. Again, the exact limitations vary among the states, but some generalizations can be made. Typically, concealed handguns are not allowed in churches; schools and school zones; police stations; post offices; local, state or federal government buildings, or buildings containing government offices; or establishments in which alcohol is served, such as bars, taverns, restaurants and the like. Carrying a firearm in violation of these restrictions is, at the very least, grounds for revocation of your carry permit, and may also cause criminal charges to be imposed against you.

Not only are there places in which you cannot carry a gun; there are also conditions under which you must not carry, such as when you have consumed alcoholic beverages.

Your right to carry will also be voided if you are indicted for a felony, subjected to certain court orders, or are convicted of a felony or certain misdemeanors.

In addition, be aware that many states have adopted a very tough prosecutorial stance regarding crimes in which a gun is even remotely involved. For example, if you should lose your temper in an argument and strike another person with your fist while you are carrying your defensive firearm, you may be charged with a more serious crime than you would have been if you had not been carrying a gun. The fact that you did not use your gun in the confrontation does not matter; you were armed.

Brandishing. Brandishing was briefly described in Chapter 28: Firearms, Self-Defense and the Law, but it deserves an expanded mention here. Brandishing was earlier defined as "displaying a firearm in a threatening or aggressive manner." Waving your firearm at a person with whom you are arguing—even in your own home—would obviously be brandishing. In most jurisdictions, brandishing is a crime punishable by a fine and/or a jail sentence.

If you display a firearm to deter an intruder—armed or not—in your own home, police, prosecutors and judges in most jurisdictions are unlikely to regard your actions as brandishing. Outside the home, however, you have much less leeway.

On the other hand, there is evidence that displaying a firearm under some circumstances may actually reduce your likelihood of being attacked. Research by University of Florida criminologist Gary Kleck, Ph.D., suggests that most of the annual 600,000 to 2.5 million defensive firearm uses do not involve the firing of a single shot. That is, in the vast majority of cases, the simple display of a firearm is sufficient to stop an attack or deter an attacker.

The decision to display a firearm to stop or deter an attack is a judgement call. You should not show your firearm to deter a person who simply might attack you, or who you merely find threatening; that may result in being charged with brandishing. You are justified in displaying a firearm only in those situations in which firing your handgun would also be justified—situations in which there is a real and imminent threat to your life or the lives of your family or other innocent persons.

You should understand, however, that even when you successfully stop an actual attack by displaying your firearm, you may still be charged with brandishing. Consult a lawyer who is familiar with the concealed carry laws in your jurisdiction for more information on brandishing.

Fig. 247. Armed citizen showing handgun to deter potential attackers.

Duty to Retreat. As discussed in the previous chapter, you will generally have a duty to retreat from a confrontation outside your home, if you can do so in safety. This duty is not always absolute, however; some states recognize exceptions to the duty to retreat. In other states, you may have a duty to retreat even in your own home. A lawyer who is familiar with the concealed carry laws in your jurisdiction can tell you more about your specific legal obligations.

As has been stated many times in this book, deadly force should be used only as a last resort, when other options, such as deterrence, avoidance or flight, are no longer available. If you use your defensive handgun against an attacker, one of the issues the investigating officers will want to resolve

is whether you could have avoided using deadly force by retreating. The same issue will be explored by a judge and/or a jury if criminal charges are filed against you, using the "Reasonable Man" ("Reasonable Person") standard. The judge or jury will try to determine whether a reasonable person, in the same circumstances, would have been able to safely retreat from the threat, or would have felt that there was no

Fig. 248. Citizen retreating before a threat.

other choice but to use force for self-protection.

As you can see, the decision to retreat is a judgement call you may have to make in a fraction of a second, under conditions of great stress, and with incomplete information. An assailant who confronts you with his hand in his pants pocket may well have a gun—and may shoot you in the back if you attempt to flee. On the other hand, if he is unarmed, you might well run away in complete safety.

Be aware that no judge or jury will be able to relive your experience of a deadly encounter. Thus, any judgement you make during the heat of a confrontation may be second-guessed later by persons sitting in the calm safety of a courtroom. This is another reason why it is always better to safely retreat if at all possible—and why it is critical to remain aware of your environment and to mentally prepare for the unexpected. In many cases, armed citizens who are involved in deadly shootings could have avoided those confrontations had they used more foresight in identifying escape routes, visualizing responses to potential threats, and avoiding unsafe places and situations.

Warning Shots. In television and motion pictures it is not uncommon to see a character fire a warning shot to deter or stop an assailant. The firing of warning shots has been prohibited by the vast majority of police departments, and should also be avoided by armed civilians, for both legal and practical reasons.

Legally, the firing of a warning shot could actually undermine your claim that you were facing a life-threatening confrontation. You can use deadly force only as a last resort against an imminent threat to your life or limb. If imminent danger did exist, you would have fired at the assailant, not have wasted a shot fired as a warning. The fact that you had the time to fire a warning shot could suggest that the danger was more potential than immediate, and your gun should never have been drawn at all.

Furthermore, don't forget that you are legally responsible for each and every round you fire, even when you are firing under the stress of a life-threatening confrontation. Finally, firing a warning shot wastes time. As has been stated, most deadly attacks occur very quickly. The time you take to fire and recover from a warning shot is time your assailant can use to launch his attack.

Power of Arrest. Some persons who have concealed carry permits may feel that having the power to effect an arrest gives them additional authority to do so. It does not. An armed citizen has no more legal authority to make an arrest than an unarmed citizen.

Note, too, that any person making an arrest may subsequently be vulnerable to criminal sanctions or a civil lawsuit. Police officers are trained to effect an arrest efficiently and safely while minimizing danger to themselves, the general public and the arrested person. Most citizens are not so trained.

In practical terms, it is always preferable, from both a legal and safety viewpoint, to call the police and let them handle a situation. The only exception to this might be when not interceding would result in an innocent person losing life or limb (as when you witness a serious attack on such a person).

Looking for Criminal Activity. A concealed carry permit gives you the right to carry a handgun on your person for the purpose of defending yourself from an attack you may innocently encounter, not to seek out and confront criminals. Care must be taken to always avoid any behavior or utterance that has the appearance of vigilante behavior; it may backfire in any legal proceeding that follows the legitimate use of that handgun in self-defense.

Dealing With Law Enforcement Officers When You Are Carrying a Concealed Handgun. On occasion, you may interact with a law enforcement officer while you are carrying a concealed handgun. For example, you may be stopped for a broken headlight or a minor traffic offense while you have a gun on your person or in the passenger compartment. More seriously, an officer may spot your gun, or may only see a suspicious-looking bulge that he or she thinks deserves investigation. Knowing how to deal with the police while you are armed is critical to prevent a misunderstanding.

If you are pulled over in your car by a police officer, you should generally sit with your hands on the steering wheel while the officer approaches. Sitting with your hands visible will lessen his or her anxiety about dealing with a potentially armed person.

When the officer comes to

Fig. 249. Pulled-over driver with ID ready, hands on steering wheel, as officer approaches.

your window, wait for him or her to ask you for your information before removing your hands from the steering wheel. Retrieve your license, registration, insurance card or other required documents using deliberate movements. When the officer returns to the patrol car, keep your hands in sight, on the steering wheel.

If you are in a state in which a concealed carry permit holder is required to disclose a concealed firearm to law enforcement, do so at this time. If there is no such requirement, you are not obligated to disclose that you have a firearm on your person. As a practical matter, however, the officer will soon learn that you have a carry permit when your information is verified on the computer in the patrol car. If you did not disclose that fact, it may raise questions or even suspicions that may affect the way in which he or she interacts with you. The decision to disclose or not to disclose a concealed firearm, in a non-disclosure state, is a judgment call the armed citizen must make at the time.

Some police officers, once they know you are carrying a handgun, may want to temporarily take possession of your firearm while they are dealing with you. This is usually a decision made by the officer to ensure safety. In all circumstances, obey the commands of the police without hesitation or argument.

Another situation in which you may interact with the police will be in the event that an officer spots your concealed firearm (something that should not happen if you follow the proper concealment techniques). In such a situation, the officer will not know that you have a permit; he or she will only see a person with a gun, who may be a violent criminal. The officer will likely want to take possession of your firearm, and perhaps even handcuff you. Again, do not argue, complain, hesitate or resist. Also, do not make any sudden moves, as to retrieve your wallet or to show the police where your concealed handgun is located. Such a move might be misinterpreted, with unfortunate results. The more compliant you are, the lower the officer's adrenaline level will be, and the more quickly and easily he or she will be convinced that you are a law-abiding citizen exercising a legal right.

Jason Davis OC
Colorday

CHAPTER 30

THE LEGAL AFTERMATH OF A DEFENSIVE SHOOTING OUTSIDE THE HOME

NOTE: This chapter is not intended to take the place of consultation with a qualified attorney, nor should it be construed as providing general or specific legal advice. The information contained herein is intended to provide broad general guidelines regarding the legal ramifications that might stem from a self-defense shooting in some jurisdictions. For more specific information, consult an attorney familiar with the laws relating to firearms, concealed carry and self-defense in your jurisdiction.

Whether it involves the acquisition and mastery of shooting skills or the development of a defensive mindset, preparedness is the key to prevailing in a violent attack. Preparedness of a different type is also essential to survive the potential legal aftermath of a defensive shooting. The prudent gun owner must become thoroughly familiar with the potential legal ramifications of defensive gun use in his or her jurisdiction.

It is important for the defense-oriented gun owner to secure legal representation before he or she is involved in a defensive shooting situation. Selecting a lawyer out of the telephone book at the police station is not likely to provide you with the kind of representation you will need. Any attorney you select should be thoroughly familiar with all applicable federal, state and local laws regarding firearm ownership, concealed carry and self-defense. The attorney should also be apprised of any particulars of your own situation that would be relevant to any police investigation that would follow defensive firearm use.

Contact your state bar association for a list of attorneys in your area, along with their specialties. Members of your gun club may be able to recommend attorneys with experience in Second Amendment and self-defense cases. Also, firearms-friendly attorneys may post their cards at gun shops or on gun club bulletin boards. As a service to its members, the NRA also offers a referral service that matches attorneys with those needing legal representation.

The following describes some of the possible legal outcomes that may be faced by a survivor of a self-defense shooting outside the home.

ARREST

In all jurisdictions, a defensive shooting will entail an investigation. It may be sufficiently clear from the circumstances of the incident that your actions were completely in legitimate self-defense; in such cases, depending upon the discretion allowed the police and prosecutor's office, you may only have to face questioning by the police. Be aware, however, that such discretion is more commonly extended in cases of self-defense in the home; outside the home, situations are often not that clear-cut.

Under other circumstances—for example, if you knew and had previously quarreled with the person you defended yourself against, or if testimony from other witnesses suggests that you are the aggressor—the police and prosecutor may consider your actions to be illegal. In such circumstances, you likely will be arrested. You may well spend a few hours in jail, and possibly several days.

FIFTH AMENDMENT PROTECTIONS

The Fifth Amendment of the United States Constitution provides you with certain rights and protections, chief among them being that you have no obligation to talk to the police until you have consulted with your attorney. The Fifth Amendment also gives you the right to have your attorney present during all questioning.

When the police arrive, you can refuse to answer their questions until your attorney is present. Of course, you should exercise some common sense in this; you may not need a lawyer to respond to such questions as "What's your name?" Also, you may want to provide police with information that they need to ensure the immediate safety of the area, such as "Which way did the assailant flee?" However, most attorneys advise that you politely but firmly refuse to discuss the actual incident until you have consulted with legal counsel. Under the stress and emotions that follow involvement in a life-threatening situation, you may not think or communicate clearly, and may utter something that could be used against you in a subsequent legal proceeding.

Even before you become involved in a defensive shooting, it is highly advisable to discuss with your attorney exactly what you may and may not say to police should you be forced to use a firearm in self-defense. Just as you prepare mentally and physically to survive a violent encounter, this legal preparation may help you better negotiate the criminal justice system.

GUN CONFISCATION

If you are arrested by the police, they will take your carry handgun and, sometimes, any other firearms you have at your home. After all, from their point of view, you may be a suspect in a felony. The problem often lies in getting them back. In some areas you may have to go to court to secure the return of your guns.

Furthermore, police departments usually mark items taken as evidence. If you are lucky, they may put their mark—a number or letters scratched or stamped into the metal—in an unobtrusive location. Also, the police may or may not treat your guns with the same care as you would. In a "worst-case" situation, you may receive your guns back with dings and scratches from careless handling, evidence marks on external surfaces, and bore corrosion from having been fired and not cleaned. (If a department suspects that any of your firearms may have been used in a crime, technicians may fire them to obtain reference bullet specimens.)

SEARCH OF YOUR HOME

A full discussion of the rules governing permissible police searches is well beyond the scope of this text. Generally, to conduct a search in your home, police need a warrant for that location specifying what is being sought. There are several exceptions to this requirement, however; consult your attorney for more information.

Any normal law-abiding person may have objects, records, and so forth that are not at all illegal, but may be of a private nature. Such objects may become public knowledge as a result of a search. Of perhaps greater concern, during a search the police will almost certainly observe and make note of (mentally, at least) any books, magazines or other items that may cast doubt on the justifiability of your defensive shooting. For example, the fact that you are a history buff and possess material relating to military firearms or operations may work against you in a court of law should you face criminal or civil charges as the result of your defensive gun use.

SUSPENSION OF CONCEALED CARRY OR GUN OWNERSHIP PERMITS

Your state carry permit likely will be suspended or revoked following your arrest for shooting your assailant, particularly if the criminal charges against you are not dropped but are pursued by prosecutors. You may have to reapply for that permit once you are cleared of all criminal charges.

CRIMINAL TRIAL

In some cases, the criminal charges against you may be pursued instead of dropped. This may occur whenever the police or the prosecutor has questions regarding your claim of legitimate self-defense. This might be the case, for example, if you had had a previous disagreement with the assailant you shot, or if the witness testimony or physical evidence is contradictory or ambiguous.

Various areas of the country differ in their support of the right of concealed handgun carry and armed self-defense. In some large cities, for example, in which both citizens and public officials may have little sympathy for these rights, you may be more likely to be put on trial for using a firearm to protect yourself than in rural areas or small towns.

CIVIL SUIT

Even if you are cleared of all criminal charges, you still may have to face a civil suit brought by your assailant or the assailant's family or estate. There are differences between a criminal and civil trial. Criminal charges can only be brought by the government, and can result in incarceration, fines, property seizure and certain other sanctions. A civil suit can be brought by anyone, and results only in the awarding of money or other non-incarceration relief, such as an order restricting your interaction with the plaintiff.

Another important difference between a criminal and civil suit lies in the standard used to determine the outcome of a trial. In a criminal case, the jury (or judge) must be convinced by the evidence beyond a reasonable doubt. In a civil case, however, judgment is made for the plaintiff or defendant based upon a preponderance of the evidence. The standard is much higher in a criminal case than a civil case because the potential sanctions of a criminal conviction, such as lengthy incarceration or even the death penalty, are much more severe than the mere money award that is typical in a civil case.

If you use your firearm in self-defense and are later tried and found not guilty of any criminal charge, you should understand that such a verdict does not preclude a civil proceeding against you. Regardless of the outcome of a criminal trial, you may be subject to liability in a civil action.

LEGAL FEES

Even in the best of outcomes, in which no criminal charges are pressed and no civil suit is filed against you, you will usually still owe your attorney at least several hundred dollars, just to represent you at a bail hearing or during police interrogation. If you are forced to defend yourself against criminal charges in a full-scale trial—or if the assailant or the assailant's family sue you in civil court—your legal bills will amount to thousands, quite possibly tens of thousands of dollars.

Even when you prevail in a violent confrontation, you will still have to go through the criminal justice system. It is not enough to prepare yourself only to thwart an attack; you must also be ready for the legal aftermath that is sure to follow your use of deadly force.

APPENDIXES

APPENDIX A

GUN HANDLING

Most defensive-oriented gun owners recognize the importance of mastering the fundamentals of shooting and the various shooting positions. Often neglected, however, are those skills collectively known as *gun handling skills*. These include reloading techniques and procedures for quickly clearing stoppages and resolving other gun malfunctions.

RELOADING

Reloading means refilling an empty gun with cartridges as quickly as possible. There are specific methods for reloading both revolvers and semi-automatic pistols, for both right- and left-handed shooters.

As was stated earlier, in situations in which you must use your handgun to defend yourself, it will be rare for you to exhaust its capacity. However, there may be times when firing multiple shots neither stops a life-threatening attack, nor allows you to flee from it. When this happens, your ability to quickly reload an empty gun may be critical.

Whenever possible, reload while you are behind cover. Reloading while out in the open exposes you to your attacker when you cannot defend yourself. Also, during reloading you must momentarily take your eyes off the target or target area. It is generally safer to do this behind cover.

In some situations you may use reloading techniques to reload a gun that is only partially empty. For example, in a situation in which you fire five rounds from a six-shot revolver and then retreat to cover, use the breathing space that cover affords to bring your revolver back to full capacity. Do not be concerned with the single live round you dump out on the ground with the five empty cases.

Reloading the Revolver With Speedloaders

The fastest way to reload a revolver is through the use of a *speedloader*, a mechanical device that holds a number of cartridges in a pattern that aligns them with the chambers of the revolver. The speed loader (pictured at right) allows the cartridges to be inserted simultaneously into the cylinder chambers, at which point they are released and the revolver is completely reloaded.

Fig. 250. Revolver speedloaders.

Revolver owners not having speedloaders must reload using loose rounds from a pocket. Right-handed shooters should put their loose rounds in a right-side pocket, while left-handed shooters should put them in a left-side pocket. Any pocket that contains extra ammunition, whether in the form of loose rounds or speed loaders, should not have anything else in it. This prevents fumbling for ammunition or inadvertently attempting to load the revolver with coins, chewing gum, lip balm, lipstick or anything else that may be in the pocket.

Reloading the Revolver (Right-Handed Technique)

Beginning with the revolver held in a two-hand firing grip in the right hand, pointed in a safe direction and the finger off the trigger (A), bend the elbows to bring the revolver back close to the body at about chest height

A

and slightly to the right of the center-line of the torso (B). Keep your eyes on the target area throughout the procedure except when you are actually inserting cartridges into the chambers.

As the gun is being brought back (just as the elbow of the firing arm begins to bend), cup the left hand underneath the trigger guard area of the frame of the revolver. Grasp the cylinder between the two middle fingers and the thumb of the left hand (C). Viewed from the rear, the thumb contacts the cylinder at the 9 o'clock position, while the two middle fingers make contact at the 3

B

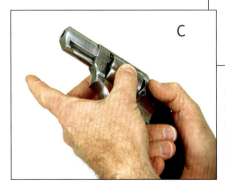

C

o'clock position. The bottom of the trigger guard is over the palm of the left hand. Care must be taken, particularly with short-barreled revolvers, to keep the left index finger clear of the muzzle.

D

With the cylinder thus firmly grasped by the left hand, the right thumb engages the cylinder release (D). Twist the right wrist to rotate the frame 90 degrees clockwise. The two middle fingers of the left hand pass through the frame; the grip is maintained on the cylinder by the thumb and two middle fingers of the left hand. It is important to rotate the frame away from the cylinder rather than simply push the cylinder out of the frame. The cylinder is held stationary by the left hand while the right hand rotates the frame away from the cylinder.

As the revolver frame is rotated away from the cylinder, roll your left wrist slightly toward you to direct the muzzle almost straight upward. Be sure to keep the muzzle angled away from you. Let go of the revolver with the right hand and maintain your hold of the cylinder with the fingers and thumb of the left hand still in the 3 and 9 o'clock positions (E). The left elbow should now be close to or touching the abdomen and the revolver should still be positioned to the right of the centerline of the body, just below the armpit.

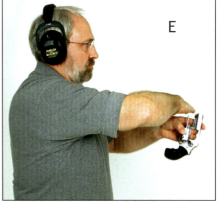

E

With the inside of the palm of the right hand, strike the ejector rod with

F

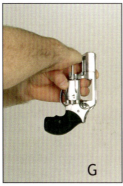

G

a straight, sharp downward blow (F, G). The rod should contact the palm at a point midway along an imaginary line between the base of the pinky finger and the center of the wrist joint.

CAUTION: Strike the ejector hard enough to throw the empty cases well clear of the cylinder with the first blow, but not so hard as to injure your hand or bend the ejector rod. In guns with dirty or scored cylinders, or when higher-pressure loads are used, the first sharp blow to the ejector rod may push the cases only part way out of their chambers in the cylinder. A second or third sharp blow may be required for full, forceful ejection.

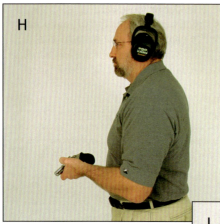

Allow the empty cases to fall free of the cylinder to the ground. Do not attempt to retrieve the cases (or any live rounds you may also eject from the cylinder).

As your right hand reaches for a speedloader, or loose cartridges in your pocket, bring the revolver in front of you at about chest height, rotating the muzzle downward and away from you (H). Retrieve a

speedloader or one or two loose cartridges from your pocket with your right hand and bring that hand to the revolver just above the cylinder.

If you are using a speedloader, look down briefly as you align the cartridges with the cylinder's chambers (I). A momentary glance to ensure that the cylinder is

indeed empty, and that the nose of each bullet has entered the chamber properly (J) is sufficient. Then release the cartridges into the chambers and drop the speedloader to the ground.

If you are loading loose cartridges, grasp them at the rim using your thumb and forefinger. Seat them with the thumb as they enter the chamber. With practice, you can load two cartridges at a time by grasping them at their rims using the thumb and first two fingers and inserting them simultaneously into adjacent chambers. When loading loose cartridges it is more efficient to remove only one or two at a time from the pocket, load them and then go back to the pocket for one or two more, rather than grabbing five or six cartridges at one time.

When reloading with either a speed loader or loose cartridges, dirty cylinder walls or a cartridge that is slightly oversize or out of round may cause you to feel some resistance while chambering one or more cartridges. It is important for all cartridges to be fully seated in the cylinder. Cartridges that protrude from their chambers can keep the cylinder from closing or rotating.

Once the cartridges are seated in their chambers in the cylinder, grasp

the grip portion of the frame in a firing grip with the right hand. Remember to keep the trigger finger along the side of the frame, out of the trigger guard. As you start to raise the revolver (still keeping the muzzle in a downward direction to keep the cartridges from falling out of their chambers), rotate the frame counter-clockwise with the right wrist while simultaneously

pushing the cylinder home with the left thumb (K). You will hear a click as the cylinder latch catches. As the cylinder clicks shut, rotate the cylinder with the thumb and middle fingers until it locks into place with a cartridge directly under the firing pin. If you fail to properly index the cylinder with a chamber under the firing pin, the gun may not fire when the trigger is pulled.

Once the cylinder is securely shut and indexed to put a cartridge under the firing pin, raise the muzzle into alignment with the target. The left hand slides back over the right into its supporting grip position and the firing position is once again assumed, and you assess the target area (L).

Reloading the Revolver (Left-Handed Technique)

Beginning with the revolver held in a two-hand firing grip in the left hand, pointed in a safe direction and the finger off the trigger (A), bend the elbows to bring the revolver back close to the body at about chest height and to the left of the centerline of the torso (B). Keep your eyes on the target area

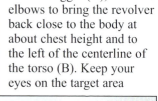

except when you are inserting cartridges into the chambers.

As the gun is being brought back (just as the elbow of the firing arm begins to bend), cup the right hand underneath the frame of the revolver in the area of the trigger guard. Grasp the cylinder

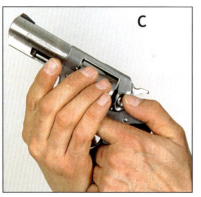

between the two middle fingers and the thumb of the right hand (C). Viewed from the rear, the thumb contacts the cylinder at the 3 o'clock position, while the two middle fingers make contact at the 9 o'clock position. The bottom of the trigger guard is over the bottom of the right hand. Care must be taken, particularly with short-barreled revolvers, to keep the right index finger clear of the muzzle.

While maintaining a firm grip with the three fingers of the left hand, bring the left thumb around to the left side of the frame and engage the cylinder release (D). Twist the left wrist to rotate the frame 90 degrees clockwise. The thumb of the right hand passes through the frame; the grip is maintained on the cylinder by the thumb and two middle fingers of the right hand. It is important to rotate the

frame away from the cylinder rather than simply push the cylinder out of the frame. The cylinder is held stationary by the right hand while the left hand rotates the frame away from the cylinder (E).

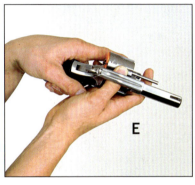

As the revolver frame is rotated away from the cylinder, roll your right wrist slightly toward you to direct the muzzle almost straight upward. Be sure to keep the muzzle angled away from you. Let go of the revolver with the left hand and maintain your hold of the cylinder with the fingers and thumb of the right hand still in the 3 and 9 o'clock positions. The right elbow should now be close to or touching the abdomen and the revolver should still be positioned to the left of the centerline of the body.

There are two methods for actuating the ejector rod. Push the ejector rod firmly with the index finger of the right hand (F), or strike it with a straight, sharp blow with the inside of the palm of the left hand (G). The rod should contact the left palm directly below the base of the index finger. The latter method is more likely to eject cases from the cylinder.

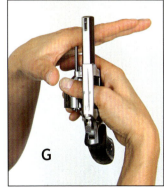

CAUTION: Strike the ejector hard enough to throw the empty cases well clear of the cylinder with the first blow, but not so hard as to injure your hand or bend the ejector rod. In guns with dirty or scored cylinders, or when higher-pressure loads are used, the first sharp blow to the ejector rod may push the cases only part way out of their chambers in the cylinder. A second or third sharp blow may be required for full ejection.

Allow the empty cases to fall free of the cylinder and hit the ground. Do not attempt to retrieve the cases (or any live rounds you may also eject from the cylinder).

As your left hand reaches for a speedloader or loose cartridges in your pocket, bring the revolver in front of you at about chest height, simultaneously rotating the muzzle downward and away from you (H). Retrieve a speed loader or one or two loose cartridges from your pocket with your left hand and bring that hand to the revolver just above the cylinder.

If you are using a speed loader, look down briefly as you align the cartridges with the cylinder's chambers (I). A momentary glance to ensure that the nose of each bullet has entered the chamber (J) is sufficient. Then release the cartridges into the chambers (K) and drop the speed loader to the ground.

If you are loading loose cartridges, grasp them at the rim using your thumb and forefinger. Seat them with the thumb as they enter the chamber. With practice, you can load two cartridges at a time by grasping them at their rims using the thumb and first two fingers and inserting them simul-

taneously into adjacent chambers. When loading loose cartridges it is more efficient to remove only one or two at a time from the pocket, load them and then go back to the pocket for one or two more, rather than grabbing many cartridges at one time (L).

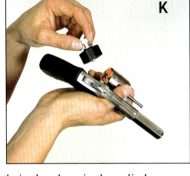

When reloading with either a speed loader or loose cartridges, dirty cylinder walls or a cartridge that is slightly oversize or out of round may cause you to feel some resistance while chambering one or more cartridges. It is important to ensure that all cartridges are fully seated in their chambers in the cylinder. Cartridges that protrude from their chambers can keep the cylinder from closing or rotating.

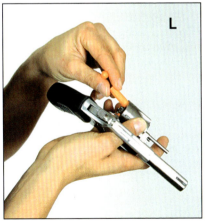

Once the cartridges are seated in their chambers in the cylinder, grasp the grip portion of the frame in a firing grip with the left hand. Remember to keep the trigger finger along the side of the frame, out of the trigger guard. As you start to raise the revolver (still keeping the muzzle in a downward direction to keep the cartridges from falling out of their chambers), rotate the frame counter-

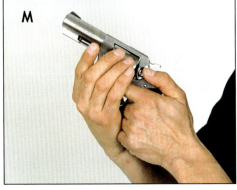

clockwise with the left wrist while simultaneously pushing the cylinder home with the right fingers (M). You will hear a click as the cylinder latch catches. As the cylinder clicks shut, rotate the cylinder with the thumb and middle fingers until it locks into place with a cartridge directly under the firing pin. If you fail to properly index the cylinder with a chamber under the firing pin, the gun may not fire when the trigger is pulled.

Once the cylinder is securely shut and indexed to put a cartridge under the firing pin, raise the muzzle into alignment with the target. The right hand slides back over the left into its supporting grip position and the firing position is once again assumed, and you assess the target area (N)..

Reloading the Semi-Automatic Pistol (Right-Handed Technique)

Beginning with the pistol held in a firing grip, trigger finger alongside the frame, and the muzzle pointed in a safe direction (A), bend the elbows to bring the pistol close to the body (B). The elbow of the shooting arm should be close to or in contact with the torso. The muzzle should point upward and away from you (or, if upward is not a safe direction, toward the target).

As you bring the pistol in close to your body, place the tip of the thumb of the right hand on the magazine release button (assuming the button is located in the usual position on the left side of the frame just to the rear of the trigger guard). It may be necessary to shift the right hand grip to allow the thumb to reach the release button. Press the magazine release button straight into the frame and hold it in while the magazine drops free of the frame (C). You should be able to glimpse the falling magazine in your peripheral vision. Do not attempt to retrieve the

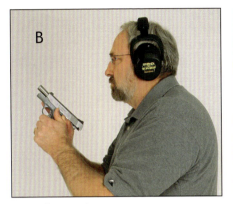

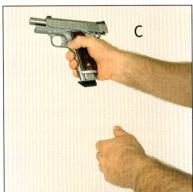

ejected magazine.

If the magazine does not fall free of the frame of its own weight, swiftly strip it from the pistol with the left hand and drop it on the ground.

At the same time, the left (support) hand reaches for a loaded magazine. Grasp the magazine between the thumb and middle finger, with the floorplate (base) of the magazine in the palm of the hand and the index finger running up the front of the magazine body, resting on or just below the tip of the bullet of the top cartridge (D).

As the firing hand continues to bring the pistol in toward the torso, rotate

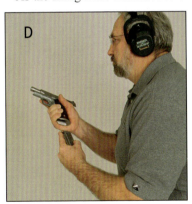

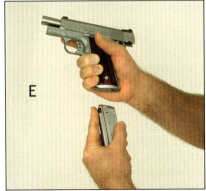

the right hand wrist 90 degrees so that the left side of the frame faces you and the pistol is just below eye level (E). At the same time, the left hand brings the magazine close to the magazine well of the pistol. Keep visual focus on the target area during these steps.

Glance down briefly at the magazine well, both to ensure that it is clear of an empty magazine and to locate it visually to facilitate magazine insertion (F). Using the left-hand index finger on the magazine to "point" toward the magazine well opening in the grip, insert the top of the magazine into the magazine well in the frame (G). Seat the magazine fully by pushing it all the way in with the palm of your hand, being sure to keep the trigger finger outside the trigger guard (H). You will usually hear or feel a click as the magazine seats and is caught by the magazine catch. Once the magazine has been lined up with the magazine well and is being seated, return your visual

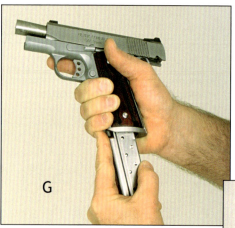

focus to the target area.

If the pistol has been shot empty and the slide is locked back, release the slide forward by either operating the slide release

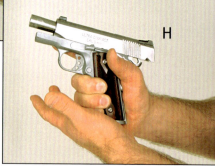

(I) or pulling the slide slightly to the rear and releasing it (J). If the gun being reloaded is not completely empty, there will be a round remaining in the chamber and no

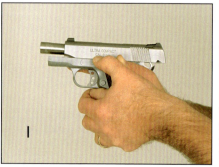

slide manipulation will be required. Note that a few semi-automatic pistols do not lock the slide back when shot empty. With such pistols, after a fresh magazine has been seated it will be necessary to fully retract the slide and release it to load a cartridge into the chamber and enable the pistol to fire.

After seating the magazine and releasing the slide forward, if necessary, the left hand slides back into its supporting position and the firing position is resumed (K).

During reloading, the eyes should remain continuously on the target or area of expected threat except for the brief moment when the magazine is

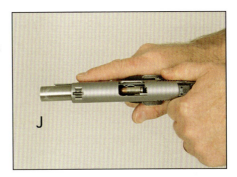

being aligned with the frame. If the threat has fled or is otherwise gone when visual focus is returned to the target area, engage the safety and lower the pistol to a ready position.

Reloading the Semi-Automatic Pistol (Left-Handed Technique)

Beginning with the pistol held in a firing grip, trigger finger alongside the frame, and the muzzle pointed in a safe direction (A), bend the elbows to bring the pistol close to the body (B). The elbow of the shooting arm should be close to or in contact with the torso. The muzzle should point upward and away from you (or, if upward is not a safe direction, toward the target).

As you bring the pistol in close to the body, place the tip of the trigger finger on the magazine release button (assuming the button is located in the usual position on the left side of the frame just to the rear of the trigger

A

guard). For some shooters, it may be necessary to use the stronger middle finger instead. Press the magazine release button straight into the frame and hold it in while the magazine drops free of the frame (C). You should be able to glimpse the falling magazine in your peripheral vision. Do not attempt to retrieve the

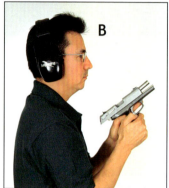

B

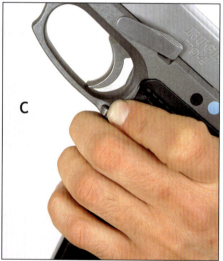

C

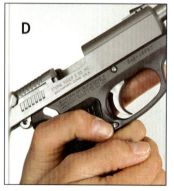

D

ejected magazine.

If your pistol has ambidextrous controls, it may be possible to release the magazine by pressing the release button with your left-hand thumb (D).

If the magazine does not fall free of the frame of its own weight, swiftly strip it from the pistol with the right hand and drop it on the ground.

At the same time as the spent magazine falls to the ground, the right (support) hand reaches for a fresh magazine (E). Grasp the magazine between the thumb and middle finger, with the floorplate (base) of the

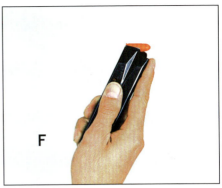

magazine in the palm of the hand and the index finger running up the front of the magazine body, resting on or just below the tip of the bullet of the top cartridge (F).

As the firing hand continues to bring the pistol in toward the torso, rotate the left hand wrist 90 degrees so that the right side of the frame faces you and the pistol is just below eye level (G). At the same time the right hand brings the magazine close to the magazine well of the pistol. Keep visual focus on the target area during theses steps.

Glance down at the magazine well, both to ensure that it is clear of an empty magazine and to locate it visually to facilitate magazine insertion

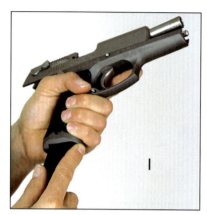

(H). Using the right-hand index finger on the magazine to "point" toward the magazine well opening in the grip, insert the top of the magazine into the magazine well (I). Seat the magazine by pushing it all the way in with the palm of your hand, being sure to keep your finger

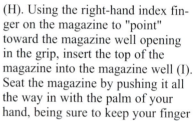

outside the trigger guard (J). You will usually hear or feel a click as the magazine seats and is caught by the magazine catch. Once the magazine is aligned with the magazine well and is being seated, return your visual focus to the target area.

If the pistol has been shot empty and the slide is locked back, release the slide forward, by either operating the slide release (K) or pulling the slide slightly to the rear and releasing it (L). You can operate the slide release with the index finger of the right hand, which will be close to the

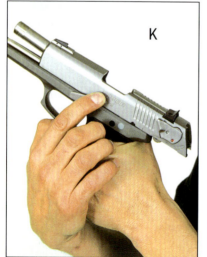

release as the right-hand palm seats the magazine (I).

If the gun being reloaded is not completely empty, there will be a round remaining in the chamber and no slide manipulation will be required. Note that

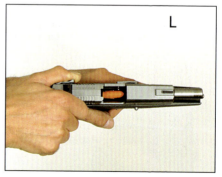

a few semi-automatic pistols do not lock the slide back when shot empty. With such pistols, after a fresh magazine has been seated it will be necessary to fully retract the slide and release it to load a cartridge into the chamber.

M

After seating the magazine and releasing the slide forward, if necessary, the right hand slides back into its supporting position, and the firing position is resumed (M).

During the reloading process, the eyes should remain continuously on the target or the area of expected threat except for the brief moment when the magazine is being lined up with the frame. If the threat has fled or is otherwise gone when visual focus is returned to the target area, engage the safety and lower the pistol to a ready position.

CLEARING STOPPAGES

Your handgun is a tool of last resort, a tool you will avoid using unless you have no other options to safely stop an attack. However, when you must use your handgun, it must work reliably. The responsible gun owner will ensure that his or her firearm functions perfectly with the defensive ammunition selected.

No matter how much ammunition testing or gunsmith tuning is done, however, there still may be rare occasions when your handgun does not fire or otherwise fails to operate properly. Gun stoppages are somewhat more common with semi-automatic pistols, but can occur with revolvers, too. A gun stoppage that occurs during a violent encounter could render you helpless to stop an assailant's attack. For this reason it is important that you learn the immediate action drills for quickly clearing stoppages, and practice these drills until they are performed in an instantaneous, almost reflexive manner whenever a gun problem occurs.

Clearing Stoppages in Open-Top Semi-Automatic Pistols

Many semi-automatic pistols have large, open-top ejection ports. Such pistols can be cleared of all three common stoppages—failure to go into battery, failure to fire, and failure to eject—using a single immediate action drill. From the point of view of the defensive shooter, being able to clear almost all stoppages with only one immediate action drill saves the time of having to analyze the malfunction, identify its cause and then decide which drill will remedy it. Having only one immediate action drill to learn and master also reduces training time and complexity, and enables you to be able to respond instantaneously anytime a stoppage occurs. The four steps of the drill are referred to as tap, invert, rack, assess.

When a stoppage occurs, your trigger finger should be removed from the trigger (A). Next, tap the base of the magazine with the palm of the support hand to ensure it is fully seated in the pistol (B). Then, invert the pistol by rotating toward the thumb of the shooting hand. Rack the slide vigorously one time by pulling it all the way to

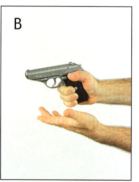

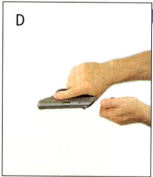

the rear (C) and releasing it to go forward (D) under spring tension. Inverting the pistol before racking the slide and shaking the gun while the slide is momentarily held all the way back will dislodge all but the most stubborn empty case or jammed cartridge. Finally, assess the target to determine if it still constitutes a deadly threat.

Note that the tap, invert, rack, assess drill will not work with all semi-automatic pistols. Experiment with the various specific immediate action drills (described below), using dummy ammunition or fired cases, to determine what works best with your handgun (see Chapter 12: Opportunities for Skills Enhancement).

Clearing Specific Semi-Automatic Pistol Stoppages

There are several types of functional problems that may occur with semi-automatic pistols. The following stoppages are the ones most commonly experienced, and each may be resolved in one or two seconds with the appropriate immediate action drill.

Failure to Go into Battery. This stoppage occurs when the slide does not return all the way forward and the cartridge is not fully seated in the chamber. Most commonly this stoppage is caused by a round that gets jammed on the feed ramp

leading into the chamber, an over-size or over-length cartridge, or an excessively dirty chamber.

If the slide of your pistol fails to go into battery (A, arrow), remove your finger from the trigger and hit the rear of the slide sharply with the heel of the hand (B). If this fails to resolve the problem, with your finger still off the trigger, retract the slide forcefully to clear the jammed cartridge. If the problem results from an oversized cartridge, any attempt to drive the slide forward forcefully may wedge the cartridge firmly in the chamber, making it extremely difficult to rack the slide or otherwise clear the stoppage.

Failure to Fire. Failure to fire can be the result of a cartridge defect, such as an improperly seated or defective primer, or a magazine that is not seated fully in the frame, which will prevent the slide from stripping and chambering the top cartridge.

The immediate action drill to resolve a failure to fire is known as tap, rack, assess. First, remove your finger from the trigger (A), tap the magazine base with the palm of the support (non-firing) hand to ensure that it is fully seated (B), rack the slide by pulling it all the way back (C) and releasing it (D), and assess the threat (E) to determine whether you need to return your finger to the trigger.

Failure to Eject. In this condition, the fired case is extracted at least partially from the chamber, but is not completely ejected from the pistol. The fired case may remain inside the slide, possibly becoming jammed into the chamber, or it may be partially protruding out of the ejection port.

This latter condition is known as a stovepipe stoppage (A).

Clearing a stovepipe is accomplished by first removing the finger from the trigger, then reaching over the top of the pistol with the support hand and forcibly sweeping that hand rearward along the top of the

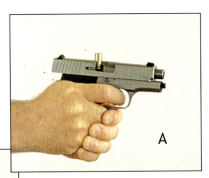

slide from a point halfway down the barrel back toward the body (B). The support hand contacts the protruding case at the knuckle of the forefinger and rips the case out of the ejection port and to the rear (C). (While clearing a stovepipe, be careful to keep the

support hand from sweeping in front of the muzzle, and keep the gun pointed in a safe direction.) At the same time, the shooting hand also thrusts the pistol forward. As the case is stripped, the support hand returns to its position encircling the firing hand, and you assess the assailant to deter-

mine whether he is still a threat before returning the finger to the trigger.

Racking the slide after sweeping the case normally is not necessary. In fact, doing so may cause a double feed, a situation in which two cartridges attempt to enter the chamber. Clearing a double feed requires time-consuming remedial action.

If a cartridge fails to be fed into the chamber after a stovepipe stoppage is cleared, perform the immediate action drill (tap, rack, assess) for a failure-to-fire stoppage (see above).

Failure to Drop Magazine. Defensive-oriented pistols generally are designed to drop their magazines freely when the magazine release is actuated. This promotes more rapid reloading, which may help save your life.

The failure to drop a magazine may have several causes. Most often a defective magazine (such as one that has a defective follower or is deformed so that it wedges inside the magazine well) is the culprit.

If this problem is observed during practice sessions with several magazines of good quality, it may result from a gun problem requiring a gunsmith's attention.

An empty magazine that does not drop free of the gun during the course of a defensive shooting situation must be immediately removed. The immediate action drill is to engage the protruding tongue of the magazine floorplate with the fingers of the non-shooting hand and, with the magazine release button depressed, sharply pull the magazine out of the gun (A). Allow the magazine to drop to the ground.

Note that some semi-automatic

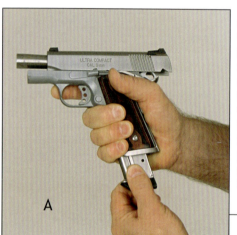

pistols feature magazine catches in locations other than the usual position just behind the trigger guard. The most common of these alternative locations is at the bottom of the pistol's butt (B). Such magazine catches require two hands for the release of a magazine, and consequently change the procedure for magazine reloading detailed earlier.

Clearing Specific Revolver Malfunctions

There are two main types of functional problems that may occur with revolvers. Each requires a specific immediate action drill to resolve the problem.

Failure to Fire. A failure to fire with a revolver occurs whenever the hammer falls on a loaded chamber (or what is thought to be a loaded chamber) and the gun does not fire. The most likely cause for a failure to fire in a stressful situation is that all the rounds in the cylinder have been fired. Another cause for a failure to fire is that the hammer has fallen on a chamber that does not contain a cartridge.

On occasion the hammer may fall on a live round and fail to fire it. If this occurs with ammunition that has previously proved reliable, this failure to fire is most commonly the result of a dud cartridge, a hangfire or misfire. If this occurs at a range while practicing, you should wait 30 to 60 seconds with the muzzle pointed downrange, in the event that the condition you are experiencing is a hangfire. On the other hand, if you are using your handgun in a defensive situation, you will not have the time to hold your fire for that period of time. The proper immediate action drill is to pull the trigger again, bringing a fresh (and hopefully functioning) cartridge in line with the firing pin.

If the firearm fails to fire a second or third fresh round, open the cylinder and look at the primers of the cartridges that failed to ignite.

Fig. 251. A faint firing pin indentation (lower case) can result in a failure to fire, and may be a sign of a problem requiring a gunsmith's attention.

A faint firing pin indentation, or no indentation at all on an unfired primer, is an indication of a firearm problem (such as a broken firing pin) that requires the intervention of a gunsmith.

Failure to Eject Cases from the Cylinder. Difficulty in ejecting fired cases from a revolver cylinder may result from oversized or high-pressure cartridges, dirt in the chambers or roughly machined chambers. If this problem is encountered during practice sessions, a gunsmith's assistance should be sought to eliminate it.

A failure to eject cases that occurs during a violent encounter can prevent you from reloading your revolver, with dire consequences. If your first strike of the ejector rod fails to forcibly eject all cases from the cylinder, strike it again with greater force. Be careful to strike in a straight line with the rod to prevent bending it with an off-axis strike. If repeated strikes do not dislodge the cases, release the rod and use your fingers to pull the fired, partially-protruding cartridge cases from their chambers, one at a time.

After Clearing a Stoppage

After clearing a stoppage in a semi-automatic pistol or a revolver, you must reassess the situation to determine whether there is still a deadly threat. In the brief moment it takes to conduct an immediate action drill, an assailant may surrender or flee. Conversely, while you are clearing a stoppage, an attacker may take the opportunity to advance on you. Avoid becoming so focused on your immediate action

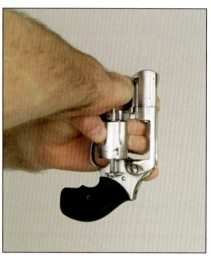

Fig. 252. If your first strike of the ejector rod fails to eject all the cases from the cylinder, strike it again with greater force. Strike in a straight line to prevent bending it.

drill that you lose awareness of your attacker's actions. Furthermore, if your efforts to clear a stoppage become time-consuming, be sure to glance at the target area every second or two to maintain awareness of the threat.

An alternative to reloading or clearing a stoppage during an ongoing attack is to carry a backup firearm. It can be less time consuming and more effective to simply jettison the empty or disabled gun and draw the backup gun than to attempt to perform a multi-step procedure under stress.

APPENDIX B

FIREARM MAINTENANCE

Virtually all gun owners recognize the value of frequent firearm cleaning, inspection, and lubrication. A gun that is properly maintained at regular intervals will function more reliably, shoot more accurately and last longer than one whose care is neglected. While a well-maintained firearm is desirable for the complete enjoyment of such activities as plinking, hunting and and competitive shooting, it is absolutely essential in a self-defense situation, in which a single stoppage can have fatal consequences.

The critical role of a self-defense firearm demands a more rigorous schedule of maintenance than might be observed with a handgun used only to plink at tin cans on weekends. This schedule includes regular cleaning, inspection and lubrication, as well as a periodic gunsmith check-up.

CLEANING YOUR FIREARM

A gun that is shot on a regular basis accumulates dirt, powder residue and other foreign matter, all of which can make a gun more prone to stoppage, wear and corrosion. Even a firearm that is left untouched on a shelf or in a drawer can accumulate sufficient dust and dirt to affect proper functioning. Removing such harmful material is critical to ensure gun reliability and readiness.

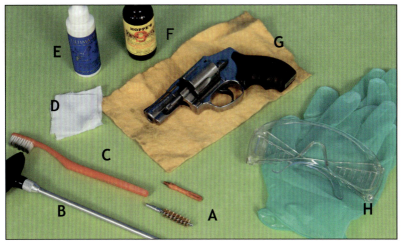

Fig. 253. The components of a basic gun cleaning kit include (A) a bore brush and slotted tip for holding cleaning patches, (B) a cleaning rod, (C) a small brush, (D) cotton cleaning patches, (E) gun oil, (F) gun cleaning solvent, (G) a soft cloth, and (H) eye protection. Also shown are thin rubber gloves, which may help protect the skin from dirt, oil and solvent.

Every gun owner should have a gun cleaning kit consisting of the following items:

- cloth patches;
- a cleaning rod and cleaning rod attachments, including a bore brush and tips to hold patches;
- a small brush (for cleaning gun crevices) ;
- gun solvent (bore cleaner);
- gun oil; and
- a soft cloth.

Kits containing all or most of these items are commercially available at any gun shop and many hardware, sporting goods and large discount stores. Make sure that any kit or individual cleaning rod, jag (a tip designed specifically to hold a cleaning patch) or bore brush is intended for a handgun in the caliber of your pistol or revolver. Also, select patches of the proper size for your bore.

In addition to the above items, you also need safety glasses to protect your eyes from cleaning solvents and spring-loaded parts that you may inadvertently dislodge from your gun. Also recommended are thin rubber gloves to protect your skin from exposure to solvents, lubricants, firing residues and lead particles. Be sure that your gun-cleaning area has good ventilation, and do not eat, drink or smoke while performing firearm maintenance.

The first step in cleaning your firearm is to ensure that it is unloaded (A). There should be no live ammunition in the cleaning area.

Next, disassemble your firearm according to the instructions in the owner's manual for the gun. If you do not have an owner's manual for your firearm, you can usually obtain one from the firearm's manufacturer. Alternatively, a professional gunsmith may be able to show you how to disassemble your gun.

With a revolver, recommended disassembly may involve nothing more than swinging out the cylinder and removing the stocks (B). Disassembling

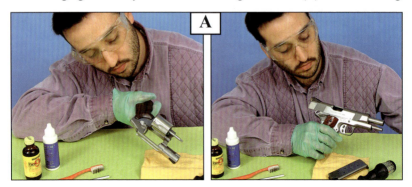

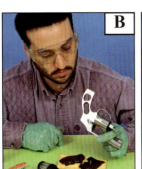

a semi-automatic pistol usually involves the separation of the slide from the frame, which also may allow the removal of the barrel and recoil spring assembly (C). On many semi-autos, caution must be exercised to prevent a compressed recoil spring from flying free when the slide and frame are disassembled. Generally, no further disassembly is needed for normal cleaning (nor is usually recommended in the owner's manual).

Actual cleaning starts with the bore. Attach a tip to the cleaning rod (D), put a clean patch onto the jag and wet the patch with gun cleaning solvent. Push the patch slowly through the bore to saturate the bore surface and loosen powder residue, lead or copper fouling, or other unwanted material. If you are cleaning a revolver, or a semi-automatic pistol whose barrel was not removed, you will probably have to push the patch through from the muzzle end (E). When cleaning from the muzzle end of the barrel, avoid rubbing the cleaning rod against the bore to prevent accuracy-robbing wear on the rifling. If you are cleaning a semi-automatic pistol whose barrel was removed as part of disassembly, push the patch through from the chamber (rearmost) end (F).

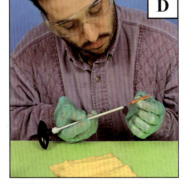

Next, attach the bore brush to the cleaning rod and moisten it with gun cleaning solvent (G). If possible, use a dropper to put solvent onto the brush; avoid dipping the brush in the solvent, as this contaminates the clean solvent

with dirt and grit on the brush.
Push the brush all the way
through the bore, then pull it back
through the bore (H). Do not try
to reverse direction with the brush
still in the bore. Run the brush
through the bore about 15-20
times, adding solvent to it as necessary.

Re-attach the jag to the cleaning rod and push a clean, dry
patch through the bore (I). This
patch will come out quite dirty
with the material that was loosened by the solvent and the bore brush. Run
more dry patches through the bore; they should come out progressively
cleaner, until virtually no fouling is visible (J). If the patches keep coming

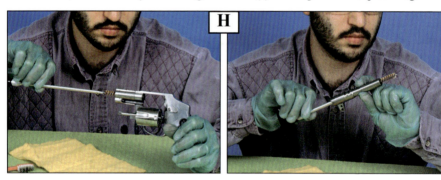

out somewhat dirty, repeat the cleaning process as outlined in the previous
paragraphs. Also, visually check the surface of the bore for any remaining
fouling, lead, or powder residue.

In cleaning a revolver, the cylinders are cleaned using much the same

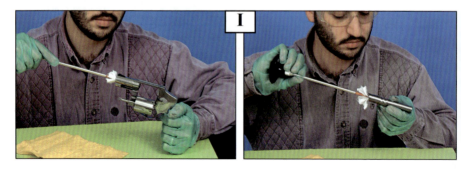

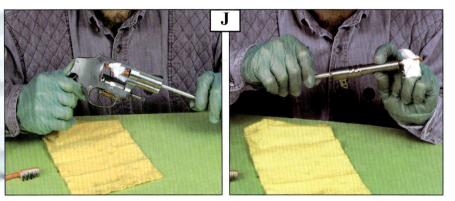

technique as is employed in cleaning the bore (K).

Once the bore is clean, residue must be removed from other gun surfaces. Use a solvent-soaked patch, cotton swab or toothbrush, as appropriate, to loosen and remove powder residue and other matter from working

surfaces. On a semi-automatic pistol, such surfaces include the interior of the slide, the slide and frame rails, and the exterior barrel surface. On a revolver, such surfaces include the crane, frame, and any action parts that are made accessible by the removal of the stocks (L).

Maintenance of semi-automatic pistol magazines is crit-

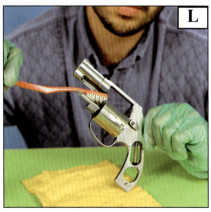

ical for proper pistol functioning. Most magazines are designed to be disassembled; instructions should be in your owner's manual. Once the magazine is disassembled, push patches through the magazine body to clean out loose dirt, powder residue and other matter (M).

In most cases, the owner's manual will present only those disassembly instructions required to perform basic cleaning and

maintenance; more complete disassembly of the firearm is usually
discouraged. However, dirt and
powder residue can also collect in
interior action areas that can be
accessed only by complete disassembly. A partial cleaning of these
inaccessible areas may be
achieved by flushing the action
with gun cleaner or a solvent that
leaves no residue, such as brake
cleaner. The solvent is sprayed
into the action in such a way as to
allow the excess to drain freely

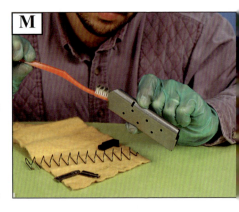

(such as with the stocks removed), dissolving and flushing away loosened
dirt and residue.

INSPECTING YOUR FIREARM

The ideal time for giving your firearm a thorough visual inspection is
when it is disassembled after cleaning. Defects are easiest to spot on parts
that are free of dirt, residue and oil. Look for cracks, burred, pitted or
indented areas, broken parts and so forth. Also be aware of screws or pins
that have worked loose, sights that have drifted from recoil forces, or parts
that seem to have shifted from their normal positions.

Additionally, every time you pick up your firearm, whether to practice at
the range, dry-fire in your basement, or clean it in your workroom, you
should give it a cursory inspection (after, of course, making sure it is
unloaded). Look for the buildup of firing residues; grips screws or other
parts that have become loose; excessive oil leaking out of the joints
between parts; and any other condition that may affect the function of the
gun. Getting in the habit of making this kind of inspection will help you
determine when cleaning or lubrication is necessary, or if there are any
conditions that may make your gun unsafe or unreliable.

LUBRICATING YOUR FIREARM

Cleaning powder residues and other foreign material from the gun usually removes necessary lubrication from working surfaces. Thus, it is essential to re-lubricate the firearm after it has been cleaned.

The owner's manual for your gun likely contains detailed instructions on
the proper method of lubrication. In general, lubricate revolvers in the

areas of the crane, ejector rod, and cylinder latch, and around the sides of the hammer and trigger. With the stocks removed, you may also squirt oil into action areas to smooth the trigger pull.

Semi-automatic pistols should be lubricated on the slide and frame rails, at the muzzle (where the barrel articulates with the slide), and in the barrel

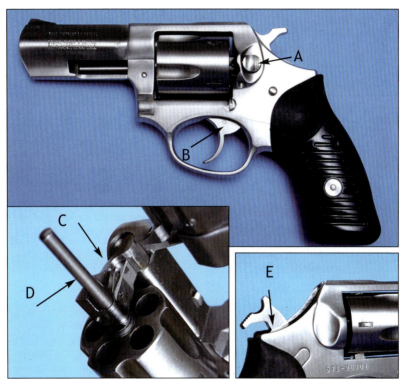

Fig. 254. Lubrication points for a revolver include the cylinder latch (A), the junction of the trigger and the frame (B), the crane (C), the ejector rod (D), and alongside the hammer where it meets the frame (E). With the hammer back, a few drops of oil may also be dripped into the action to lubricate internal action parts. Internal parts may also be accessed for lubrication by removing the stocks.

locking area. Also apply a small amount of oil to the sides of the trigger and hammer where they enter the frame, to smooth their movement. Additionally, drip a small amount of lubricant into action areas, particularly around the trigger and hammer pins. If you desire, you may put a very light film of oil on the exterior surface of the magazines to prevent rust and to help insertion and removal from the pistol. It is critical not to allow oil to be transferred to the cartridges carried within the magazine. Oil on

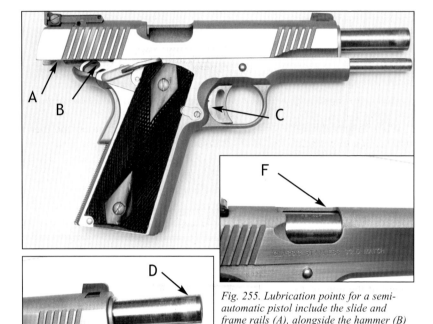

Fig. 255. Lubrication points for a semi-automatic pistol include the slide and frame rails (A), alongside the hammer (B) and trigger (C) where they enter the frame, the muzzle end of the barrel (D) and guide rod (E), and the top of the chamber end of the barrel (F).

cartridge cases can penetrate to the primer, making its ignition less reliable, and may have other deleterious effects on gun functioning as well.

It is important to use only those lubricants designed expressly for use in firearms. Over time, improper lubricants may become gummy, impairing proper gun functioning, or may be too thin or runny to provide lasting protection. Also, firearms that are used in climates that are extremely hot, cold, wet or dusty often have very special lubrication needs, as do firearms that will be stored for extended periods. Consult with a gun shop or gunsmith to determine the proper lubricants to be used with your firearm.

It is also important to avoid over-lubricating your handgun, or leaving oil in certain areas. For example, while a thin film of oil should coat the bore of a firearm that is to be stored, all oil must be removed from the bore before the gun is fired. Also, excess lubricant can penetrate wood stocks and cause them to deteriorate, and too much oil left inside the magazine of a semi-automatic pistol or the chambers of a revolver cylinder can contaminate cartridge primers and lead to misfires.

FUNCTION CHECKING YOUR FIREARM

After cleaning, inspecting and lubricating the firearm, the final stage is reassembly and function checking. The inspection process alluded to previously should continue during reassembly. Be aware of parts that do not go together as they should, a sudden increase in the play or looseness of pins and other components, and so forth.

When the firearm is reassembled, make sure that it is unloaded and then dry-fire it a few times to see if there are any changes in the feel of the trigger or the functioning of the controls. With a revolver, swing the cylinder out and test the action of the extractor rod. Rack the slide of a semiautomatic and ensure that its various safety controls are functioning. Don't just look with your eyes; listen with your ears. Sometimes the sound of the gun as it is cycled or dry-fired can reveal a functional problem.

Similarly, when firing live ammunition at the range, be aware of any changes in the gun's function or feel. A sudden tendency of the gun to misfire, jam, or change the tightness or location of its groups may be a sign of a mechanical problem.

Changes in gun function are sometimes the result of a buildup of dirt, powder residue, congealed lubri-

Fig. 256. Always function check a firearm without ammunition after it has been disassembled for cleaning or repair. Here a shooter works the slide of a semi-automatic pistol.

cant and so forth. This is especially true of jams or sluggishness in cycling that occur gradually when many rounds have been fired without maintenance. In such cases, proper functioning is often restored by a thorough cleaning and lubrication.

On the other hand, problems in functioning that appear suddenly or are not rectified by cleaning may indicate a broken part or other serious condition. In such cases, consult a gunsmith.

OTHER MAINTENANCE

Firearm maintenance involves more than just cleaning, inspection, lubrication and function testing. Both semi-automatic pistols and revolvers are powered by springs, which can, over time, fatigue and impair functioning. The springs that power revolver hammers generally last for many years

Fig. 257. Performing regular maintenance, such as the replacement of fatigued recoil springs (above), is a part of responsible firearm ownership.

before they weaken enough to cause problems; however, revolvers having a tendency to produce light hits on the primer may be suffering from weak springs. A gunsmith can help diagnose and remedy this problem.

Recoil springs on semi-automatic pistols should be replaced at regular intervals, usually every several thousand rounds. Your owner's manual should have specific recommendations regarding recoil spring replacement, as well as directions for installing new springs. A gunsmith can also assist you in replacing recoil springs.

The weak link of the semi-automatic pistol is its magazine. While most magazine springs are designed to retain their stiffness for long periods, even when left compressed, some magazine springs will fatigue over time. Some feeding problems may result from improper magazine spring tension; a gunsmith can diagnose this condition.

GUNSMITH CHECK-UP

In addition to the normal maintenance you can perform, it is important to periodically have a gunsmith completely disassemble, clean inspect and lubricate your firearm. This is also an opportunity for an experienced eye to look for wear, breakage or other conditions that may affect your gun's ability to defend you or your loved ones.

The frequency of this kind of gunsmith examination depends upon your shooting habits. In general, if you practice regularly with your firearm, an annual check-up is indicated.

APPENDIX C

OPPORTUNITIES FOR SKILL ENHANCEMENT

The NRA Personal Protection Outside the Home course should not be regarded as the endpoint of the training experience, but rather as the first step in the development of skills and abilities that will contribute to the personal safety of you and your family. There are many ways in which the knowledge, skills and attitude you have acquired in the Personal Protection Outside the Home Course can be enhanced, from individual practice to formal training and official competition. The selection of the appropriate activity is based on your needs, resources and time schedule.

DRY-FIRE PRACTICE

Dry-fire practice is an inexpensive, safe and time-efficient way to enhance shooting fundamentals, improve coordination and speed of pre-sentation, and practice the various shooting positions. Dry-firing involves practicing every phase of the firing process using an *unloaded* firearm.

All dry-fire practice must be performed in accordance with the following safety rules:

- The firearm must be completely unloaded
- All dry-firing is done in a dedicated dry-fire area having a safe backstop at which the gun is pointed
- No live ammunition is allowed in the dedicated dry-fire area
- Reloading drills are performed only with dummy ammunition
- Eye protection must always be worn

Of course, even though the firearm is unloaded, it is important to still observe the first rule of Safe Gun Handling—**<u>ALWAYS</u> keep the gun pointed in a safe direction.**

Dry-firing can be used to practice a variety of skills:

- Drawing from a holster, with or without concealment
- Reloading a revolver or semi-automatic pistol;
- Clearing stoppages (using dummy ammunition)
- Assuming various shooting positions (kneeling, squatting, prone, etc.) after drawing the pistol
- Mastering the shooting fundamentals (aiming, breath control,

Brownel's

hold control, trigger control and follow-through) as well as grip, position and NPA (Natural Point of Aim)
• Practicing movement and the use of cover

The ways that dry-firing can be used to enhance your defensive shooting skills are limited only by your imagination. For example, you could set up several targets in a basement area providing a good backstop, and practice engaging the targets as you draw from a standing position to positions of cover. Maintaining a focus on the handgun's sights enables you to verify proper sight alignment and sight picture.

A variation on traditional dry-fire techniques has been afforded by laser technology. Several firms currently market target systems allowing a standard unmodified firearm to "fire" a beam of laser light at a target sensor, which emits a visual or audio signal when hit. These systems normally involve the insertion into the gun's chamber of a cartridge-shaped laser emitting unit that is activated by the strike of the firing pin.

Fig. 258. Dry-fire practice in the home, using concrete wall as backstop.

LIVE-FIRE PRACTICE

Although dry-fire practice, as well as the review of books, videos and other materials, can add considerably to your knowledge and ability, there is no substitute for live-fire practice in improving defensive shooting skills.

Initially, the novice shooter should concentrate upon mastering the shooting drills presented in this course. Later, as both speed and accuracy improve, more challenging drills may be attempted. It is imperative that you always observe the three main rules of Safe Gun Handling—
ALWAYS keep the gun pointed in a safe direction; ALWAYS keep your finger off the trigger until ready to shoot; and ALWAYS keep the

gun unloaded until ready to use—during all live-fire exercises.

Safety is never sacrificed or compromised for the sake of speed or for any other reason. This is especially true when your practice involves drawing from the holster.

If multiple target arrays are used, they must be positioned so as to allow all rounds fired to hit a suitable backstop.

It is often useful to have a shooting partner during live-fire exercises. Not only does this give you an additional incentive to practice; a shooting partner can help you better assess your progress. For example, a partner can time your exercises with a stopwatch or an electronic shooting timer. The latter device is an especially useful tool. Typically, when the "start" button of a shooting timer is pressed, an audible signal is emitted after a random two- to three-second delay. Each shot fired after this start signal is sensed and timed by the device. After the particular string of shots is completed, you can review your times for each shot. Although a shooting timer is ideal for use with a shooting partner, you can also use it alone.

During a live-fire practice session, a shooting partner can also observe and give you feedback on your draw, stance, grip, and shooting fundamentals. For a detailed, objective record of your practice session, have your partner videotape you while you shoot. (Always ensure that the video camera is behind the firing line, and that the camera operator is not exposed to danger from other shooters.) Videotape, especially when played back in slow motion, allows you to

Fig. 259. Live-fire practice with a shooting partner.

identify areas for improvement in your draw technique and shooting form that the naked eye might miss.

SELF-DEFENSE SCENARIOS

In addition to assisting you during live-fire practice at the range, a shooting partner can also help you role-play various confrontational scenarios

outside your home. Typically, one person takes the role of the defender while the other is the attacker. While you can perform such role-play in the home with a non-firing firearm simulator made for training use, do not use such simulators outside the home. They may be mistaken for real guns by passersby, and in any event, many people may be made uncomfortable by the sight of people practicing such scenarios with anything that resembles a firearm.

Fig. 260. Armed citizen and partner practicing self-defense scenarios outside the home.

Even without firearm simulators, there are many aspects of street self-defense that you can still practice, including maintaining proper awareness of your surroundings, identifying escape routes, and planning and executing unarmed responses to potentially threatening situations. Interestingly, the experience of persons doing such role play is that, even though they know it is only a pretend situation involving friends or family members, they will experience an elevated level of stress. Learning how to perform under such conditions will help better prepare you for the stress of a real encounter.

NRA QUALIFICATION PROGRAM

You can develop your skills and gain recognition for your level of proficiency in the NRA Handgun Qualification Program. The NRA Handgun Qualification Program is a self-paced recreational shooting activity that provides shooters of all skill levels with both fun and a sense of accomplishment. The Program consists of seven different skill ratings which are earned by attaining the required scores on a series of increasingly challenging courses of fire. Shooting is done with two hands and within specific time limits to help build shooting skills having real-world applicability. For more information on the NRA Handgun Qualification Program, see Appendix D: Information and Training Resources.

NRA Bullseye 50 meters
Action Pistols target moving
IPSC
USPSA
IDPA - Prado $30

COMPETITION

Handgun competition is an excellent way to sharpen shooting skills, and the NRA offers matches open to beginner and expert alike. NRA Bullseye competition provides an opportunity to refine the shooting fundamentals—aiming, breath control, hold control, trigger control and follow-through. For competition that hones many shooting skills relevant to concealed carry and self-defense, try NRA Action Pistol. In this sport, varied target arrays are presented that must be shot within relatively quick time limits, drawing the gun from the holster. In most Action Pistol events, a large light-color target is used, with imprinted scoring rings in its center that are virtually invisible to the shooter. This helps the shooter develop the ability to accurately place shots in the center of target mass.

Fig. 261. Practical shooting competition.

Practical handgun competition, such as that sponsored by USPSA/IPSC (United States Practical Shooting Association/ International Practical Shooting Confederation), IDPA (International Defensive Pistol Association) and others, is another fun and exciting way to improve shooting and gun handling skills. In these sports, the shooter is presented with a virtually unlimited number of handgun challenges, and all firing is done against the clock; most stages start with the gun in the holster. Most stages incorporate speed, movement and decision-making, thus giving the shooter practice in shooting accurately and quickly under stress.

For information on NRA-sanctioned matches, as well as other forms of competition, see Appendix D: Information and Training Resources.

ADDITIONAL TRAINING

The NRA Personal Protection Outside the Home course provides a thorough grounding in the fundamentals of defensive shooting and concealed handgun carry. Extensive practice and rigorous application of the techniques introduced in this course will make the shooter interested in self-defense more capable of defending his or her life and family. The high number of rounds fired, and the diversity of skills taught, make this NRA course comparable to courses offered at elite shooting schools.

Some people, however, may wish to obtain additional training to learn new shooting techniques or increase their proficiency in the techniques already learned. These individuals can avail themselves of the training available at numerous facilities throughout the country. Note that the instruction provided at such facilities may vary in terms of length, quality, type and cost.

Shooters contemplating enrolling at such a facility to enhance their skills should consider at least the following factors:
- Reputation of facility
- Geographic location
- Cost
- Credentials of instructors
- Student-teacher ratio
- Safety record of institution
- Types of courses offered
- Availability of nearby lodging (for multi-day courses)

EDUCATIONAL MATERIALS

In recent years there has been a great increase in the amount of educational materials related to defensive shooting. You choose from among hundreds of pamphlets, books and videos to gain information on virtually every aspect of gun ownership and use, from maintenance and disassembly to advanced firing techniques for self-defense and safe gun storage methods for the home. Appendix D: Information and Training Resources contains a sample of the available materials.

Note that the NRA does not necessarily approve or endorse the information contained in any of the materials listed in Appendix A. While much of the content of those materials is in agreement with official NRA training guidelines and policy, some content may differ from what is taught in NRA courses. You are urged to glean as much information as possible from a wide variety of sources, but always with a critical eye toward the effectiveness and safety of the techniques being taught.

APPENDIX D

INFORMATION AND TRAINING RESOURCES

The following is not meant to be an exhaustive list of the books, magazines, videos and training opportunities available to today's gun owners. Instead, it is only a representative sampling of these resources. Inclusion of a resource in the list below does not imply NRA endorsement of its contents. Consult an NRA Certified Instructor for further information on additional resources that may be available to you.

BOOKS

Armed and Considered Dangerous: A Survey of Felons and Their Firearms, by James D. Wright and Peter H. Rossi. Aldine de Gruyter, Hawthorne, NY, 1994. ISBN 0-202-30542-2

Armed and Female, by Paxton Quigley. E.P. Dutton & Co., New York, NY, 1989. ISBN 0-225-24742-4

Armed Response: A Comprehensive Guide to Using Firearms for Self-Defence, by David Kenik. Merril Press, 2005. ISBN 0-936783-45-1

The Basics of Pistol Shooting. National Rifle Association of America, Fairfax, VA, 1991. ISBN 0-935998-00-4

Best Defense: True Stories of Intended Victims Who Defended Themselves with a Firearm, by Robert Waters. Cumberland House Publishing, Nashville, TN, 1998. ISBN 1-888952-97-0

Concealed Handgun Manual, by Chris Bird. Privateer Publishing, San Antonio, TX, 2000. ISBN 0-9656784-6-6

Defensive Shotgun, by Louis Awerbuck. Desert Publishing, El Dorado, AR, 1989. ISBN 0-87947-412-2

Defensive Shooting for Real-Life Encounters, by Ralph Mroz. Paladin Press, Boulder, CO, 2000. ISBN 1-58160-094-1

Effective Defense—The Woman, The Plan, The Gun, by Gila May Hayes. FAS Books, Onalaska, WA, 1994. ISBN 1-885036-01-9

Fight at Night, by Andy Stanford. Paladin Press, Boulder, CO, 1999. ISBN 1-58160-026-7.

The Freedmen, The Fourteenth Amendment and the Right to Bear Arms, 1866-1876, by Stephen P. Halbrook. Greenwood Publishing Group, Westport, CT, 1998. ISBN 0-275-96331-4

Gun Control and the Constitution: Sources and Explorations on the Second Amendment, ed. by Robert Cottrol. Garland Publishing, Inc., Hamden, CT. ISBN 0-8153-1666-6

Guns, Bullets and Gunfights, by Jim Cirillo. Paladin Press, Boulder, CO, 1996. ISBN 0-87364-877-3

Guns, Crime and Freedom, by Wayne Lapierre. Regnery Publishing, Washington, DC, 1994. ISBN 0-89526-477-3

Hidden in Plain Sight, by Trey Bloodworth and Mike Raley. Professional Press, Chapel Hill, NC, 1995. ISBN 1-57087-168-X.

Home Firearm Safety. National Rifle Association of America, Fairfax, VA, 1996.

Kill or Get Killed, by Rex Applegate. Paladin Press, Boulder, CO, 1976. ISBN 0-87364-084-5

More Guns, Less Crime, by John Lott. University of Chicago Press, Chicago, 1998. ISBN 0-226-49363-6

NRA Firearm Sourcebook: Your Ultimate Guide to Guns, Ballistics and Shooting. National Rifle Association, Fairfax, VA, 2006. ISBN 0-935998-26-8

NRA Marksmanship Qualification Program (booklet). National Rifle Association, Fairfax, VA.

Origins and Development of the Second Amendment, by David Hardy. Blacksmith Corp., North Hampton, OH, 1986. ISBN 0-941540-13-8

Principles of Personal Defense, by Jeff Cooper. Paladin Press, Boulder CO, 1988. ISBN 0-87364-497-2

Smart & Safe: Handling Your Firearm (booklet). National Rifle Association of America, Fairfax, VA.

The Street Smart Gun Book, by John Farnam. Police Bookshelf, Concord, NH, 1990. ISBN 0-936279-06-0.

Street Smarts, Firearms and Personal Security, by Jim Grover. Paladin Press, Boulder, CO, 2000. ISBN 1-58160-067-4.

Stressfire, by Massad Ayoob. Police Bookshelf, Concord, NH, 1986. ISBN 0-936279-03-6

Tactical Advantage, by Gabriel Suarez. Paladin Press, Boulder, CO, 1998. ISBN 0-87364-975-3

Tactical Pistol, by Gabriel Suarez. Paladin Press, Boulder, CO, 1996. ISBN 0-87364-864-1

Tactical Reality, by Louis Awerbuck. Paladin Press, Boulder, CO, 1999. ISBN 0-58160-051-8

That Every Man Be Armed: The Evolution of a Constitutional Right, by Stephen P. Halbrook. Independent Institute, Oakland, CA, 1994. ISBN 0-945999-38-0

The Truth About Handguns, by Duane Thomas. Paladin Press, Boulder, CO, 1997. ISBN 0-87364-953-2

Up To Speed, by John Mattera. Zediker Publishing, Oxford, MS, 1998. ISBN 0-9626925-8-1

MAGAZINES

All titles below published monthly by the National Rifle Association of America, Fairfax, VA.

American Rifleman
America's 1st Freedom
American Hunter
InSights
Shooting Illustrated
Shooting Sports USA

VIDEOS

Fundamentals of Gun Safety: The Basic Rules of Safe Firearm Ownership. National Rifle Association of America, Fairfax, VA, 1991.

A Woman's Guide to Firearms. Lyon House Productions, Hollywood, CA, 1987.

Personal Protection in the Home. National Rifle Association of America, Fairfax, VA, 2001.

TRAINING

Consult an NRA Certified Instructor for information on further training opportunities to enhance your knowledge, skills and attitude.

COMPETITION

The following competitive activities (listed with their sanctioning organizations) are among those that will develop shooting and gun handling skills that are relevant to defensive shooting.

NRA Action Pistol: Competitive Shooting Division, National Rifle Association of America, 11250 Waples Mill Road, Fairfax, VA 22030, (703) 267-1486.

IDPA (International Defensive Pistol Association): 2232 CR 719, Berryville, AK 72616, (870) 545-3886.

USPSA/IPSC (United States Practical Shooting Association/International Practical Shooting Confederation): P.O. Box 811, 702A Metcalf St., Sedro Wooley, WA 98284, (360) 855-2245.

FACTS ABOUT THE NRA

Established in 1871, the National Rifle Association of America (NRA) is a non-profit organization supported entirely by membership fees and by donations from public-spirited citizens.

Originally formed to promote marksmanship training, the NRA has since reached out to establish a wide variety of activities, ranging from gun safety programs for children and adults to gun collecting and gunsmithing. Hundreds of thousands of law enforcement and civilian personnel have received training from NRA Certified Instructors in the firearm skills needed to protect themselves and the public. In addition, clubs enrolled or affiliated with the NRA exist in communities across the nation, teaching youths and adults gun safety, marksmanship, and responsibility while also providing recreational activities.

The membership of the NRA has included eight Presidents of the United States, two Chief Justices of the U.S. Supreme Court, and many of America's most outstanding diplomats, military leaders, members of Congress, and other public officials.

The NRA helps train shooters to compete in numerous forms of shooting competition at the local, state, regional, national, and international levels.

The NRA provides numerous training and educational programs. The NRA, also cooperates with federal agencies, all branches of the U.S. Armed Forces, and state and local governments that are interested in training and safety programs.

The basic goals of the NRA are to

- Protect and defend the Constitution of the United States, especially in regard to the Second Amendment right of the individual citizen to keep and bear arms
- Promote public safety, law and order, and the national defense
- Train citizens and members of law enforcement agencies and the armed forces in the safe handling and efficient use of firearms
- Foster and promote the shooting sports at local, state regional, national, and international levels
- Promote hunter safety and proper wildlife management

The NRA does not receive any appropriations from Congress, nor is it a trade organization. It is not affiliated with any gun or ammunition manufacturers, or with any businesses which deal in guns or ammunition.

To join NRA today, or for additional information regarding membership, please call 1-800-NRA-3888. Your membership dues can be charged to VISA, Master Card, American Express or Discover.

INDEX